The Rise of the
Virtual State

The
Rise of the
Virtual State

Wealth and Power
in the Coming Century

Richard Rosecrance

BASIC
BOOKS

A Member of the Perseus Books Group

Published by Basic Books,
A Member of the Perseus Books Group

A catalog record for this book is available from the Library of Congress.
ISBN 0-465-07141-4

Designed by Rachel Hegarty

99 00 01 02 03 / 10 9 8 7 6 5 4 3 2 1

For Herman A. Benjamin
Ex uno multi et multa

"All that is, comes from the mind; it is based on the mind, it is fashioned from the mind."

—Suttapitaka Dhammapada, ch. I, verse I

"It may be said that, so far from having a materialistic tendency, the supposed introduction into the earth at successive geological periods of life—sensation, instinct, the intelligence of the higher mammalia bordering on reason, and lastly, the improvable reason of Man himself—presents us with a picture of ever-increasing dominion of mind over matter."

—Sir Charles Lyell

Contents

Part Four
The New System of International Politics and Economics

Preface

Once again the world's path appears troubled and unclear. Growth in the center of the world economy contrasts with poverty on the fringe; peace between major nations is offset by internal conflicts and strife on the periphery; diplomatic failures in the Balkans and Afghanistan belie gains in East Asia and Latin America. There would appear to be no consistent trend in international relationships; indeed,the central tendency often is lost in the noise of the day's events.

This book asserts that, despite retrogressions that capture our attention, the world is making steady progress toward peace and economic security. It argues that as factors of labor, capital, and information triumph over the old factor of land, nations no longer need and in time will not covet additional territory. Instead they can concentrate on the most remunerative factors of production: high-level manufacturing and services, which depend most strongly on a highly trained labor force.

In the past, material forces were dominant in national growth, prestige, and power; now products of the mind take precedence. Nations can transfer most of their material production thousands of miles away, centering their attention on research and development and product design at home. The result is a new and productive partnership between "head" nations, which design products, and "body" nations, which manufacture them. Despite its apparent resemblance to territorial dominion in the past, however, the relationship between designing and producing nations does not entail a new imperialism of north over south. Body nations rapidly develop new ganglia that in time create heads of their own, as South Korea has done. Producing countries can also range head nations against each other to compete for the use of their production capability. China—today the world's leading body nation—knows how to win concessions from head nations such as Japan, Germany, and the United States.

A new phenomenon, the virtual state, has arisen. Lodging production abroad enables this new kind of state to specialize in higher-valued, intangible goods: products of the mind. The trend to service-based economies is of relatively recent origin. Since 1945, as commodities deriving from land have increased slowly in value and manufacturing prices have risen relatively rapidly, the value of services has grown more steeply still. The countries that have focused on high-level services—Hong Kong, Taiwan, Singapore, and increasingly Korea, Switzerland, Belgium, and Holland—have done better than their industrial producing colleagues. The United States, with over 70 percent of its GDP in services and only 18 percent in manufacturing, stands on the threshold of virtual status.

Western nations sometimes bemoan this loss of production—the "great sucking sound" with which Western capital and industrial jobs move to Third World locations. The jobs thus lost, however, are in less advanced manufacturing; nor does it appear that the economy suffers. Real wages, which declined in the United States after 1973, are now dramatically rising. Increased employment in services, most in middle- to high-level jobs, has compensated for unemployment in certain industries. As educational standards mount and industry demands greater technology, the United States and other countries find better jobs to replace those lost to the Third World, where a concern for world welfare suggests these jobs should move in any event. Not only does Western employment not decrease as a result, it can signally increase, as it has done in the United States.

Nor do "virtual states" suffer by specializing in the products of the mind, which include research and development, product design, financing, marketing, transport, insurance, and legal services. The return on these "concept" occupations, as the skyscrapers in Hong Kong readily attest, is much higher than the return on manufacturing. This is not to suggest that Taiwan cannot create its own Silicon Valley (soon to be replicated in Malaysia), but it does mean that more and more of Taiwan's production will be done on the mainland. Singapore has turned to Malaysia, Johore, and China for its manufacturing. In the aftermath of the financial crisis all these economies have come back strongly.

The idea of production abroad is a radical step for the world economy. When Jean Bodin wrote *The Republic* in 1590, the sovereign state was supposed to gather its resources, crops, and people into one locale. The duty of the sovereign was to prevent religious strife and thus concentrate political power at the center of the state. After the Peace of Westphalia in 1648 states became even more centralized, and international war replaced civil war as the dominant political route to power. With Napoleon and Clausewitz in the nineteenth century, countries became mobilization bases from which assaults on other countries could be launched. This again entailed having the resources, population, and military assets in one place. Territorial expansion was the means to achieve this mastery.

A century ago metropolitan nations sometimes produced goods in their colonial tributaries, but not in each other's. Despite the burgeoning international trade of the later nineteenth century, World Wars I and II represented a complete reconcentration of national economies, cutting the ties with erstwhile trading partners.

Now, however, production takes place in completely independent states with no political connection with the head nation. How is such radical economic and political change possible? It occurs because foreign direct investment is now secure abroad. Unlike the 1960s and early 1970s, producing countries do not nationalize their foreign plants but rather compete for them. Unlike the *dependencia* period, when southern nations sought to decouple themselves from the north, many southerners now want to become the north. It is a sometimes unremarked paradox that Mexico—long a prickly nationalist bastion of Central America—is now part of the North American Free Trade Area; and a hemispheric free-trade zone is possible. Fernando Cardozo, once one of the primary *dependistas*, is now leading Brazil toward incorporation with the world economy. Argentina, once the haven of Perón, now seeks to institute the American dollar as its currency. The links between north and south have become solid and indefeasible.

The new dependence on productive assets that are located within someone else's state represents an unprecedented trust in the integrity and peacefulness of strangers. Economic reliance on other countries also partially vitiates the military insistence on concentration of assets. The security of virtual states rests on the assumption that trade routes will be kept open and that flows of factors of production will generally not be interrupted. They remain technologically viable because the Internet provides instantaneous means of communication with subsidiaries in any part of the globe. A plant in Brazil can be identical to a plant in Eastern Europe and can be managed remotely by Western or Japanese corporations.

The countries that have made these improbable leaps of faith have become enriched. Interdependent states have grown far more rapidly than autarchic economies. Those that have spread their industry to different countries and markets have gained greatly over those that produce only at home. The nations that have placed their bets on peace have done much better than those that have predicated war. The warlike regions— Eastern Europe, the Balkans, the Middle East, and to some degree Southern Asia—have wallowed in stagnation, while peaceful realms— Western Europe, East Asia, North and South America, and Oceania— have moved ahead. Peace has been eminently profitable.

This does not mean that major war is ruled out for all time. The factor of land might stage a resurgence and territory become more significant. A dramatic spurt of population growth could increase the demand for basic materials, although the demographic forecast is for a decline in the world birth rate. A major depression might sever the trading and productive ties that link nations together. Balance of power conflicts could resume. Ethnic hatreds could spill over into international violence as they did at the time of World War I. Where land and its products still remain the vital factor of production—in the agriculture of Eastern Europe, the oil of the Caspian or the Middle East—territory will continue to exert a delusive influence. For the world as a whole, however, such tendencies will be retrograde and atavistic. Indeed, the efforts at peace in the Middle East, the Balkans, and Northern Ireland are a harbinger of the universal urge to join the international economy and to participate in its growth. South Africa is tentatively resuming its long foregone economic development, and islands of growth are emerging elsewhere in Africa. In Asia, Africa, and the Middle East, the countries that have funneled their investment capital into armaments have been punished by the market and by international investors.

Ecological outcomes also favor the virtual state. As information becomes an increasing component of GDP, the weight of exports and the products of national income grows lighter—easier to carry and transmit—because their knowledge component is higher. At the ultimate stage competition among nations will be competition among educational systems, for the most productive and richest countries will be those with the best education and training. As countries strive to improve their human resources in worldwide competition, they will also concurrently improve their own societies. The rise of the virtual state thus inaugurates a new epoch of peaceful competition among nations, promising a cooperative transition to the new millennium.

———————

This book has been a long time coming. I have been assisted at every stage by my colleagues, students, and family. I have learned a great deal from international economists, particularly Deepak Lal, Ed Leamer, Richard Cooper, and Gary Hufbauer. I benefited from discussions with Barry Michels, Alan Kessler, and Kerry Chase. Norman Richardson and John Edmunds offered helpful insights. A series of research assistants have made important contributions to the work, including Carolina Wieland, Gitty Amini, Mike Blakley, and Peter Thompson. My colleagues John Mueller, Carl Kaysen, Ron Rogowski, Alan Alexandroff, and Art Stein have argued with me, greatly to my benefit. Robert Gilpin, David Lake, and Joseph Grieco usefully disagreed with me. In Europe I learned a great deal from François Duchêne, Roger Morgan, and Ivan

Zielonka, in Asia from Stephen Cheung and C. K. Law. Becky Carrera, Karen Cun, and Grace Han rendered the text more readable. William Frucht, my editor at Basic Books, has made important contributions to the style and thought of the book, enabling me to extend the analysis. Herman A. Benjamin not only contended with his recalcitrant son-in-law but brought the insights of the *Wall Street Journal* to bear upon my arguments. My greatest debt, however, is to Barbara Benjamin Rosecrance, who modestly refused joint authorship of this volume despite her major contributions to its form and substance. My debt to her is far greater than I can acknowledge here. I need not add that all errors remain my own.

—— Part One

The Theory

chapter 1

A New Kind of Nation

Amid the worldwide clamor of ethnic politics, regional conflict, and financial crisis, a new reality is emerging. Developed states are putting aside military and territorial ambitions as they struggle not for political dominance but for a greater share of world output. In the process, nations are shrinking—in function if not in geographic size. The nation-state is becoming a tighter, more vigorous unit capable of sustaining the pressures of worldwide competition. We are entering a world in which the most important resources are the least tangible—where land is less important than an educated populace, where stockpiles of goods, capital, and labor are less important than flows, and where parochial interests are less important than the international economy as a whole.

It is true that the ambitions of lesser states to gain territory still engage the world's attention. Serbia's Slobodan Milosevic extended ethnic cleansing to Kosovo. Several years ago Radovan Karadzic tried to create an independent Serbian province in Bosnia with allegiance to Belgrade. In 1990 Iraq's Saddam Hussein aimed to corner the world oil market through military aggression against Kuwait (also aimed at Saudi Arabia); control of oil, a product of land, represented the acme of his ambitions. India and Pakistan, both possessing nuclear capabilities, are vying for territorial dominance over a Kashmiri population that neither may be fully able to control. Ethnic rivalries beset Hutu and Tutsi in Rwanda, Albanians and Serbians in Kosovo.

These examples look to the past. Developing countries, which still produce goods derived from land, continue to covet territory. But where the products of land no longer determine market and power relationships, a new form of state is being born: the virtual nation, a nation based on mobile capital, labor, and information. The virtual state is a political unit that has downsized its territorially based production capability and is the logical consequence of emancipation from land. Virtual states and their associates would rather plumb the world market than acquire territory.

In its pure form—an ideal model toward which many states are tending—the virtual state carries with it the possibility of an entirely new system of world politics. In the past, when military conflict and the desire for territory determined relations between nations, the main flow between countries consisted of armies. Future flows will be largely economic as capital, technology, manpower, and information move rapidly among states. In the long term, national access to international factors of production can replace the need to control additional land.

This does not mean that states will be abolished as territorial entities, that conflicts over land will never occur, or that politics can take place without geographic space. Geographic concerns reassert themselves in Eastern Europe. States require a certain minimum of territory to conduct political business and establish representative institutions differentiated from those of other countries. As the success of Singapore has demonstrated, however, huge open spaces are scarcely necessary for economic competence, nor are preexisting competitive products.[1] Singapore does not produce a single commodity in which it had a prior comparative advantage. It does not have oil, tin, or rice—the typical products of its neighbors. Its economic position rests on "created" comparative advantages in semiconductors, textiles, and important service industries. The countries now entering the international system are much smaller than their imperial forebears, yet they can achieve stunning economic capacity.

Transferring the bulk of their home production overseas, and shifting most of their economy to high-level services, virtual nations reshape both productive and international relationships.[2] They inaugurate a world based on mastery of flows of production and purchasing power rather than stocks of goods. They emancipate labor from routine mechanical tasks and offer new employment in technical or creative services.[3] They usher in a world based on education and human capital rather than machines and physical capital.[4] They offer nations the opportunity to forge international links of production that are difficult if not impossible to break. Like the headquarters of a virtual corporation, the virtual state determines overall strategy and invests in its people rather than amassing expensive production capacity. It contracts out other functions to states that specialize in or need them. Imperial Great Britain may have been the model for the nineteenth century, but Hong Kong (now the Special Administrative Region of China) will be the model for the twenty-first.

The virtual state is a recent evolution, based on the prior ascent of a different form: the trading state.[5] Led by Japan and Germany after World War II, the most advanced nations shifted their efforts from controlling territory to augmenting their share of world trade. In the 1960s and 1970s, when goods were more mobile than capital or labor, selling abroad was the name of the game. As capital has become increasingly mobile, however, advanced nations have come to recognize that exporting is no longer the only means to economic growth; one can instead produce goods overseas for both foreign and domestic markets.[6]

Today as more production by domestic industries takes place abroad, and technology, knowledge, and capital become more important than land, the function of the state is being further redefined. The state no longer commands resources as it did in mercantilist yesteryear; rather, it negotiates with foreign and domestic capital and labor to lure them into its own economic sphere and stimulate its growth. The virtual state also locates production overseas so that it can concentrate home efforts on high-level services: research and development, product design, financing, marketing, and transport. A nation's economic strategy is now at least as important as its military strategy; its ambassadors have become foreign trade and financial representatives.[7]

Major foreign trade and investment deals command the executive attention that political and military issues received two decades ago. The new type of international crisis is apt to resemble the frantic two weeks in December 1994, when the White House outmaneuvered the French to secure for the Raytheon Company a $1 billion deal for management of rain forests and air traffic in Brazil.

The virtual state relies on mobile factors of production. Of course it houses virtual corporations and presides over foreign direct investment by its enterprises. But more than this, it encourages, stimulates, and to a degree even coordinates their activities. Unlike nineteenth-century territorial behemoths—the United States, Russia, and Germany, which aimed at omnicompetence—the virtual state does not seek to excel in all economic functions, from mining and agriculture to production and distribution. Rather, the new kind of state specializes in modern technical and research services and high-level production techniques, and derives its income not only from manufacturing but from product design, marketing, and financing. The rationale for its economy is efficiency attained through productive downsizing. Size no longer determines economic potential. Virtual nations and their associates hold the competitive key to greater wealth in the twenty-first century. In time they may supersede the continent-sized and self-sufficient units that prevailed in the past.

From Territorial to Trading States

States have traditionally been obsessed with land. The international system, with its intermittent wars, was founded on the assumption that land is key to both production and power. States could improve their position by building empires and invading other nations to seize territory. Before the age of nationalism, a captured principality willingly obeyed its new ruler; conquered provinces contained peasants and grain supplies, and their inhabitants rendered tribute to the new sovereign. The Hapsburg monarchy, Spain, France, and Russia became major powers through territorial expansion between the sixteenth and nineteenth centuries.

With the Industrial Revolution, however, capital and labor assumed new importance. Great Britain led the way in discovering sophisticated uses for the new factors of production. British machine capital turned out textiles for the world market, and English financial capital was invested abroad. At the same time, natural resources—especially coal, iron, and later oil—fueled the Industrial Revolution. Agricultural and mineral resources stimulated the development of the United States and other fledgling industrial nations such as Australia, Canada, South Africa, and New Zealand in the nineteenth century.[8] Capital and labor—mobile factors of production—did not become paramount for these countries until late in the twentieth century.

By that time land had declined in relative value and had become harder for nations to hold.[9] Nationalist mobilization of colonial populations has dismantled all of the nineteenth-century empires and now impedes most imperialist or invader attempts to extract resources. A nation may expend considerable effort to occupy new territory without gaining proportionate economic benefits.[10]

Nationalist resistance and the shift in the basis of production have reduced the benefits of war. Land, which is fixed, can be physically captured, but labor, capital, and information can slip away like quicksilver after an attack.[11] The Iraqi Army ransacked the computers in downtown Kuwait City in August 1990, only to find that the cash in bank accounts had already been electronically transferred. Even though it had abandoned its territory, the Kuwaiti government continued to spend billions of dollars to resist the invasion.

Today, for the wealthiest industrial countries such as Germany, the United States, and particularly Japan, the investment in land no longer pays the same dividends. Since midcentury commodity prices have fallen nearly 40 percent relative to manufactured goods.[12] Returns from the manufacturing trade greatly exceed those from agricultural and commodity exports. As a result, the terms of trade for many developing nations have been deteriorating, and in recent years the rise in prices of international services has outpaced that for manufactured products. Land prices have been steeply discounted.[13]

With this decline a new political prototype, the trading state, emerged in the 1970s and 1980s.[14] Rather than territorial expansion, the trading state sought its vocation through international commerce. The shift in national strategy was driven by the declining value of fixed productive assets. States for which a military-territorial strategy was not feasible, either because of size or because of their recent experience with conflict, also adopted trade-oriented strategies. Small European and East Asian states, Japan, and West Germany all moved strongly in a trading direction after the Second World War.

In recent years a further stimulus has hastened this change. Faced with enhanced international competition in the late 1980s and 1990s, corporations have engaged in pervasive downsizing. They have trimmed the ratio of production workers to output, saving on costs. The resulting productivity increases have lessened the widely noted gap between manufacturing and services.[15] The corporations that survive and grow worldwide are those that can maintain or increase output with a steady or declining amount of labor.[16]

A new kind of corporation emerged. The virtual corporation, economic analogue of the virtual state, has become increasingly pervasive. Focusing on product design, marketing, and financing, it has left production to someone else. The virtual corporation disperses its production around the world.

This new company originated in Silicon Valley. Corporations there recognized that they could enhance cost cutting, productivity, and competitiveness still further by using the production lines of other companies. The old model of fully integrated headquarters, design offices, and production lines exemplified by Ford's huge plant at Willow Run in Michigan gave way to lighter, smaller models. The comprehensive integrated structure is expensive to maintain and operate, especially in lean times when it can't run at full capacity; a firm that employs someone else's production line, however, can cut costs dramatically. Such a firm does not have to buy land and machines, hire labor, or provide medical benefits to the workers who produce its goods. It capitalizes on what are called *economies of scope*—turning out more than one product on the assembly line, and leasing assembly lines from other firms. The company may even design particular products for a specialized firm that performs exacting operations, such as the surface mounting of miniaturized components directly on circuit boards without the need for soldering or conventional wiring. In either case the original equipment manufacturer contracts out its production to other companies. Without a large investment sunk into a fixed manufacturing capacity, such a company can adapt quickly to changes in the market.[17]

The virtual corporation is research, development, design, marketing, financing, legal, and other headquarters functions with few or no manufacturing capabilities—a company with a head but no body. It represents the ultimate achievement of corporate downsizing, and the model is spreading rapidly from firm to firm. It is not surprising that the virtual corporation should catch on. Concept or head corporations can design new products for a range of different production facilities. Strategic alliances between firms (whether or not embodied in formal mergers), such as American and US Airways, Ford and Mazda, or Citicorp and Travellers, are also very profitable. According to the *Financial Times*, firms that actively pursue strategic alliances are 50 percent more profitable than those that do not.[18]

From the Virtual Corporation to the Virtual State

The newly pruned corporation has facilitated the emergence of the virtual state. Downsizing has become a path to corporate efficiency and productivity gains. Now the national economy is also being downsized—not in dollar output but in productive base. Among the most efficient economies are those that possess limited production capacity at home. The archetype is Hong Kong, whose production facilities even before the transition to Chinese rule were located in southern China. Hong Kong's GDP comprises 83 percent services and about 8 percent manufacturing production. The model of the virtual state suggests that political as well as economic forces push toward downsizing at home and a relocation of production facilities abroad. In Singapore, for in-

stance, the successors of Lee Kuan Yew keep the country on a tight political rein but still depend economically on the inflow of foreign factors
of production, while moving local production to Malaysia and Indonesia as well as China. The virtual state is in this sense a negotiating entity that depends as much on economic access abroad as on economic
control at home. Despite its past reliance on domestic production,
Korea no longer manufactures everything at home, and Japanese production is increasingly lodged abroad. In Europe, Switzerland is the
leading virtual nation. One example of its new focus on headquarters
functions is that roughly 98 percent of Nestlé's production capacity is
located elsewhere. Holland now produces most of its goods outside its
borders. Britain's foreign direct investment in 1994 was almost as large
as that of the United States. Even the United States participates in this
trend. A remarkable 20 percent of the production of U.S. corporations
now takes place outside the country.

A reflection of how far these tendencies have gone is the growing portion of GDP consisting of high-value-added services such as concept,
design, consulting, and finance. Services already constitute 70 percent
of American GDP. Indeed, the decision to produce abroad is also a decision to concentrate at home on more highly remunerative services. In
the case of the United States, 63 percent of service production occurs in
the high-value category and is growing rapidly. Of course manufacturing matters, but it matters much less than it did.[19, 20]

Manufacturing for these developed nations will continue to decline in
importance. If services productivity continues to increase, it will greatly
strengthen U.S. competitiveness abroad. The United States can no
longer assume, however, that services face no international competition. Efficient high-value services will be as important to a developed
nation as manufacturing of automobiles and electrical equipment once
was.[21] Since 1959 services prices have increased by twenty-five times,
industrial prices by sixteen times.[22] This means that countries with a
very creative and educated labor force will move increasingly into services and leave manufacturing production to emerging nations. Given
highly trained labor, some nations may be able to skip the manufacturing stage and still prosper.

FIGURE 1.1   Value added as a share of GDP at current prices.

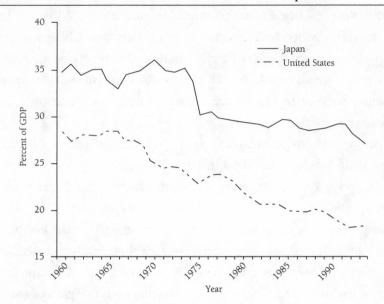

A: Manufacturing sector.

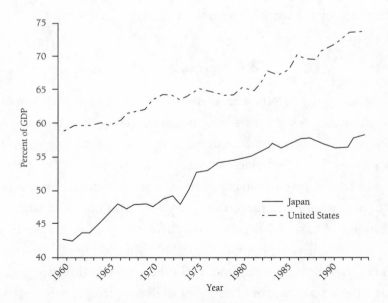

B: Services sector.

SOURCE: OECD Historical Statistics, 1960–1994; and Robert Rowthorn and Ramana Ramaswamy, "Deindustrialization: Causes and Implications," International Monetary Fund Working Paper WP/97/43, April 1997.

The world may become further divided into head and body nations, or nations representing some combination of the two. While Australia and Canada stress the headquarters or head functions, China will be the twenty-first-century model of a body nation. Although China does not innately or immediately know what to produce for the world market, it has found success in joint ventures with foreign corporations. China will be an attractive place to produce manufactured goods, but only those designed, marketed, and financed by other countries. China cannot yet chart its own industrial future.

Neither can Russia. Focusing on the products of land, the Russians are still prisoners of territorial fetishism. Their commercial laws do not yet permit the delicate and sophisticated arrangements that ensure that body manufacturers deliver quality goods for their foreign heads. Moreover, Russia's transportation network is primitive. The Russian mafiosi are too entwined with the country's government and legal system. The Moscow government has been unable to collect enough taxes to provide basic services or to make payments on the national debt; but these are temporary obstacles. Russia, China, and India will in time serve as important loci for the world's production plant.

Economic Success and the Emancipation from Land

The world's progressive emancipation from land as a determinant of production and power gives new opportunities to emerging nations. Structures of comparative advantage that were unchangeable can now be overcome through the acquisition of a highly trained labor force.[23] Africa and Latin America may not have to rely on exporting raw materials or agricultural products; they can develop an educated labor force such as India has in Bangalore and Ireland in Dublin. Investing in human capital, nations can substitute for trying to foresee the vagaries of the commodities markets and avoid the constant threat of overproduction.[24] Meanwhile, land continues to decline in value. Recent studies of 180 countries indicate that despite overpopulation in a few countries, population density is positively correlated with wealth. The economist Deepak Lal observes that investment and growth per capita are inversely related to land holdings.[25] This conclusion particularly derives from the current successes of small East Asian, Japanese, and European economies.[26] Though China and India are beginning to grow rapidly, their population density does not yet approach that of smaller, highly industrialized nations. The United States and Russia have substantial endowments of raw materials, but population density is much lower, and economic growth has been variable.

These findings represent a dramatic reversal of past theories of international power. In the 1930s international relations textbooks ranked the great powers in terms of their possession of land and endowments of key natural resources: oil, iron ore, coal, bauxite, copper, tungsten, and manganese. Analysts presumed that the state with the largest stock of raw materials would prevail. CIA estimates of the strategic importance of various regions during the cold war were based on similar assumptions. It turns out, however, that countries with a negligible stock of natural resources are often the most prosperous.[27] Japan, for instance, accomplished its economic miracle with little coal and no iron, bauxite, or oil. Except for rice, it imports most of its food. But Japan is richly endowed with human capital.

The implications for the United States are equally striking. As capital, labor, information, and knowledge become more important than land for economic success, America can influence and possibly reshape its pattern of comparative advantage. The New Trade theory articulated by the economist Paul Krugman focuses on path dependence: the degree to which initial design choices condition later technological development, the so-called QWERTY effect. The present QWERTY keyboard, which became standard for typewriters in the 1920s, was not the arrangement of letter-coded keys that produced the fastest typing. In fact, one of its virtues (perhaps its only one) was that by slowing typists down, it prevented keys from sticking. Now computers have succeeded typewriters, but everyone who types is trained in QWERTY; we're stuck with it. In the same way, path dependence—the way initial choices determine next steps—can influence success in developing industrial products. Nations that made the first investments in the 16-kilobyte computer memory chip used what they learned to achieve advantages in the 4- and 16-megabyte chips. Intervention at an early point in the chain of development can determine results later on;[28] this suggests that the United States and other nations can and should deliberately alter their patterns of comparative advantage and choose their focus of economic activity.

American college and graduate education, for example, has sustained research in high technology and contributed to a very wide range of U.S. industrial choices. It has supported the decisive American role in the international services industry in research and development, consulting, design, packaging, financing, and the marketing of new products. Mergers and acquisitions are American subspecialties that draw on the skills of financial analysts and attorneys. The American failure has been in the first twelve years of education. Unlike those of Germany and Japan (or even Taiwan, Korea, and Singapore), U.S. elementary and secondary education falls well below the world standard. This has not yet affected American advantages in high-level services, but it has influenced U.S. prowess in advanced manufacturing.

Economics teaches that products should be valued according to their economic importance. For a long period, education was undervalued socially and economically, despite productivity studies done by Edward Denison and others at The Brookings Institution that showed its long-term importance to U.S. growth and innovation. Recent studies have underscored this importance. According to the World Bank, 64 percent of the world's wealth consists of human capital.[29] Yet the social and economic valuation of primary and secondary education has not appreciably increased in light of these findings. Educators, psychologists, and school boards debate how education should be structured. Administration officials bemoan the deteriorating physical plant in education. Neither invests more money in it. Corporations have sought to upgrade the standards of teaching and learning in their locales, but municipalities and states have lagged behind, as has the federal government. Elementary and high school teachers should be rewarded as patient creators of high-value capital in the United States and elsewhere.[30] In Switzerland, elementary school teachers are paid around $70,000 per year, near the salary of a starting lawyer in a New York firm. In international economic competition, human capital is the means by which states liberated from the confines of their geography have been able, with appropriate education, to transform their industrial and economic futures. A nation can choose its comparative advantage as a result of the prowess of its graduate schools, but it can only carry out its choices by better secondary education.

Land, Trade, and the Decline of Warfare

What will a world of virtual states be like? The angry and dispossessed will continue to launch isolated episodes of terrorism against other countries and their own governments. There may be biological or chemical attacks on particular countries. But in general, interstate violence should decline. In the process of downsizing and moving production outside their borders, corporations and nation-states will have to get used to relying on others. Virtual corporations need other companies' production facilities. As a result, economic relations between states will come to resemble nerves connecting heads in one place to bodies elsewhere. Producer nations will work quickly to become the brains behind emerging industries in other countries. In time, few nations will contain within their borders all the components of a technically advanced economic existence. To sever the connections between states would thus undermine the organic unit.

The new values and interconnections these states espouse and live by set the standards for international behavior. Such values become international norms—accepted paths to success and power. Countries tend to imitate those that are most successful and powerful. Many states followed in the wake of Great Britain in the nineteenth century; in recent decades, numerous states seeking to improve their lot in the world have emulated Japan and South Korea. Under Mikhail Gorbachev in the 1980s even the Soviet Union sought to diversify its strategy away from military spending and territorial expansion. In the past, international norms underlying the balance of power, the Concert of Europe, or even rule by the British Raj helped specify appropriate courses of action for parties in dispute. The international economy also partly rested on normative agreement. Free trade, open domestic economies, and more recently, freedom of capital movement were normative notions. In the Far Eastern financial crisis, the International Monetary Fund acted as a norm-setting agency that inculcated market economics and impartial regulation of banks among nations not yet fully ready to accept all international obligations. While these norms have not always been accepted, they define what is approved.

The persistence of norms depends on the success of the nations using them. In the nineteenth-century British pantheon of virtues, free trade was a norm that could be extended to other nations without self-defeat. Success for one nation did not undermine the others' prospects for industrialization and growth—but the acquisition of empire caused congestion. Once imperial Britain had taken the lion's share of colonial territory, little was left for others. The inability of all nations to live up to the norms Britain established brought conflict. The imperial norm was inappropriate because it created instability in the very system it aimed to promote.

In a similar vein, Japan's trading strategy could be emulated by many other countries. Its pacific principles and dependence on world markets and raw material supplies have engendered greater economic cooperation among states. At the same time, Japan's insistence on maintaining a quasi-closed economy and a foreign trade surplus cannot be successfully imitated by everyone; if some achieve this result, others necessarily will not. In this respect, Japan's practices and norms stand athwart progress and emulation by other nations.

President Clinton rightly argued that the newly capitalist developmental states, particularly Korea, have modeled themselves on restrictionist Japan. If this precedent were extended to China, the results would endanger the long-term stability of the world economic and financial system. Accordingly, the 1997–98 financial crisis usefully stressed the need for greater openness in trade, finance, and the unhindered movement of factors of production among states. Appropriate norms reinforce economic incentives to reduce conflict among nations.

As long as the international system of nation-states lasts, there will be conflict among its members. States inevitably see events from a national perspective, and competition and struggle are endemic. The question is, in what ways will conflicts express themselves? Within a domestic system, conflicts between individuals need not escalate to the use of physical force. Law and settlement procedures usually reduce outbreaks of violence. In international relations, however, no sovereign, regnant authority can discipline feuding states. International law sets a standard, but it is not always obeyed. The great powers constitute the executive committee of nation-states and can intervene from time to time to set things right. Yet as Kosovo, Bosnia, and Rwanda show, powers intervene with great reluctance if at all, and countries virtually never intervene in the absence of shared norms and ideologies.

In these circumstances, the economic substructure of international relations becomes exceedingly important. This structure can either impel or retard conflicts between nation-states. When land is the major factor of production, the temptation to strike another nation is great. The resources to be gained lead directly to increased wealth and power. When the key elements of production are less tangible, the situation changes. Real estate does not bring knowledge, and aggressors cannot seize the needed capital. Workers may flee an invader. Electronic funds may vanish in a moment. Wars of aggression and wars of punishment lose their impact and justification.

Critics such as Paul Ehrlich, however, contend that land will become important once again. Oil supplies will be depleted; the quantity of fertile land will decline; water will run dry. Population will rise relative to the supply of natural resources and food. This process, it is claimed, could return the world to the eighteenth and nineteenth centuries, with clashes over territory once again the engine of conflict. Such a conclusion, however, is far from inevitable. The natural resources on which the world currently relies may run out, but as before, there will be substitutes. For instance, whale oil, once the most common fuel for lighting, became largely unavailable in the 1840s. The harnessing of global energy and the production of food do not depend on particular bits of fluid, soil, or rock. The question, rather, is how to release the energy contained in abundant matter.

Ehrlich's scenario assumes that the productivity of land will begin to decline, but the long-run trend has been the opposite: the yield of commodities per square mile of the earth's surface has steadily increased. In effect, the supply of land-based productivity has been expanding, causing a gradual fall in the prices of food and raw materials, relative to financial capital, human capital, and information. Given the rapid technological development of recent years, the continued primacy of the latter seems more likely. Few trends have altered the historical tendency toward the growing intangibility of value in social and economic terms. It scarcely seems possible that in the next century this process would suddenly reverse itself.

Small nations have attained efficiency and competitiveness, and even large nations have begun to think small. If reliable access to assets elsewhere can be assured, the physical need to possess them diminishes. Norms are important reinforcements of such arrangements. Free movement of capital and goods, substantial international and domestic investment, open and impartially regulated markets, and high levels of technical education have been the recipe for success in the industrial world of the late twentieth century. Those who depended on others did better than those who depended only on themselves.

Can the result be different in the future? Virtual states, corporate alliances, and essential trading relationships augur peaceful times. They may not solve domestic problems, but the economic bonds that link virtual and other nations will help ease security concerns.

The Civic Crisis

Though peaceful in its international implications, the rise of the virtual state portends a crisis for democratic politics. Western democracies have traditionally believed that political reform, extension of suffrage, and economic restructuring would solve their problems. In the twenty-first century none of these measures can fully succeed, because national governments have insufficient jurisdiction to deal with global problems. Economic restructuring in one state does not necessarily affect others—and the political state is growing smaller, not larger.

If ethnic movements are victorious in Canada, Mexico, Kosovo, and elsewhere, they will divide their states into smaller entities. Even existing states are seeing their powers circumscribed. In the United States, if Congress has its way, the federal government will lose authority. In response to such changes, the market fills the vacuum, gaining power.

As states downsize, malaise among working people is bound to spread. Employment may fluctuate and sometimes decline. President Clinton once observed that Americans had fallen into a "funk." The economy can be prosperous and the stock market ebullient, but there is no guarantee that favorable conditions will last. For most countries, the flow of international factors of production—technology, capital, and labor—will swamp the stock of economic power at home. The state will become just one of many players in the international marketplace and will have to negotiate directly with international factors of production to solve domestic economic problems.[31] Under appropriate conditions, countries will need to invest abroad or they will lose foreign markets. They must also induce foreign capital to enter their domain. To keep such investment, national economic authorities will need to maintain low inflation, rising productivity, a strong currency, and a flexible and trained labor force. These requirements will sometimes conflict with domestic interests that want more government spending, budget deficits, and more benefits. That conflict will result in continued domestic insecurity over jobs, welfare, and medical care. Unlike the remedies applied in the insulated and partly closed economies of the past, purely domestic policies can no longer solve these problems.

Globalization may increase inequality between skilled and unskilled workers in developed countries even as it reduces conflicts in Third World nations. The movement of production overseas employs labor in new countries. The emigration of people from the Third to the First World increases real wages in their country of origin. In the developed world, however, it may lead to a surplus of unskilled workers.

The state can compensate for its deficient jurisdiction by seeking to influence economic factors abroad.[32] The domestic state therefore must not only become a negotiating state but also become internationalized. This lesson, already learned in Europe, is well on its way to codification in East Asia in the aftermath of the financial crisis. Among the world's major economies and polities, only the United States remains, despite its vigorous economic sector, essentially introverted politically and culturally. Compared with their counterparts elsewhere, citizens born in the United States know fewer foreign languages, understand less about foreign cultures, and live abroad reluctantly, if at all. In recent years British industrial workers who could not find jobs at home migrated to Germany, learning the language to work there. They had few American imitators.

The virtual state is an agile entity operating in twin jurisdictions: abroad and at home. It is as prepared to mine gains overseas as in the domestic economy. In large countries, however, internationalization operates differently. Political and economic decision makers have begun to recast their horizons, but middle managers and workers lag behind. They expect too much and learn too little. This is why the dawn of the virtual state must also be the sunrise of international education and training. The virtual state cannot satisfy all its citizens. The state's ability to support wages and prices and sustain employment and industries by legislative fiat has greatly declined.[33] Displaced workers and businesspeople must be willing to look abroad for opportunities. In the United States they can do this only if American education prepares the way.

Sunrise or Sunset?

The operations of the virtual state and of nations concentrating on high-level services are fundamentally progressive. In the past, national leaders sometimes concluded that they could alleviate domestic grievances by successful military expansion. Louis XIV, Napoleon, Hitler, and Stalin sought territorial solutions to domestic problems. Since the virtual state relies on flows of information and capital, technology and labor, it does not have to expand its territorial confines to cope with economic or political difficulties. Mastery of *flows* is more important than possession of large fixed territorial *stocks* of resources. This is why countries that relied simply on existing stocks have recently done so badly. Soviet Russia pursued heavy industry on the basis of existing resources and agriculture, but it could not keep up with changes in technology and capital on a worldwide basis. India built a hothouse industrial plant designed to replace imports, but it remained behind the curve of technological development in other parts of the world. Brazil has only recently begun to upgrade its industries on the basis of inflows of foreign capital and technology.

Domestic outcomes have become more uncertain. A government cannot guarantee particular inflows or the success of its corporate investments overseas. Domestic labor cannot be sure that the influx of foreign labor will only supplement rather than supplant its role. Workers and businesspeople will need education, training, and energy to adjust to the challenge. The world stands at the threshold of changes like those of the Industrial Revolution. But the Industrial Revolution was a revolution in tangibles: machines, railways, textiles, and products of the assembly line. The technological revolution of today and tomorrow is a revolution of intangibles: ideas, knowledge, technique, software, new creative products, and capital.[34]

Knowledge innovations may or may not catch on. In Silicon Valley new intangible innovations have a success rate of 5 to 10 percent. Biotechnologists cannot be sure that their genetically engineered products will work or that the Food and Drug Administration will approve their sale; but venture capitalists still make money, because their stipulated returns are set accordingly.

Each generation is more dependent than its elders on intangibles. Those who will reach adulthood in the twenty-first century face the demanding task of making high-level services pay on a heretofore unparalleled scale. They will need much better training than their predecessors; but the world is beginning, in every country, to recognize this need. The future is still opaque, but it is brightening.

The Partnership of Politics and Economics

To succeed, a virtual state requires a partnership between politics and economics operating in both domestic and international realms. It must arrange domestic patterns of regulation and benefit so that factors of production can flow easily from one nation to another. For this to happen, market and state must accommodate each other's interests. If the market dictates all political results, policy outcomes will be the result of bribery and the sale of offices; government decisions and judicial outcomes will be sold to the highest bidder. On the other hand, if the state governs all economic activity, efficient allocation of resources will be sacrificed,[35] and political and military values will take precedence over economic gain. Finding a proper balance between politics and economics is not easy. The example of Russia illustrates excesses in both directions. During the cold war, Soviet Russia acted as a military state that ultimately sacrificed economic and welfare values. More recently, however, post-Communist Russia has permitted economic influence peddlers to buy policy outcomes. The drive for individual economic gain has undermined its national economy as well as its political stability.

The same tensions exist internationally. If economics is totally subordinated to power politics, the international market languishes. Tariffs rise, and economic exchange suffers. Yet international trade and finance still need the protection of political states—to enforce contracts internationally and to ensure the unhindered movement of commerce on the high seas. Unless great powers agree, the obligations of international trade will not be sustained on a worldwide basis.[36] Thus in both domestic and international arenas, market and political influences must align to foster international trade and the movement of factors of production.

The age of the virtual state presages a decline of major warfare and a general improvement in world prosperity—but this advance comes at a price. Individuals may feel insecure as their state fails to buffer them against the winds of economic change. Those with intelligence, adaptability, and the drive to succeed, however, will "seize the day" and fashion a more intricate trading network in which previously detached cultures will be increasingly linked together.

The virtual state is an entity that prospers from dependence on others. It does not rely on the products of land or on manufacturing capacity, most of which has been shifted abroad. It focuses on creative and management services, designing new products to be made in the factories of other nations. In so doing, it reaps a profitable return, as do its industrial associates. This mutual profit can only be sustained, however, if international relations permit the untrammeled flow of factors of production between economies. Developing the concept of the virtual state, this book investigates the probability and success of that requirement, and of the institution of the virtual state itself.

Plan of the Book

Chapter 2 begins by examining the long process of historical evolution that has led to the rise of the virtual state. Simply put, it tells the story of the increasing dominance of flows over stocks. At the same time, mobile factors of production such as capital, labor, and information have begun to take precedence over fixed factors such as land. In time an international economy dominated by virtual states will arise from our present world. The process of virtualization will be uneven, however, affecting some countries more than others, and leaving many considerably short of the model of the virtual state. Most developed nations will move toward services, retaining a limited though still powerful manufacturing capacity at home. At the other end of the spectrum, a number of states in the emerging world will augment their production capabilities, becoming essentially manufacturing or body nations. The United States, Japan, and Germany are not virtual states in that they maintain substantial manufacturing capacity; they represent an intermediate political and corporate form. Thus it is important to ask, what happens in a world where less than full virtualization occurs? This topic is treated in chapter 3.

The theory this book offers is fundamentally optimistic. It sketches a future with an ever-widening zone of international peace. This zone, however, may not be large enough for virtual relationships to develop and prosper. There is a case that conflict as usual will continue to determine world politics. This major counterargument will be considered in chapter 4.

Part II examines the market and the state and discusses the implications of the view that states moving toward virtuality must seek a domestic and international balance to sustain their economies. Chapter 5 asks whether states can achieve an appropriate domestic balance between market and regulatory processes. Chapter 6 addresses the even more complex question of whether international political ties can become sufficiently strong and enduring to enforce contracts and facilitate movement of factors of production on a worldwide scale. If the international system cannot maintain such ties, commerce based on globalization will shrivel and subside. (This issue is also addressed in the Appendix, which proposes changes in the traditional theory of international politics to accommodate stable and profitable international orders.)

Part III depicts the impact of virtualization on key nations in world politics: the Far Eastern virtual states, Japan, the United States, Russia and Europe, and China and emerging nations. In each case the process of virtualization is one influence shaping the balance between economic and power motivations in national policy. Political forces are also important in bringing states together or setting them against one another. Chapters 7 through 11 chart this process for key nations whose role will shape the course of the twenty-first century.

Part IV seeks a balance between the factors making for international conflict and those fostering peaceful relations. Only enhancement and growth of the latter factors can sustain virtual ties among countries. If these prerequisites are met (a provisional but feasible assumption), the international and domestic orders will be further remolded in a virtual direction. Within domestic societies, as chapter 12 seeks to show, new intangible products will increase in variety and value. Chapter 13 argues that throughout the world the move to intangibles and virtual connections will revolutionize the relationship of worker and workplace, state and world, politics and economics, education and capital. A virtual world will not be without conflict, but it will represent a step toward a world free of war.

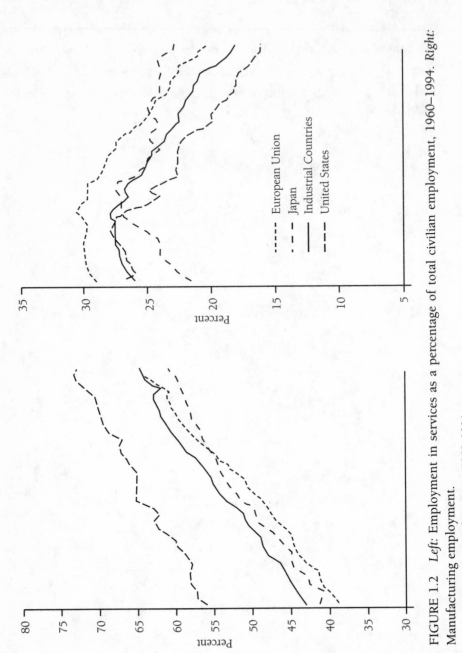

FIGURE 1.2 *Left:* Employment in services as a percentage of total civilian employment, 1960–1994. *Right:* Manufacturing employment.

SOURCE: *OECD Historical Statistics, 1960–1994.*

chapter 2

The Shift from Stocks to Flows

The world economy did not always serve as an adhesive among nations. Historically, economic factors caused war more frequently than they fostered international cooperation. This was particularly true when military operations could capture another nation's productive base. World commerce has evolved through distinct stages, which can be termed *primordial*, *industrial*, and *virtual*. In the primordial phase, land provided the essential ingredients in all economic enterprise.[1] Grain was the primary product. Grown on local plots, it was at first scarcely traded even between neighboring villages. Later, regional political units exchanged grain and other agricultural goods—first locally and then on the high seas.[2] Cities and then states engaged in this trade.

Trade in specialty agriculture produced even greater returns. In the Aegean and the Mediterranean seas at the time of Greece and Rome, oils and wines commanded higher prices than grain, and they could be grown on smaller plots.[3] Later, Venice and Genoa traded oil and wines for the products of northern Europe: herring, iron, hardware, cotton-linen cloths, and silver. The silver could be exchanged for exotic products from the Far East—spices, tea, porcelain—or sugar from the Caribbean. Trade in the products of land assumed ever increasing importance over historic time.

Trade, however, presumed a recognized medium of exchange. It also required a legal framework uniting the trading units. Before the Christian era Roman law regulated merchant exchanges between Rome and outlying societies in Europe. Extended to other nations, the *jus gentium* facilitated international transactions; but distant foreign states, particularly those of different cultures, were often tempted to seize goods rather than trade for them.

To safeguard its control of key products, a rising country frequently sought to establish trading colonies on the shores of the region containing needed commodities.[4] Trade then could become internal—between outpost and metropole of the same country. One did not have to trust foreigners.[5] Venice, Genoa, Portugal, and Holland established such colonies, and their trade benefited accordingly. Britain and France did the same in the eighteenth and nineteenth centuries.

Colonial peoples, however, frequently resented foreign rule as an unwelcome intrusion.[6] Even as they expanded their colonies, trading powers sought other ways of assuring trust at both ends of a trading relationship. The more organized the trading partner in legal and political terms, the more likely that trade could be officially sanctioned between parties with contracts upheld in local courts at both ends of the link. Beginning with Hugo Grotius in the seventeenth century, international commercial law developed to protect this trading relationship.

Countries also used ethnic merchant communities—Jews in Europe, Indians and Chinese in the Orient—to guarantee delivery and payment.[7] The coreligionist or conational in the foreign country would assure his colleague at home that the goods would be received, sent, or paid for in accordance with the contract. When Christianity initially prohibited usury (the lending of money at interest), merchants would arrange payment in a foreign currency that included a premium for the transaction. For a time, foreign interest-bearing transactions were easier to arrange than domestic ones.

Even if local courts in each jurisdiction guaranteed fulfillment of the contract (and they often do not do this even now, especially where courts, as in China, play a political role), shipments still needed to be insured. Regular trade through the Straits of Gibraltar to northern Europe was not established until the fourteenth century. Navigation was complex and uncertain. Latitude calculations were difficult enough, but longitude proved an even more intractable problem until the invention of the chronometer in the eighteenth century.[8] At the beginning of the fifteenth century, captains had to stay in sight of land to find their way. By 1492 they could roughly calculate latitude and navigate at considerable distance from land—to the New World, India, and the Orient. Even then, however, ships were vulnerable to storms, calms, pirates, and uncharted currents. Cargoes might arrive late or not at all. Douglass North observes that one of the important developments in Western trade involved transforming "uncertainty" into "risk" (which could be quantified and thus insured against). Insurance was invented to ameliorate the vicissitudes of commercial transport on the high seas.

Initially a financier shared the risk with a captain in the Italian *commenda* system, with the two dividing profit shares. In the fourteenth century the Venetians began using their informal stock exchange to set premiums for formal maritime insurance. Lloyds of London emulated Venetian practice after 1700. Lloyds and others knew that setting low premiums for a single individual's risky venture would be foolhardy. According to the law of large numbers, however, if an insurance agency combined many such risks together (assuming the risks were unrelated), it could greatly reduce the overall uncertainty and generally lower premiums. As the risks of trade lessened over the centuries, nations became more willing to rely on it—a very important trend, as we shall see. The law of large numbers also became the principle of bank lending as it emerged from Renaissance Florence.

At first the trade thus insured did not inhibit war but rather provided an incentive to wage it. Since exotic products could only be grown in certain locations, the capture of tropical or subtropical land promised great economic returns. Trade in the products of land in this way stimulated the development of empires. By expanding territorially, a large imperial country could acquire the products in greatest demand and thereby enrich itself. Countries fought one another to annex productive land in Europe and overseas. Spain, France, and Britain competed for territory in North and South America, the Far East, and India.[9]

The situation changed when the products of land were challenged by the machine-made goods of the Industrial Revolution. This marked the second stage in the evolution of world commerce. As new textiles and machinery poured from English and continental factories and railroads proliferated, the incentive to acquire new land lessened to some extent. Capital (and machine capital) rose in value relative to land as a factor of production.

Factories could be placed almost anywhere, presuming that transport could carry raw materials to them and take finished goods away. Particular parcels of land thus became somewhat less important. But machine production depended on energy. Mills ran on water power, but factories usually needed steam power, which came from burning coal. Machinery, moreover, was made of iron or steel, and thus countries building factories needed sources of iron ore. The products of land thus ultimately turned out to be very important in the industrial age. As factories converted from coal to oil power after the mid nineteenth century, possession of key minerals became even more important. In World Wars I and II highly developed industrial nations battled over the possession of land. They needed oil, coal, iron, and even sources of food. Few countries had sufficient supplies within their own national territory. The two most internationally pacific and isolated major powers in 1939—the United States and Russia—were those that already possessed key raw materials, agriculture, and oil. The aggressors, Germany and Japan, were countries that needed to import scarce raw materials to sustain their industries. Thus the partial shift to capital and machine capital as factors of production did not produce peace among nations.

Consider the following example. Suppose the products nations wanted derived from factors of production that were entirely mobile. Would they engage in military combat to get these products? One rarely hears nowadays of a war caused by an attempt to capture the funds of another country. Unlike gold, today's money can be transferred away in the blink of an eye. Only occasionally do nations seek to capture the labor force of another nation. Captured peoples are likely to emigrate when they can or work sullenly and ineffectively for the foreign occupier, a problem Israel, for instance, faces with the Palestinian populations of the West Bank and Gaza. If nations sought a particular piece of information, they might attempt a quick military raid or seek to spy on an opponent in possession of the vital secret—but one does not make war to capture information as a generalized factor of production. Microsoft and Intel are national assets, but unlike gold, they cannot be seized and manipulated for foreign purposes without their consent.[10] Their creative originality must be uncoerced.

If the most important factors of production are so much more mobile than armies or navies, they are a deterrent to war. Invaders cannot seize and hold mobile factors: they slip away. As the importance of territory lessens relative to other factors, the incentive to engage in military operations becomes smaller. We are now entering such an age. The third phase is the process of virtualization.

This does not mean that raw materials are no longer important, only that they are less significant than they once were. We have already seen that commodities—goods derived from land—have fallen in value relative to industrial goods and services. When commodities were highly valued in the nineteenth century, trade took place primarily between industrial and agricultural producers. Today the highest valued trade takes place between industrial producers. The inter-industry trade of yesteryear has given way to intra-industry commerce. In the process, agriculture and minerals have become relatively less valuable while manufacturing and services have risen to new heights. As tariffs have declined, the number of commodity and oil producers has increased, creating competition in world markets. As long as countries have faith in their easy access to commodities through world trade, they do not have to possess them at home. Thus three distinct but reinforcing trends reduce the incentive to wage war for land: the rise of services relative to manufacturing as a source of wealth; the broad and increasing availability of agricultural and mineral commodities reflected in their falling real prices; and the increasingly fluid and mobile character of the major factors of production.

Stocks and Flows

When capital's importance rises relative to land and service industries rise in importance relative to manufacturing (in the sense that the return to service industries is higher than the return to manufacturing),[11] we lay the basis for virtualization. Yet there is another important point that differentiates the present from the past. In the past, nations wished to hold stocks of goods. Adam Smith, the great eighteenth-century economist, believed that national wealth was measured by a country's possession of such stocks. Attacking his mercantilist opponents, Smith argued that imports added to national prosperity by augmenting stocks. He did not favor enhancing exports and minimizing imports. Following Smith and later economists, many national leaders sought to expand their access to stocks. One means of doing so, of course, was through international trade—but it could also be accomplished by war. To be sure, warfare destroys goods. Industrial equipment, populations, and buildings may be devastated by military operations. If trade does not produce the desired access to stocks, however, war remains an option.

Japan faced this choice in 1940. Having invaded much of northern and eastern China, Japan could not sustain its occupation without additional resources. But because of the invasion, Europe and America had embargoed Japan from trade in scrap steel, oil, and raw materials. So Japan decided to strike Southeast Asia to find the necessary sources of energy and minerals to maintain its position in China. It occupied Malaya, the Philippines, the Dutch East Indies, French Indo-China, and Thailand.[12] To prevent an American challenge to this expansion, Japan also struck Pearl Harbor—the base of the U.S. Pacific fleet—thereby bringing the United States into the war. It never seriously considered withdrawing from China.

Japan wanted command of large stocks of raw materials, food, and oil. Since World War II, however, open trade has made possession of large stocks less important. If a country could be sure of getting stocks through international commerce, it would worry less about maintaining huge stockpiles at home. When nations came to understand this, the security of flows began to take precedence over the physical possession of stocks. For modern nations this has emerged as an important truth. The key issue then became how to influence the flows of stocks in and out of the country. Today the countries with the greatest influence in world politics are those that command flows of purchasing power, goods, and factors of production into and out of their economies. Nations' views about stocks have come to resemble the Japanese just-in-time system of inventory management: they prefer speedy delivery of needed goods over the cost of maintaining large standing inventories. Rather than insisting on unencumbered possession of stocks, nations have settled for access to flows.

The Virtualization Process in Modern History

This shift represents a milestone in the evolution of the world economy. For many countries in the fifteenth to eighteenth centuries, trade flows were far less important than national possession of raw materials, population, and factors of production. There were periods in which countries thought briefly about becoming *trading states*—nations whose vocation was the pursuit of trade rather than military-political expansion, but these interludes did not last.[13] At the end of the eighteenth century, for instance, the conquest of empire encountered a temporary blockage. The American colonies revolted against Great Britain. France could not conquer more territory in the New World and indeed assisted the colonists in their struggle for independence from England. For a brief moment trade—rather than empire—beckoned.

The French Revolution and the rise of Napoleon, however, completely changed the equation. French nationalism sanctioned new military techniques that allowed French armies to conquer much of Europe. Though France did not expand abroad, Napoleonic militarism brought French metropolitan rule to other countries. Local conquest was very successful for a time.

After the defeat of Napoleon in 1814–15, Great Britain installed a new system of international relations. Following the British example, countries aimed at industrialization at home and cooperation abroad. These objectives were partly enshrined and protected in the Concert of Europe, which functioned from 1815 to 1848. Continental nations following the British model underwent domestic political transformation, and a series of new liberal states emerged from the revolutions of 1830 and 1848. But these revolutions were not universal, and they left Europe with conservative unreformed governments in Prussia, Austria, and Russia confronting more liberal regimes in France and England. These ideological differences prevented the Concert of Europe from functioning effectively after 1848.

Equally important, conservative regimes found new means of waging war—means that did not cause domestic disruption. The lightning offensive sustained by railway transport of troops to the front allowed victors to defeat their enemies in a few weeks with limited domestic strife. Successful nationalist wars forged German unity between 1864 and 1871. Dynamic new offensive measures cemented the conservative hold on power in central and Eastern Europe. This was the age when increasing trade and industrialization only made the need for markets and raw materials more compelling. After 1874 nations returned to the imperial quest with a vengeance, seeking markets and raw materials overseas. Even England abandoned Disraeli's previous view that colonies were "a millstone 'round our necks." Trade did not become a surrogate for empire; the pursuit of trade also fostered the acquisition of colonies. Trading states, which had abjured military preoccupations, succumbed once again to the lure of territorial expansion.

World War I did not change this equation appreciably. Though war now became anathema for some states (principally France and Britain), not all renounced it. The inequities of the Versailles settlement allowed Italian and German leaders to rage against its injustice. When economic depression undermined liberal government, Germany embraced a nationalist, not a Marxist, remedy. Hitler came to power on a platform of overturning the international status quo. At the same time, new military techniques of blitzkrieg made it possible to surmount the defensive stalemates of trench warfare; local territorial expansion became feasible once again. Fascist and Communist regimes, moreover, sought to monopolize sources of raw materials and industry. They substituted control of land areas for reliance on a liberal trading order.

After World War II, liberal trade was reinstated on one side of the ideological fence. Within a group of Western and industrial nations led by the United States, a number of countries were able to improve their welfare and economic growth by trade with other nations. Japan and West Germany pioneered in this effort, developing export-led growth strategies that had not been used since England's initial version in the nineteenth century. Within the Western international economy, the protection of trade routes and domestic stability provided a favorable climate for reliance on exports.

This did not occur within the Communist camp. Rather, Russian needs determined trade with its East European satellites. The East European satellites were kept as tributaries to the Soviet economy and did not generally participate in exchange with the West.

After the end of the cold war, an essentially Western and industrial economy extended into the old Soviet and Chinese blocs. China became a Western trading partner. Vietnam was recognized and included. The new countries of Kazakhstan, Uzbekistan, the Ukraine, and the Baltic states reentered the international economy. Key Eastern European countries joined not only NATO but also the European Union.

The expansion and generalization of the trading world at the end of the cold war was not the only transformation. For the first time in world history, countries began to put significant amounts of their domestic production into the territorial confines of other states. Foreign investment had proliferated in the nineteenth century, but between the great powers it was largely portfolio investment. In very few instances did nineteenth-century great powers lodge their production within the economies of other major nations.

Beginning in the 1960s, however, the United States for political as well as economic reasons deliberately put significant amounts of U.S. manufacturing production into Europe. In the 1970s and 1980s Europe and Japan returned the favor, placing production and assembly plants in the United States. In the 1980s the United States further diversified its production to East Asia, with large investments in Singapore, Taiwan, Hong Kong, Malaysia, and Indonesia. Japan moved in the same direction. This process was expanded to include China in the late 1980s and 1990s. Now, at the end of the century some virtual states have most of their production located abroad, and even the United States and Britain—intermediate cases—have sent 20 percent or more of their production abroad. How can this have occurred?

Virtualization is based on the growing importance of capital and capital flows (particularly foreign direct investment) in the world economy. In the nineteenth century, countries invested abroad in stocks and bonds, but (except in their own colonies) they did not generally own foreign manufacturing plants.[14] Today foreign direct investment (the measure of foreign production) has increased much more rapidly than domestic GDP. Carried further in the twenty-first century, these flows offer unprecedented opportunities for economic progress and peace.

There are good economic reasons for downsizing at home. Production abroad guards against the possibility of tariffs in the new manufacturing country and secures access to overseas markets. Labor forces in other countries may be cheaper or more flexible than those at home, though this does not entirely account for the large amount of foreign direct investment in the United States. Investment goes to countries where productivity times labor cost equals or improves on the figure attainable at home. So overseas labor must be productive as well as cheap.

Strictly economic reasons are only part of the story. Investment abroad can always be nationalized—taken over by the host country. Trade routes can be interrupted by military conflict on the sea-lanes. The receiving country may not enforce contracts undertaken with foreign business enterprise. Those who establish production abroad risk their manufacturing assets and the returns they might have earned at home. In other words, foreign direct investment represents a huge gamble on stability and peace within and among countries, both domestically and internationally. It is even more of a gamble because productive investments cannot be sold on a stock exchange. It may take months or

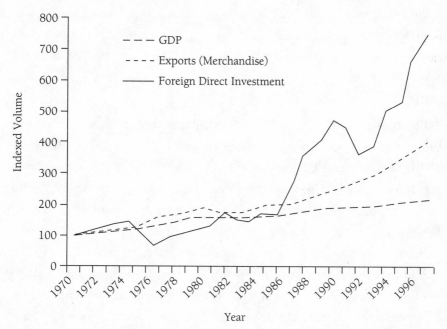

FIGURE 2.1   Relative growth of worldwide GDP, manufacturing exports, and foreign direct investment since 1970.
SOURCE: WTO, UNCTAD and *The Economist,* June 20, 1998, p. 5.

years to find a buyer for foreign tangible assets that have not yielded an appropriate return. That nations could have moved so strongly and forcefully in this direction suggests an atmosphere of domestic and international peace in many parts of the world.

Can such a gamble be sustained? The answer isn't yet clear, but one interesting trend is that the information revolution makes possible corporate control of production at some remove. Factories in the nineteenth century were means of centralizing the control over workers who previously worked in widely disseminated cottage industry. Unless workers were put in one place, their output could not be fully accounted for and monitored by managers or foremen. Now we have indirect control or control by information.[15] We have *virtual foremen* as well as human managers. If local workers communicate with their bosses by phone and E-mail, so can overseas workers and plant managers. Differences in time zones may actually be turned to one's advantage. Subordinates overseas can work "overnight" to produce results ready for the morning meeting in the home office.

The Futility of Size

Yet there is another reason for the emergence of the virtual state and for virtual connections among nations. All states are now too small to control their economic fates. No country's jurisdiction is worldwide. Even the former Soviet Union, with eleven time zones and eleven million square miles, was not large enough to control its economic destiny. In fact despite its vast resources, the Soviet economy by the 1980s was an isolated and ignorant backwater, unable to keep up with the march of technology in the world economy. Nor were Soviet military forces strong enough to conquer and occupy the world or even Afghanistan. The nation's near-continental dimensions did not serve a functional purpose.

Stalin's Soviet Union was not the only elephant in world politics. Great Britain's nineteenth-century empire was large but decentralized. Even as a colony, the government of India did not always agree with the British government and sometimes pursued an independent economic policy. In time, so did the dominion governments of Australia, New Zealand, and South Africa. When the empire gave way to the British Commonwealth of (independent) Nations, it only recognized what long had been the fact.

Hitler's Germany and Napoleon's France also aimed at gigantic empires, at least for their times. Both failed in attempts to conquer Russia. Neither could absorb the Middle East or North Africa. Nineteenth-century U.S. attempts to occupy most of North America reached its limit at the 49th parallel and the Rio Grande. Despite several military victories over Mexico and the cession of California to America, the United States could never occupy Mexico. Great powers attempted to get bigger from the seventeenth century through the first half of the twentieth, but they never got big enough. The increasing industrial might needed to sustain world power made self-sufficiency an ever-receding goal.

In the early modern period the world was a profusion of proto-states: duchies, principalities, bishoprics, as well as kingdoms. More than 500 autonomous units existed within Europe alone. As Charles Tilly shows, by 1900 this number had declined to about twenty-five, with another twenty-five or so in the rest of the world.[16] Since 1900, however, there has been a huge increase in the number of states and a corresponding decline in their size. Almost 200 states inhabit contemporary world politics. How could the size of the state be declining when the problems it faces require an enlarging territorial jurisdiction?

A partial answer to this question has been the pervasive momentum of decolonization together with the national self-determination of peoples. Separatism and nationalism have made foreign rulership less effective than ever. Another partial answer is that as states have become more and more dependent on trade with others for key items of their complex existence, the area that a country would have to control to guarantee possession of everything it needs has become unmanageably large. If minerals, fashions, exotic foods, specialty timbers and textiles, art objects, and energy sources are spread throughout the world, only the conquest of the world will give the requisite satisfaction. Despite the intricate development of weapons of mass destruction, this is impossible. Nations cannot even fully defend themselves against such instruments, let alone use them to extort additional large chunks of land. As economic interdependence has vastly increased the territory one would need to engross, it has also correspondingly diminished the possibility of any single state achieving mastery.

Here the new process of virtualization fully asserts itself. Virtualization is the recognition that territorial size does not solve economic problems. If this is indeed the case, economic access must become the substitute for increasing domain. Rather than augmenting the local scope of political authority, states seek to improve their economies by influencing (and sometimes employing) productive processes in other nations. Instead of enlarging the political scope of the state, leaders now aim to increase the scope of their economies by encouraging them to operate among and within those of other states. This is a difficult and uncertain process, but it is far more cost-effective than trying to conquer the world. It also locks economies together in ways that mere trade did not. Interdependence of production creates a far more solid relationship than interdependence of trade. It forges a tie that is very difficult to break.

The Triumph of Flows

Until the 1980s industrial capital had not transformed the old reliance on stocks into a concern to maximize flows. Although few wars were started to acquire physical capital—machines and factories[17]—and none succeeded in capturing mobile capital, industrialization and foreign trade did not successfully substitute for military force to acquire land.

Yet as self-sufficiency became impossible for even the largest states, land became less important as a factor of production, and isolation became increasingly inimical to industrial competitiveness, the stockpiling strategy grew less and less effective. As long as mastery of stocks was the prime national objective, flows and also the national welfare deriving from them would inevitably be slighted.

Countries began to realize dimly that no nation could get big enough militarily to bring all needed resources within its own national frontiers. As we have seen, for a brief time at the end of the nineteenth century successful imperialism taught that territorial expansion was still possible; yet even the vast British Empire did not enjoy self-sufficiency. Britain was still heavily dependent on trade with regions outside the empire, such as the United States and Latin America.

For a time it appeared that vast agglomerations of power and economic strength would emerge as European nations took over the rest of the world; but the trend toward larger states reversed after World War I. Empires broke up, and colonies were freed after World War II. New nations broke off from older multinational societies. A trend toward political smallness set in, and nearly 200 nations emerged as autonomous units in world politics. These smaller states could not sustain their domestic industry and employment merely by selling at home. They had to export abroad, and they also needed goods that foreigners provided.

Economic openness ultimately contributed to this trend. When the high tariffs and exchange controls of the 1930s finally petered out at the end of

World War II, a whole series of new economic institutions emerged: the International Monetary Fund (IMF), the World Bank (IBRD), the General Agreements on Tariffs and Trade (GATT, now the World Trade Organization, WTO). These organizations opened up trade and payments among nations. Capital controls were gradually dismantled in many developed countries in the sixties, seventies, and eighties, and the European Union moved to install a single currency (the Euro) in 1999.

Military invasion and occupation no longer succeed, and countries can achieve international economic access without force. Land has also ceased to be the most important factor of production. Under these conditions international flows take on new significance. Stocks at home are no longer sufficient. Even the largest countries need flows of capital, goods, and labor to make ends meet.

Nor has this transformation been unprofitable. Investment abroad frequently yields higher returns than investment at home. Labor may sometimes gain a higher return working in another country. Thus we have witnessed the movement of capital to southern and eastern regions of the globe as labor has surged north and west.

In the 1930s industrial growth at home outpaced the growth of international trade and the flow of capital. After World War II the growth of international trade increased much more rapidly than national gross domestic product. In recent years the flow of foreign direct investment has risen even faster than the international trade in goods and is much higher than the growth in GDP. The income from international flows is rising more rapidly than that from purely domestic stocks. Information technology carries this process even further. Increasingly the most important factors of production—the mobile factors—have created more value than the fixed factors; and the most mobile—information—has created the greatest value. It is therefore not surprising that international flows are beginning to dwarf the importance of domestic stocks.

Flows and the Virtualization Process

The virtualization process reflects the history of political, military, and economic developments described in this chapter. As states become smaller relative to the problems they must surmount, economic flows partly come to substitute for governmental dictates. National jurisdictions are too small to solve international economic problems. For military as well as political reasons, states cannot generally become larger. If states cannot grow, they can nonetheless use the productive capacities of other nations. Virtualization is the result, with the risky placement of production within the confines of other nations. Since this placement is becoming more reciprocal, however, no single state emerges as master of its fate. As nations invest abroad, they also seek to lure relevant foreign factors of production into the home economy. The result has been far greater returns than if the factors had stayed at home. The world economy and also national states have prospered as a result.

chapter 3

How States Become Virtual

All major developed economies have moved toward becoming virtual states—centralizing headquarters functions at home and production abroad—but most have not gone all the way.[1] Three possible outcomes exist along the virtualization continuum. The first is the attainment of virtual status. Some countries will move most of their manufacturing overseas. The Southeast Asian tigers—Hong Kong, Singapore, and Taiwan—will largely manufacture their products in mainland China and in nearby Malaysia and Indonesia. At home they will concentrate on research and product design. Many states, however, will not go this far. A second group of countries—including the United States, Germany, France, and Britain—will begin more and more to specialize in high-level international and domestic services while retaining considerable production capacity at home. The returns from such services are rising relative to manufacturing. In these countries corporate downsizing has already focused production on higher return or specialty manufacture, with a consequent rise in the service sector. In the diversified and extremely sophisticated manufacturing that continues, these increasingly service-oriented countries are seeking economies of scope to accompany or transcend the old economies of scale.[2] They will move to shift lower-end production overseas. Thus even "intermediate" countries will begin to use foreign direct investment to establish production in another country.[3]

A third group of nations—principally in the developing world—will drop their previous focus on raw materials and agriculture and create major manufacturing capabilities.[4] China, Brazil, Mexico, and India will be among this group. These countries will constitute a cadre of body nations that will do the producing for the rest of the world. Such countries require new infrastructure—power grids, transportation links, port facilities, highways, and communication networks—to make manufacturing possible. They will need to develop energetic workforces with enough training to operate the sophisticated Western and Japanese plants that will spring up in their midst. Africa will at some point join this group. Thus three different results emerge from the virtualization process: (1) full virtualization, (2) an intermediate form, and (3) the development of new manufacturing nations. This chapter will concentrate on the second and third outcomes.[5]

The Forms of Offshore Manufacturing

Though they are not fully virtual, intermediate nations work hand in hand with their own corporations, labor, and education systems to achieve greater effectiveness and competitiveness, both nationally and internationally. The partly virtualized state also works with foreign corporations. The corporations that enter one's economy are Janus-faced. To a degree, foreign corporations operating in a country are an extension of foreign state interests in that they seek to achieve purposes of their home governments. Yet they also have to respond to the policies and market conditions of the host society. Foreign corporations are subject to influence by the host government, which through them can affect the policy of the home government. Direct investment abroad represents a corporate belief in the success of the host country's economy. It reflects a basic consistency between the international policy of home and foreign governments. Though foreign corporations reflect foreign influence, they also contribute to the host country's prosperity. As Robert Reich points out, they are a part of "us," in that they contribute to domestic employment, purchasing power, and the technology base.[6] Foreign businesses represent an essential input into domestic economic and technological learning. They train workers and employers in the host country on new methods of production.

What is true of Japanese or French firms in the United States is also true of American corporations abroad. U.S. corporations and work-forces are American-oriented wherever they may be operating, but they are also economically constrained to reflect host economic interests. Corporations operating overseas are the essential link between head nations and body nations; they are transmission belts that provide for mutual influence between design nations and production nations. They also represent incipient political as well as economic stakes in the well-being of a foreign country. Factor flows of capital, labor, technology, and information between nations lay the basis for reciprocal influence.[7]

Manufacturing may move to other countries in four different ways. First, a firm can make a deal with another corporation to manufacture its products, forming an industrial alliance, as GM and Toyota did at their NUMMI plant in Fremont, California. Second, one firm can take over or merge with another, creating joint production facilities. Third, corporations may simply set up manufacturing subsidiaries overseas. Finally, in a novel industrial development corporations may create *foundries*, or generalized production facilities, to manufacture for more than one other company. In each instance shared production sites come to represent the leading edge of economic innovation. In many areas of manufacturing, including automobiles, textiles, and memory chips, worldwide production capabilities exceed current demand. This over-capacity fosters a further consolidation of producing facilities.[8]

INDUSTRIAL ALLIANCES

Industrial alliances permit one company to benefit from the manufacturing talents and markets of another. Associations between different international companies do not always last, particularly if they are competitors in other product lines. Nevertheless, industrial alliances are usually highly profitable, and firms wish to avoid duplicating production if they can. Cummins Engine, for example, maintains several international alliances to spread the large costs of engine development. It has joint ventures in China and India and a joint production agreement to make large engines for electricity generation with Wartsila of Finland; it also makes small engines in partnership with Komatsu of Japan. Industrial alliances nonetheless do not always succeed in producing goods abroad. Companies must have a great deal of trust in each other for such alliances to prosper over the long term.[9] Company alliances depend on and help to create national alliances.

MERGERS

Another means of saving on production capability is the creation of formal mergers between foreign and domestic firms. Mergers are a radical solution; they eliminate competition and usually give one firm direction of the newly consolidated unit. The 1998 merger of Chrysler and Mercedes (Daimler-Benz),[10] for instance, left Mercedes in the driver's seat even though joint headquarters were established in both Detroit and Stuttgart. The merger served the needs of both companies. Chrysler needed a radical injection of cash and new markets. It had given up making cars in Europe more than a decade earlier and wished to develop new markets there. Mercedes had significant luxury car sales in the United States but no product line of medium-priced cars or sport utility vehicles. Chrysler's vans and U.S. markets offered Mercedes a new opportunity in America; Mercedes' markets and production facilities gave Chrysler new possibilities in Europe. The merger made it unnecessary for either company to build new production facilities in the other country.[11]

Ford and Jaguar, GM and Saab, and Ford and Volvo also found synergies in shared production and markets. Volkswagen (VW) and Rolls Royce (Vickers) seized on similar common interests in merging their firms, though BMW got the Rolls Royce name. With its new Bentley automobiles, Volkswagen will begin to compete with Mercedes and Lexus for the high-end luxury market in the United States and Europe. Rolls–Bentley gained new market outlets on the continent. In Ford's case, Jaguar added a luxury and sporty dimension that its Lincoln marque had not provided. Saab offered GM a specialized performance vehicle for American and worldwide markets. As GM moved to acquire Saab, Ford moved to purchase the auto production of Volvo. Jaguar, Saab, and Volvo had not been able fully to penetrate the U.S. market on their own. In each of these cases we see attempts to come to terms with overcapacity in the auto industry as a whole. All of these mergers allowed companies to convert underused facilities to manufacture different brands, rather than build new factories. Mergers thus allowed these firms to expand their global reach with relatively little risk.

Given the research and design skills of modern companies, the development and marketing of new products presents no insuperable problem. Yet building additional production lines where acceptance of your product is not assured is a big gamble. For these reasons, return on equity is greatest and risk is less if companies take over or merge with other firms. Mergers also solve the problem of trust between independent competitors; one leadership emerges to direct the merged firm.

SUBSIDIARIES

Sometimes a company decides against merger and opts to set up producing plants within a foreign market, but without a partner. Typically these subsidiaries achieve lower costs than at home. They also avoid tariffs around the export market. Honda operates subsidiaries in Marysville, Ohio, and Toyota in Frankfort, Kentucky. GM has its Vauxhall subsidiary in Britain and Opel in Germany. It is building new subsidiaries in Brazil and Eastern Europe. Ford has German Taunus, Ford/UK, and factories in Spain. Both companies are seeking to create new subsidiaries in Latin America and East Asia.

As a subunit of the home firm, subsidiaries avoid the complications of mergers. They work best in countries with a similar legal and commercial system and allow parent companies to extend an efficient and cheap producing mechanism to new markets. Since economies of scale are attained at fairly low production rates and components can be sent from the parent plant, the home firm can monitor and control costs better than when they are relying on the production of a partner company.

FOUNDRIES

The establishment of foundries represents still another solution to the problem of competition between allied industrial units. Foundries have no proprietary product but exist as production facilities for design firms. Few publishers own their own manufacturing facilities. Available printers in such places as Kingsport, Tennesee, Slovenia, Hong Kong, and Bangladesh manufacture books from text and design specifications provided by publishers in New York, Frankfurt, and London. The same is true in computer chips. Taiwan has pioneered in the establishment of foundries for semiconductor companies. Working on a contract basis for Silicon Valley firms, Taiwan foundries turn out specialized semiconductors made to designer specifications. The advantage of mergers and foundries is that they increase trust and reduce the uncertainty involved in industrial alliances. The issue of trust is an important one,[12] and companies go to great lengths to be sure they can rely on their foreign associates. Given the difference in corporate cultures, companies understand that the establishment of long-term concord is not always an easy process.

Body Nations: Where Manufacturing Will Be Located

While many developed nations are focusing more on services, an opposite trend proceeds among some emerging countries. Economies that once depended on coffee, cocoa, timber, or banana exports are now diversifying toward manufacturing. São Paulo is one of the major manufacturing centers in Latin America, and it will become more powerful still as Brazil opens up to foreign direct investment. Mexico is now adding inland factories to the *maquiladoro* assembly plants sited along the Rio Grande. Guandong, Dalian, and other coastal provinces used to represent the main production locations in China for Western and Japanese factories. These coastal strips boasted an energetic and not untrained workforce that could be mated with Western capital. Created initially as "new economic zones," they had considerable latitude and freedom from Beijing's control. Now, foreign investment is moving inland to find new workforces at cheaper wage rates. As Chinese state-owned industries are restructured, closed, or sold to the public, a worker surplus will emerge to staff even more foreign and Japanese plants, thereby insuring China's future as the quintessential body nation.

After Brazil, Mexico, and China will come India, Bangladesh, and perhaps, ultimately, Burma. In East Asia the tiger nations will further shift their production to regional body nations: from Singapore to Indonesia and Malaysia, from Hong Kong and Taiwan to China. Korea will produce more in India. As it becomes more service-oriented, Thailand will diversify some of its production to Burma or even Cambodia. Body nations will have to keep their currency values low to stay competitive. The Far Eastern financial crisis put a great deal of pressure on the Chinese yuan, as the baht (Thailand), the ringgit (Malaysia), the rupiah (Indonesia), and the Korean won were devalued. Japan's devaluation of the yen also made it difficult for Far Eastern body nations to maintain their efficient manufacturing plants at full employment.

In time Africa will discover new manufacturing possibilities. South Africa already has a well-developed but high-cost industry; it will have to be modernized if it is to serve other nations. As government policy stabilizes, Ghana, Nigeria, Uganda, Kenya, and Zimbabwe will in time offer productive bases for Western and Japanese firms. Mauritius is already operating as a manufacturing unit. In Latin America, Brazil and Argentina have moved beyond specialty crops such as coffee, grain, and beef to produce manufactured goods for foreign firms. Chile and Peru also will join their number. In Asia, Bangladesh ultimately will join India as a manufacturing powerhouse.

This is not to say these nations will not also acquire some service industries. India is developing new service industries in Bangalore and elsewhere to serve clients in Silicon Valley and Texas. Indian programmers are much cheaper than their Western counterparts. Indeed, what India is doing shows the difficulty of making fine distinctions between services and manufacturing. Technically India "manufactures" software, but the knowledge component of the product is so high that Bangalore computer programming firms almost can be categorized as a service industry.

The Importance of Trust

All three forms of states—head nations, mixed environments, and body nations—rely on trust between foreign and domestic corporations and foreign and domestic governments. It is not enough for companies in different countries to develop lasting relationships. These ties will not endure if their home countries become enemies. For industrial alliances, mergers, or subsidiaries to succeed links between states must duplicate and reinforce those between companies. Governments hesitate to promote corporate linkages until political relationships have become well developed and predictable. They may require formal military alliances between investor and recipient nations or a de facto settlement of past international disputes between the two. Similarly, investors require political stability to sustain their willingness to invest.

The most effective international relationship is probably that between the United States and Europe. America invested in Europe on a large scale after the North Atlantic Treaty Organization (NATO) had established a protective shield against attack, and European states had learned to trust the United States. As American confidence in Europe rose in the 1960s, the first wave of U.S. foreign direct investment entered the continent. Reciprocally, however, European investment in the United States awaited a fall in the value of the dollar and greater understanding of the vagaries of the U.S. market. Large-scale European investment in the United States began only in the 1970s and 1980s. By then European companies knew how to please state governors and legislatures who in turn would pave the way for their plants, and local politicians readily reciprocated.

Other regions of the world evidence similar requirements. U.S. and European foreign direct investment in Latin America required greater political and economic stability there, which only emerged in the second half of the 1980s. While United Fruit, Coca-Cola, and other companies had long-term investments in Latin America, Mexico and Brazil did not want foreign manufacturing counterparts. Undemocratic Latin governments pursuing high-tariff industrialization rebuffed American and European political and economic overtures.

Foreign investment in the Far East also depended on an end to the Vietnam war and a settlement of rivalries in Southeast Asia. These only occurred in the late 1980s and early 1990s. From the Asian side as well, ex-Communist nations and even liberalizing Communist regimes had to be willing to seek external investment. This did not happen until the Association of Southeast Asian nations reached out to new members and forged stronger political ties among countries. By the early 1990s East Asian economies including China were ready to receive productive investment from America and Europe. Only Korea and Japan held back.

More dependable security relationships made this investment possible. During the bipolar era that arose after World War II, foreign bases were necessary to protect one side or the other in the global contest. After 1990 the end of the cold war led the Philippines to request American troops to leave. Yet this did not occur in Northeast Asia, where the possibility of a new Korean War led South Korea and Japan to continue the U.S. base structure. Even China saw U.S. Pacific bases as a long-term reassurance against the rebirth of Japanese militarism. As Russia dropped its former Communist satellites in East Asia, particularly Vietnam, they needed to find other means of support. Gradually, the Association of Southeast Nations (ASEAN) and the Asia-Pacific Community (APEC), which included the United States, Canada, and Australia as well as China and Japan, emerged to forge a Pacific-wide consensus on peaceful relationships. By the beginning of the 1990s there was no danger of war limiting economic ties.

This did not mean setbacks could not occur. Indian and Pakistani nuclear tests resulted in official sanctions on the two countries' loans, investments, and trade; but they also signaled to private investors that the Indian subcontinent could become less hospitable, politically and militarily. An arms race between Pakistan and India leading to greater deficits and inflation in both countries would not reassure foreign money managers.[13] In 1998 both nations were already spending too much on arms and debt service, and Pakistan was nearly bankrupt. In a different way, political turmoil and change in Indonesia also temporarily scared investors away and toppled successively the stock market, the rupiah, and then General Suharto. It would not be until political stability was restored—internally in the Indonesian case and internationally in the Indo-Pakistani case—that foreign investments would be resumed on a significant scale. The establishment of the Euro as the European currency in 1999 had a further stabilizing effect. Foreign investors could go into fringe areas like southern Italy and Spain because the returns would come in the form of hard currency Euros, not lire or pesetas. Again, political agreements among eleven European Union countries paved the way for a deeper economic association with the outside world.

The Worldwide Trend Toward Services

As nations move production overseas, their domestic industrial establishments are downsized. We see this throughout the developed world. Service production is rising, and manufacturing is declining in relative terms in every major developed country. This is not because developed countries can no longer produce goods efficiently; it is because services offer a higher return on investment. IBM, GE, Ford, and even GM have become more highly involved in design, consulting, and financial services. Daimler, Siemens, and Asea-Brown-Boveri (ABB) are in part information companies. Public relations, entertainment (films, music, broadcasting), and consulting firms reap large profits from services. Software, CDs, and video disks can be physically shipped, but the intangibles of creative design and programming embedded in them are what determines their value. The cost of manufacturing and packaging a CD disk is about fifty cents, but one can pay $50 for it in the megastore. The recompense to knowledge and creativity is thus vastly increasing on a worldwide basis.

As the auto industry illustrates, in some realms of manufacturing there is already abundant capacity, indeed overcapacity. In these sectors, countries and corporations are extremely reluctant to add production lines. Thus new corporate relationships that allow existing production facilities to be shared for different purposes are a logical and economic outcome. Companies then can concentrate on designing and marketing new products. Service functions increase proportionately.

Many economists once believed that services were nontradable items, furnished entirely by the home country. This has turned out to be false.

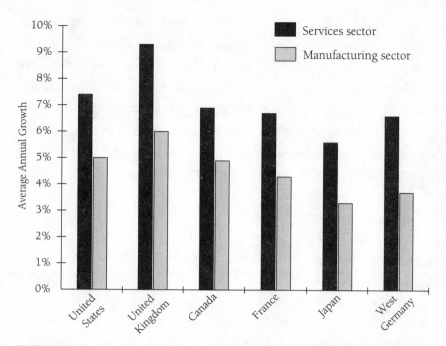

FIGURE 3.1   Average annual growth in value added by sector, 1984–1995.
SOURCE: *United Nations Statistical Yearbook*; *OECD Directory of National Accounts*, Vol. 2, 1997; World Bank, World Tables, 1995.

The GATT Uruguay Round focused a great deal of attention on opening the markets of developing countries to service exports from the developed world.[14] Developing countries initially resisted this pressure, but as they developed service exports of their own in software, programming skills, billing, and office management, they became more sympathetic to free trade arguments. In return, developing country markets will increasingly host foreign direct investment in services. Western service exports in banking, finance, and insurance will spread to East Asia, Japan, and China. The Far Eastern financial crisis has spurred this process by opening up partially closed economies to purchases by Western firms.

Laggard Countries

Service exports, foreign direct investment, and production abroad can flourish if the countries involved enjoy political stability and dependable relationships. Where political and economic conditions are uncertain, however, foreign investors hesitate. They invest in mineral or oil production, commodities that easily can be sold on world markets. Russia's natural wealth and the resources of Kazakhstan, Azerbaijan, and Uzbekistan have attracted foreign capital even though commercial, legal, and police systems to protect those investments remain primitive. In China investors have concentrated on short-term projects executed in the coastal provinces and hopefully insulated from political pressures, but they have shied away from long-term projects. In the short term, foreign companies can build power plants and other infrastructure, extract early returns, and then hand over the completed facility to the Chinese government. Hong Kong entrepreneurs have specialized in such BOT (build, operate, and transfer) arrangements with China. Beyond Hong Kong, however, China will enjoy similarly enduring economic relationships with foreign countries only after it has begun to establish long-term political, legal, and economic stability both domestically and in its relations with its neighbors.[15] Domestic problems are the main reason countries lag economically. Modernizing political and legal systems takes time, but regional and international bodies can sometimes assist in the process. By specifying the internal economic and political conditions for countries wanting to join, the European Union exerts a powerful reforming influence on potential member nations in Eastern Europe. The North Atlantic Alliance has done the same. Before they can join, new members of NATO have been required to settle disputes with other countries. ASEAN members do not engage in force regionally or with one another. The International Monetary Fund, sometimes too strictly, lays down the economic requirements for receiving assistance from international lending agencies.[16] Private investors do not come in until they receive a go-ahead from the IMF. Thus, international pressures exerted by political alliances and financial agencies encourage reform and economic stability in emerging nations. Without these organizations, internal change and development would take much longer.

─────────

The virtualization process has a range of outcomes. At one extreme it creates the virtual state, a nation that lodges most of its production outside its borders. Yet large industrial countries that retain significant manufacturing capabilities also are affected by virtualization. Such nations recognize the advantages of performing their low-cost manufacturing abroad and want to gain the new profits to be made in service industries. At the same time, emerging states are beginning to forego commodity production and are moving to manufacturing. Thus a new partnership evolves as head nations forge new relationships with body nations to produce abroad. The process of virtualization depends on existing international relationships and also strengthens them. Not only has the national market become the international market, domestic production has now become international production.

chapter 4

The Conflict-As-Usual Thesis

While this book offers a fundamentally optimistic view of economic and political relations in the twenty-first century, this does not mean that peace will prevail among all nations.[1] In continents and regions where land remains the major factor of production and power, war will continue; but where virtualization takes hold, conflict should moderate.

Some do not accept this view. Certain political and military critics see traditional rivalries recurring as they did after World Wars I and II. They believe nuclear weapons will continue to spread. Changes in the pattern of comparative advantage and international trade will accentuate, not retard, economic conflict among nations.[2] Some conclude that the two leading international powers, whoever they are, are destined to struggle for primacy by waging war.[3] Others think unstable domestic systems will contribute to international conflict. One version of this argument contends that inequalities within nations will lead to domestic upheaval or political revolution. (The traditional Marxist argument, for example, makes this claim.) Still others believe that economic nationalism will prevent the dispersal of a country's manufacturing plant.[4] Domestic uncertainties, mercantilism, or conflict will then generate international tensions that will accelerate if the inequality between states continues to grow. Sooner or later, it is said, there will be military conflict between poorer and richer nations.[5] Finally, critics claim that economic and technological vulnerabilities stem from participation in a globalized international system, perhaps paving the way for international terrorism. We will examine all of these arguments in the second part of this chapter.

First, however, there is an important contention that needs to be addressed. Some observers claim that the promise of the virtual state will be thwarted by conflicts between corporations and governments and between governments and people.[6] In this view corporations will not follow or work with their governments, nor will governments be influenced by their companies. Liberal democrats sometimes reject the notion that business and political leaders can work together to improve international economic outcomes.[7] They believe governments must control profits, regulate working conditions and other labor matters, and stimulate the economy to ensure full employment. Corporations are seen as the enemies of this strategy. Some remember that President Franklin Roosevelt renounced government cooperation with "economic royalists." (Of course, Roosevelt also famously cooperated with them in his National Recovery Administration.) Furthermore, many conservatives also find government–business cooperation implausible. Free marketeers denounce government intervention and do not expect business leaders to offer cooperation to political leaders. (The same corporate leaders of course also expect acquiescence and facilitation of their activities by governments.)

These arguments are mistaken. In every modern country alliances are gradually being forged between those who direct flows of factors of production and those in the political realm.[8] A country's economic success is now as important as its military success once was. Since economic progress cannot depend only on selling at home, further economic growth requires penetration of foreign markets. In these circumstances government officials have become economic ambassadors. As numerous U.S. Commerce Department missions have attested, government helps business to attain its objectives overseas.[9] French, German, and British businesses also rely on their governments for crucial assistance in selling abroad. In turn, in all these countries the political state also encourages foreigners to move operations into the country, creating favorable economic conditions for their entrance. The econo-mization of the political state already has begun.

Because it sees itself as a loser in this process, the labor movement has not fully understood its benefits. Labor organizations in such societies are much less internationalized than are business and government. Instead of considering new and positive opportunities for their own working people in other countries, labor unions resist inflows of foreigners. Instead of moving up the manufacturing chain to higher-level production jobs, labor wants to maintain its hold on lower-level positions. Until very recently at least, the labor movement in developed societies has been the least prepared of modern factors of production to respond to new economic opportunities at home and abroad. At the same time, foreign labor in emerging countries is quite ready to emigrate to take advantage of jobs in developed nations.

In the end, the forces propelling such shifts seem virtually irresistible.[10] Economic incentives inexorably pull in new migrants.[11] At the same time, the attraction of overseas jobs for domestic labor will begin to generate an outflow of manpower. When opportunities beckon abroad, well-trained labor and middle management will consider pulling up stakes, as capital has long done. Labor shortages in any area are likely to be made up: first, through international flows; second, through retraining and education of new generations of worker-managers. As labor grows increasingly mobile, the old incentive to acquire new labor supplies by conquering territory eventually will disappear. Factor mobility will begin to compensate for the fixity and permanence of state frontiers.

This does not mean that labor will send many of its workers abroad; some of its ties will be virtual ones. Accountants, data clerks, and software producers do not have to leave their country to serve foreign employers. They can work on international communication and data networks. American computer and software companies can transmit their work to Indian programmers to complete overnight. U.S. insurance companies can do their paperwork in Dublin with no movement of personnel. Foreign companies can also use U.S. programmers and databases.

If this is true, the state can work with factor flows to improve its population's living standards; but three countertrends must still be addressed. The first is that conflicts within states may limit any movement toward domestic prosperity and international peace. The second is that international terrorism may disable or prevent domestic gains. Finally, domestic conflict or not, it always is possible that new hostilities will break out among states, using up economic products in wasteful expressions of international violence.

The Prospect of Internal Conflict

The virtual state cannot prosper or extend its leadership if social conflict cuts its economic links with other nations. There are at least two different versions of the domestic conflict thesis. According to one, ethnic and cultural differences will cause civil strife between population groups. If this spreads, nothing short of a new imperialism will contain it.[12] According to the second, increasing economic inequality and repeated recessions will put richer and poorer citizens at odds.[13] The danger of terrorism by political groups would rise in either instance. In both cases chronic domestic tension and violence would disable governments and ultimately foment international as well as internal conflict. Then factor flows to other nations would be cut back or terminated altogether. Are these prospects likely to be realized?

DOMESTIC ETHNIC CONFLICT

In the world of the 1990s no one needs to be persuaded of the dangers of ethnic conflict. In Kosovo, Rwanda-Burundi, Bosnia, Somalia, the Sudan, India, and Pakistan, ethnic conflict has roiled internal and external politics. In Afghanistan contending Muslim factions cannot agree on a division of the country. Indian peasants in Chiapas resent their rule by Mexico City. Chechnya Muslims have won de facto autonomy from Moscow. Even Quebecois seek a separate state within or apart from Canada, and the Inuit people want independence from Quebec. How did these apparently similar events occur? Are they likely to be replicated on a wide scale elsewhere?

Ethnic conflict rises when federal arrangements linking ethnic groups collapse or when economic conditions deteriorate, affecting parties differentially. In Yugoslavia and Bosnia, both occurred.[14] The loss of income in the old federal Yugoslavia imposed burdens on the constituent republics of Slovenia, Croatia, and Bosnia that they did not want to bear. Thus they seceded, one after another. Their minorities, however, protected under the multinational federal government of President Tito, now lost that protection.[15] This posed few problems in Slovenia, with a largely homogeneous population, but it caused ethnic conflict in both Croatia, which had a large Serbian minority, and Bosnia, where a slight majority of Muslims confronted Croatians and Serbians. The rump Yugoslav government initially helped the Serbs militarily, and they were able to take over 49 percent of Bosnia. Croatia, though, largely triumphed over the Serbs in its own territories. In each case an ethnic population questioned whether it could be fairly ruled by an alien cultural group.

An equivalent process took place in Rwanda-Burundi. When the economy went sour in Rwanda, the majority Hutus took vengeance on the Tutsi group, which previously ruled in Kigali. When Tutsis rallied their forces and expelled many of the Hutu killers, the latter lingered in refugee camps, readying their forces to strike again. After Tutsis from Burundi, abetted by the Ugandan leader Musuveni, took up their cause the Tutsis carried their ethnic thrust all the way to Zaire, installing Laurent Kabila to succeed General Mobutu Sese Seko.

In 1989 Slobodan Milosevic revoked Kosovo's autonomy and reimposed Serbian rule on the majority Albanian Muslim population. People resisted, and dissident elements took military action against rule from Belgrade. In response to NATO bombing Milosevic carried ethnic cleansing to a new height, expelling the Muslims and destroying their homes.

In Sri Lanka the majority Sinhalese population has discriminated, economically and politically, against the minority Tamils in the eastern part of the island. The Sinhalese government has not yet been able to find a formula to reconcile Tamils with the existing order; it has neither permitted the Tamils independence nor accommodated their economic demands.

Some observers have claimed that these communal conflicts portend a worldwide "clash of civilizations." Now that cold war tensions are over, the argument goes, the future dividing lines in world politics will be between religions and cultures, with Western Christianity left as a minority backwater among world civilizations.[16] Muslims, Confucians, Orthodox Christians, and perhaps Hindus will represent the coming spearhead of ethnic change. In particular, a Confucian-Muslim alliance will unite China with the Middle East, creating a huge multicontinental challenge to Europe, Japan, and the United States. Although they may not unite against a common enemy, dissenting cultural groups cannot be drawn together by economic linkages, so it is argued, because economic interests take a distant second place to cultural and religious concerns. By implication, then, countries of one culture or ethnic background cannot expect to produce their goods within the society of a different background. Trade between ethnic rivals will be curtailed or terminated.

Others claim that new tectonic clashes will take place between cultural factions in small and weak states, necessitating the rise of empire to discipline their outbreak.[17] The United Nations, NATO, the European Union, and the United States will be powerless to stem the flood of such conflicts. This explosion of hatred will not be contained by rational means but only by imperial political force.

The "clash of civilizations," however, has been greatly exaggerated.[18] First, conflicts within cultures occur as frequently as those among civilizations. The cold war itself was a conflict between different halves of Western civilization—but it was no less significant for occurring within the ambit of Western cultural and economic precepts. Marxism and communism were as distinctive Western offshoots as democracy and free markets. The same is true within other cultures. In Muslim civilization the conflict between Sunnis and Shi'ites is deep and pervasive, as reflected in the tension between Afghanistan and Iran. Divisions exist among Muslim states as well. Indonesia and Malaysia—two large Muslim-dominated nations—actively support the international and Western world economy, while states such as Iran, Iraq, and Sudan oppose it. Other nations, such as Turkey and Bangladesh, have not fully chosen their orientations. Nations of the same civilization can and do have important differences, however, economically and politically.

Second, nations of different civilizations have frequently joined the single world economy. Many non-Western societies that initially resisted inclusion in the international economy have decided to become members. China and India, once insular economies promoting inefficient industrialization strategies based on import substitution, have begun to open to foreign trade and investment.[19] States with distinctive Third World cultures such as Mexico and Brazil have decided to participate in the wider economic world. Many African states are now readying themselves for structural adjustment, exports, and foreign investment; cultural differences between them and Europe or Asia do not seem to have precluded their joining the world economy. Japan, a Shinto-Buddhist country, decided after World War II to become an exporting nation and to participate in world trade. Culture did not impede its economic success. Gradually other states such as Russia and Bosnia are taking hesitant steps to join the Western economic world. Russia has deflated its economy to prop up the ruble, and Bosnia has gradually reopened consumer markets and is seeking foreign investment. In sum, the embracing links of international markets and sources of capital have brought many culturally disparate nations within their bounds.

As nations come to rely on foreign investment and exchange, factors of production may flow between economies regardless of ethnic orientations. Self-confident nations can place their production within the territorial confines of other nations without worrying that links will be cut. With production overseas, they can further develop their service industries at home. The key ingredient supporting this faith is economic gain on both sides.

It is too early to conclude that cultural differences will not impose limits on international cooperation. Unless cultural conflicts are capped by the international community, they might spread. Nations of disparate ethnic coloration have shown, however, that they can participate together in the rising international flow of factors of production. Differences of civilization have not stopped the movement to high-level services as an economic vocation or prevented countries from lodging their production overseas.

Finally, intervention by international agencies or military alliances has offered a partial remedy to domestic cultural conflict. In Bosnia, NATO and the two successive international forces (IFOR and SFOR) have prevented local conflict between contending groups and reestablished a domestic government enjoying tolerable legitimacy. The UN or NATO did not intervene in Rwanda in 1994, and international intervention was too limited and too short-lived to succeed in Somalia in 1990. The United Nations provided an international mandate for intervention in Haiti in which a legitimate government was returned to power. International pressures and humanitarian intervention have helped governments enjoying some degree of support to be returned to power in El Salvador and Cambodia. Precautionary intervention has so far succeeded in preventing an extension of ethnic strife in Macedonia and Slovakia, though not yet in Kosovo.[20] The international record is not perfect, but it appears increasingly clear that early intervention can go a long way in preventing burgeoning ethnic conflict.[21]

DOMESTIC CONFLICT

Cultural differences are not the only cause of conflicts within and between countries. Even states that are ethnically homogeneous may still become vulnerable to tensions between income groups. These domestic differences could then spill over into conflict with neighboring states. In some countries the resurgence of capitalism and high technology has increased domestic inequality.[22] There is a larger difference between top and bottom income groups in the United States and Britain, for instance, than in Japan or Scandinavia. At the extreme, "winner-take-all societies" compensate the most successful and neglect second finishers in sports, business, and entertainment.[23] Those farther down the achievement pyramid receive even less. Lagging competitors may not remain satisfied. In Weimar Germany, when workers and the lower middle class were thrown out of jobs and unemployment reached 25 percent in the 1930–32 economic depression, their rebellion expressed itself in votes for the National Socialist German Workers (Nazi) party that brought Adolf Hitler to power. This victory in turn directed hostility toward nations on Germany's borders, some of which held erstwhile German territory. Internal conflict thus stimulated external conflict. This result could occur even today in the absence of social safety nets for the worst off.

Are lower-class or suddenly dispossessed populations likely to become dissatisfied? In answering this important question one must know how fluid the dividing lines are between upper and lower groups. Is it possible to move up from last to first in one generation? Do citizens believe that upward mobility is possible?[24] If the answers to these questions are negative, in time the society is likely to become unstable. If, on the other hand, people generally believe that hard work and intelligence are rewarded in their country, they can accept a considerable degree of inequality. Although social classes remain, accents differ, and inherited privilege continues, the influence of past inequality is gradually eroding in most modern societies. Present income can compensate one for social barriers in the past. New ideas can earn a present and substantial return.

It is perhaps noteworthy that people frequently remain optimistic even where inequality exists.[25] While this may be true, dynamic trends may be moving in a retrograde direction. Real wages and job security may decline.[26] Households may not be able to keep up with expenses unless they have two workers. People may get less well-paying jobs and hold them for shorter periods of time. Economic insecurity may rise.[27] Ultimately, recessions may occur more often or last longer, throwing more people out of work. If overcapacity exists in many industries, profits will fall and some firms will become insolvent.[28] Others will be subject to mergers or takeovers. Some workers will lose their jobs. Lower incomes will translate into lower consumption. Particularly today, a sudden fall in world stock markets could have a devastating effect. Losers would call in their loans or sell their assets, contributing to further declines and perhaps to a downward economic spiral affecting many nations.

A sharp fall in living standards, uncompensated by two-worker incomes, could have destabilizing effects. As long as incomes are rising, however, people will tend to tolerate inequalities. If a world recession hit, throwing many out of work, unrest would rise; but even then, social outcomes would depend on the success of international "rescue operations" to combine domestic economic reform with a massive inflow of foreign capital.

Recessions cannot be prevented in capitalistic economies.[29] There is a periodicity to economic swings that has never been fully predicted, yet it always occurs. Business cycle theory remains the least developed branch of modern economic knowledge, partly because it militates against the pervasive belief that economic outcomes are perpetually in equilibrium.[30] If prices should be higher or lower, demand or supply will instantly adjust. If stockholders are willing to hold assets, it is because they believe in the assets' continuing value.

There is a growing belief in the industrial world that departures from equilibrium should not be long enduring. Thus economic forecasters in 1999 believe that a sudden fall in stock market values will be more like the 30 percent correction of 1987 than the 90 percent collapse after 1929. Today profits are not greatly out of line; full employment in many countries allows consumers to continue to purchase goods. Governments do not hesitate to intervene to bolster demand. Even more important, major states and international agencies such as the IMF are ready to assist countries in trouble, preventing default on their loans. They have already done so to limit the effects of the Far Eastern financial crisis of 1997–98.

Most contemporary economists do not believe in John Maynard Keynes's idea of an "underemployment equilibrium" that could keep capitalist economies from rebounding from a crisis.[31] If they are right, recessions in the twenty-first century need not resemble the long downturns of 1873 to 1896, or 1929 to 1940. The short-lived fall in the stock market in 1987, rather, should become the typical case. Assets may decline, but they should rebound quickly, leaving underlying economic values less affected. Buoyant consumer sentiment also sustains markets.[32] Factor flows might abruptly leave an economy, but they should rush back in when basic assets become undervalued.

Nor will nations neglect countries in trouble. As foreign direct investment assumes a greater proportion of the investment dollar on a worldwide basis, countries and companies are less likely to react to a crisis by selling their production stake within other economies. Factories—plant and equipment—are illiquid assets. They cannot be sold on a stock exchange. Companies need months or years to find a buyer. Under economic stress, external countries and companies are likely to move to reflate the afflicted foreign economy in order to prop up the values of their investments. As one example, Japan could not ignore a foreign crisis in China, just as it did not neglect its East Asian position in the aftermath of the financial crisis of 1997–98. Japan offered funds to assist the affected country to pay its debts in an effort to prop up asset values. These contributed to restabilization in both Korea and Thailand.

Japan also helped the United States. In 1987 Japan propped up the U.S. stock market by retaining and even buying U.S. Treasury bonds.[33] Nor would the result depend on the actions of one country alone. Central banks act together in a crisis to prevent a contagion affecting other markets. Few countries would respond to a future financial debacle as many did in 1931 by halting capital flows, denying loans, rationing foreign exchange, or upping tariffs.[34] These efforts to insulate national economies from the rest of the world proved futile. As soon as one prominent member of the system failed, as Austria and then Germany did in 1931–32, the whole system came down with them. This is why international monetary agencies since World War II have stressed financial intermediation as well as national banking reform. If banks are sound and well supplied with capital, depositors will not panic at the first hint of downturn. They will keep their assets in institutions and not demand cash to stuff into mattresses. Then the circular flow of goods and assets can continue.[35] Financial assistance from outside can soften the blow.

Business downturns occur when economic inequality becomes so great that consumers cannot afford to buy the produce of industry.[36]

When a slump takes place, the first losers are often holders of capital, and the first effects of recession can reduce inequality.[37] Wage labor need not be affected greatly if the recession is short. If underlying conditions are favorable—low inflation, low government deficits, manageable debts, low unemployment,[38] high or growing productivity—factor flows will reflate the economy within a short period. This does not mean that the world cannot suffer recessions and perhaps even depressions once again; the conjunction of circumstances that could produce such an outcome cannot be ruled out. On the other hand, unlike the situation in the 1930s, all major economic players—central banks, finance ministries, and governments—are resolved to act together to prevent contagion and to reflate major markets. "Beggar thy neighbor" policies are no longer respectable reactions to world problems. If this is true, world economic crises are unlikely in themselves to engender international conflict. They are more likely to stimulate cooperation among major states to reflate asset values and put people back to work.

Yet state interest may prevent the dispersal of a country's production plant. Some ask why countries should act like virtual corporations. If they permit their production to be lodged outside their borders, they reduce GNP unless returns from foreign investment compensate for a balance of trade deficit and decrease employment at home.[39]

There are three rejoinders to this argument. First, as we have seen, the trend to services and the transfer of production is occurring worldwide, not just in virtual states. This is because the returns on service investments are growing more rapidly than the returns on manufacturing. Switching economic resources from manufacturing to services is likely to raise, not lower, GDP. This holds for key European countries as well as for the United States.

Second, production should take place where the combination of productivity and labor costs is most favorable. Aside from high-value manufacturing, production will increasingly take place in Mexico, East Asia, and other places where labor is competent and also inexpensive. In pure economic terms, if production capital does not move to areas of labor abundance, labor should be free to flow to areas of capital abundance.

The failure to produce abroad will generate immigration pressures to move labor to Europe, North America, and Japan. If international inequalities are a spur to conflict, production abroad helps to reduce income disparities between countries.

Third, particular countries also benefit. Low-cost overseas production means that home consumers can purchase goods at lower prices—a direct improvement in living standards. If technical GDP is lost through production abroad, it can be made up through returns on foreign investment. Britain followed such a strategy in the nineteenth century, compensating for its deficit in the balance of trade by surpluses in service exports (financial services, income on foreign investment, insurance, and shipping). Other countries, including the United States, can and will move toward the export of service "invisibles" to remedy balance of trade problems.

Consider, however, the counterargument. Would the United States or other countries be better off forcing their manufacturers to operate entirely at home? In a closed economy without foreign competition, this might be possible. As the fate of the Soviet Union demonstrates, however, closed economies do not prosper in the longer term. Forcing U.S. or German industry to produce at home, the state would simply cause a decline in its manufacturing competitiveness, involving losses in both revenue and market share. It would be much better to use government tax policy to increase foreign earnings.[40] Such changes are unlikely to cause domestic conflict.

The Threat of Terrorism

Even if internal conflict does not increase, dissatisfied individuals or groups could raise the specter of terrorism on a worldwide scale. Modern terrorists do not explicitly make demands that might reveal who they are. They act to punish previous transgressions by established governments. Only later, sometimes years later, can they be identified. Thus Iranian and Libyan terrorists reacted against the United States for shooting down an Iranian airliner in the Gulf by bombing Pan Am

Flight 103 over Lockerbie, Scotland, in 1988. The Egyptian terrorists who bombed the World Trade Center were seeking to punish the United States and Egypt for actions against their compatriots in the Middle East. Aum Shinrikyo laced the Tokyo subway with Sarin gas in retribution for the actions of Japanese capitalists and the Japanese government. This sect also attempted to spray anthrax bacteria from the roof of a building in Tokyo. Israeli and Arab terrorists routinely bomb, shoot, or poison their opposite numbers and sometimes their own leaders.[41] For more than a half century the IRA and Northern Ireland Constabulary have waged covert and sometimes open war on one another. Free market societies are extremely vulnerable to these attacks.

In addition, as Aum Shinrikyo demonstrated, biological and chemical weapons are available to terrorists. A variety of poisons can be introduced in water supplies or air-conditioning ducts. Planes can spray enemy troops or villages with chemical toxins. It is difficult for governments to respond to these attacks because the perpetrators are not typically enemy states. Crazed, isolated individuals and small terrorist cells with antigovernment mentalities can create disruption without revealing their base of operations. On whom does one then retaliate? The explosives used in the bombing of the Murrah Federal Building in Oklahoma City in 1995 were made from ordinary fertilizer and diesel fuel. Bomb manuals to guide terrorists are available for sale.

So far, terrorists have shown only limited interest in launching biological attacks. Biological materials are difficult to disperse, and they can be countered by inoculation of the targeted population. Up to now, only states have been able to develop aerosol capacities to attack cities. Even these, while very dangerous, have not yet been capable of destroying even one large city.[42] Biological attacks on water supplies can be countered by chemicals in the water that can kill such toxins. Contamination of food is difficult and unreliable. Nonetheless, the threat of biological and chemical terrorism must be taken seriously and may be growing.

To stop or deter these attacks, governments need better intelligence on malcontents in their midst. Terrorism and internal threats are now greater menaces than the danger of external war. Perhaps suicide bombings can ultimately be deterred by retaliation on another group or country, but dissidents within one's own society are another matter. The Unabomber was not part of an international conspiracy. Cooperation among national police forces in Interpol and other agencies provides a partial answer to these problems, but it does not yet offer a complete response.[43]

In the longer term it seems that societies will have to accept such attacks on an episodic or occasional basis. Cities may become targets for terrorists dissatisfied with the status quo. People will be killed, though not many. As terrorism expert Brian Jenkins points out, the terrorist wants lots of people watching, not lots of people dead.[44]

Will this violence stop the movement of factors of production between states and cause a breakdown of the world economy? It scarcely seems likely. International flows are now enormous; foreign exchange transactions alone may total more than $2 trillion per day. World GDP will soon exceed $100 trillion, an increasingly large proportion of which is generated through international exchange and trade. Foreign direct investment is rising more rapidly than trade and far more than GDP.[45] Random attacks on individuals or facilities will not prevent its continuing. The regions where terrorism has the capacity to inhibit or prevent economic flows are sites of chronic unrest, where recurrent terrorist attacks may be seen as the warfare of the weak. In some of these regions the reestablishment of legitimate governments in previously authoritarian societies, the spread of economic welfare, and reintegration of fringe groups in mainstream society will reduce the problem. Terrorism has been halted in Argentina and Uruguay with the establishment of legitimate governments in both countries. The Dublin agreement of 1997 may reintegrate the IRA into the domestic politics of Northern Ireland. The Palestinian leadership may achieve a détente with Hamas, and perhaps with Israel. Where strife continues, as in Colombia, southern Italy, and the Middle East, international cooperation among police and military agencies will help limit its scope. Terrorism, however, will continue as a phenomenon in some countries, though some experts worry that we may be spending too much on counterterrorism and too little on economic improvement in many modern societies.[46]

There is finally the prospect of cyberterrorism, which goes to the very heart of the vulnerability of modern economic societies. Computer codes that govern the operation of billing systems, power grids, and communications networks are sometimes written in foreign countries. Even where they are not, existing control programs are frequently vulnerable to outside penetration. A Defense Department official testified recently that thirty-five specialists recruited from the National Security Agency to test the integrity of U.S. systems had been able, using commercially available hardware and technology, to penetrate the American power grid and the telecommunications backbone of the Department of Defense. Communications and control systems connected to the Internet are vulnerable to outside disruption and interference. The official concluded: "We screen kids for using drugs, but we ignore the fact that a fraudulent company can operate in the United States and on its own sweet time develop an economic order of battle against this country."[47]

At the national level we are protected by the global awareness that if one nation starts tampering with the cybernetworks of others, it will also be vulnerable to penetration and interruption of its own control systems. Defense does not exist, but the threat of retaliation is a deterrent. Countries thus have a great incentive to seek to prevent terrorists using their domains as a base of operations against others. Perhaps an equal deterrent to harboring terrorists is the knowledge that an attack on the computer systems of one state is an attack on the world economy as a whole. There is no telling who will ultimately be affected. This consideration of course means little to states not well integrated into the virtual economy. For them, nations will need to develop new norms to work together to prevent terrorist threats—threats that could in time threaten the global economic system.

External Conflict

Many commentators believe that international conflict derives primarily from the multiplicity of separate national interests in the international system.[48] Conflict among states has been chronic in Western and international history even when domestic peace prevailed. World War I emerged out of a century of economic progress, cultural enlightenment, and political liberalization. Relations among states were antagonistic even when those among peoples were not. If this is true, many believe that separate states pursuing nationalistic interests will always fight one another.

Sometimes an even balance of power can mute conflict in international relations, but as war is a typical method of enforcing a balance, these mechanisms by themselves do not ensure peace.[49] Even if this were not true, balances of power do not always take hold.[50] Another method of conflict control is hegemonic leadership by one strong and benevolent state, such as nineteenth-century Britain or late twentieth-century America. America's leadership will undoubtedly continue well into the twenty-first century. The problem with this method is that hegemonic leadership has an intrinsic tendency to decline.[51] Britain, though strong, could not lead the international system at the end of the nineteenth century. The United States is stronger still, but it cannot pay the costs of deterring or defeating all conflicts at the beginning of the new century.[52] It needs support from other great powers such as the European Union, Japan, China, and even Russia. Leaders must be supported by their own populations as well as by the cooperation of other countries. While the British public generally endorsed the foreign policy of its leaders, the American public has sometimes imposed an isolationist stance on U.S. foreign policy. It is not certain today that the American people will continue to support an energetic U.S. role in foreign affairs now that the cold war is over.

Aside from domestic support, however, leaders of the system must win the cooperation of other states. Britain did not secure the cooperation of Germany in 1914, and it is far from certain that the United States will win the cooperation of Russia and China in the coming century. If these two large states demur, cooperation cannot be achieved on arms control, preventing the spread of nuclear, chemical, and biological weapons, and maintaining sanctions against rogue states.

If the leadership structure declines or dissolves, the world is back to conflict as usual, with nations jockeying for relative advantage. Such an international competition for power would not prevent war; rather, nations would employ conflict and so-called defection strategies to secure an edge. The history of the competition for power among states does not generate confidence that major conflict can be avoided.[53] These contentions require further analysis.

THE ANGLE OF INTERNATIONAL INFLUENCE

First, one of the factors exacerbating international conflict in the modern era is that national ambitions have tended to be embodied in ideological terms.[54] Thus during the cold war Russia clothed its national interests in the ideology of communism. During the French Revolution French interests were proclaimed to include liberty, equality, and the rights of man, while the continental opposition fought to retain the eighteenth-century conservative social order. Thus the French revolutionary wars were fought not just over state interests but over contending doctrines and ways of life. World War II was equally based on ideological conflict. The war was harder to avoid and more uncontrolled because Germany and Italy propounded national socialism and fascism while America and Britain fought for democracy and freedom. In this period ideologies had captured a state entirely in the sense that all state actions had to be justified in terms of an abstract ideological principle. International relations thus pitted one state's doctrine against another's. Conflict could scarcely be limited in these circumstances.

Is this the problem today? Not obviously. At present the *isms* are international rather than national; the ideological differences that remain mostly are differences within states, not among them. Every society contains a middle class, and almost all countries face internal pressure for further liberalization and democratization. The differences among nations have to do for the most part with their degree of democratization. Some nations are still military or feudal autocracies. Some possess liberalizing coalitions seeking to influence a military or statist regime. Others have democratic institutions without the traditional and liberal practices of democracy.[55] Under these circumstances outside states that seek to influence a country must press for internal reform through internal politics. Domestic political competition is much more likely to resolve issues than international war.

Methods are correspondingly different. In the past, when nation-states embodied a noxious ideology, it was necessary militarily to defeat and occupy a state in order to eradicate the ideology. Horizontal conflicts—lateral conflicts between nations—might involve onerous military obligations.[56] Today military methods are less necessary. Conflicts can be at least partly addressed by political and economic means. A foreign nation seeks access to the societies of other countries to exercise a degree of influence on domestic economics and politics. Sometimes this succeeds. Japan, for instance, holds a large amount of American debt. If Japanese bond holders dumped U.S. Treasury bonds, interest rates in the United States would rise. Business loans, mortgages, and auto loans would be more expensive. Thus the American government pays attention to Japanese interests. Similarly, the United States is the greatest market for Japanese exports and Japan's leading trading partner. Japan cannot neglect the way American economic policy affects the Japanese economy.

The influence that twenty-first-century countries seek is not nineteenth-century control. They do not want and could not establish dominion over another state. Nations gave that up when imperialism was discredited as an international phenomenon half a century ago. They desire, rather, to open countries up to outside economic and political influences, furthering open markets and growing liberalization. The IMF, the Bank for International Settlements, and the World Bank are the surrogate warriors of the next century. If military intervention is *horizontal* influence, we may think of this liberalizing as *vertical* influence.

Because states were cordoned off from one another, the angle of interventionist influence in the nineteenth century was about 90 degrees. A country had to expand horizontally against another state to have influence on it. If one country could have influenced another without lateral extension, that is, entirely by effecting social change from within, the angle of influence could theoretically have been 0 degrees—all vertical.[57] Such a complete shift has not yet occurred. States today must combine vertical with horizontal influence measures. Political and economic techniques still must be accompanied by military strategies. The former are exercised by the market and by international agencies. Thus the angle of influence today is nearer to 45 degrees, and it may be decreasing.[58]

To take but one of many examples: during the cold war the United States, having no direct influence in Soviet internal politics, was condemned to oppose Russia externally and militarily (horizontally). After the cold war Russia became a more open if not yet fully liberal-democratic society. American political consultants could help President Yeltsin win reelection in 1996. U.S. and IMF financial assistance could seek to assist the reform of the Russian economy, the control of weapons of mass destruction, and establishment of an efficient bureaucracy to collect taxes, thereby supporting the ruble. Greater Russian economic success could make relations between Washington and Moscow more friendly. This does not mean that military measures are not still important, that Russia and America will put aside their previous doctrines of nuclear deterrence, or that relations cannot become adversarial again. Each nation remains on its guard; but the main avenue of influence proceeds through internal politics and economics, despite the profound differences between domestic systems.

It appears that the most promising way to make angles of influence between nations more nearly vertical is to seek to spread democracy to all nations. The democratic peace theory asserts that democratic states rarely fight one another, however much they may be involved in conflicts with autocratic nations.[59] Even democratic societies, however, may have their differences. As Michael Doyle demonstrates, there were many more conflicts (short of war) between liberal democracies in the nineteenth century than after World War II.[60] The process of democratizing may also be full of uncertainty and conflict, both internationally and domestically.[61] Some countries can be democracies in form or name without acquiring the liberal or constitutional traditions that fully protect individual rights.[62] The formal institution of democracy may not succeed in bringing peace or stability if there is no "liberalizing coalition" to infuse and motivate it.[63]

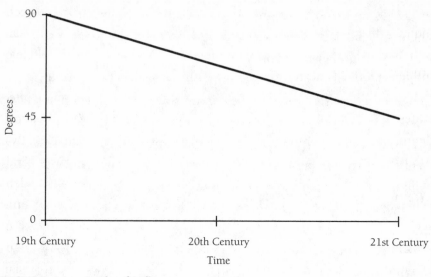

FIGURE 4.1   Angle of influence.

Yet even formally democratic states are more open than their auto-cratic or military predecessors and counterparts. The operation of a tol-erably free press, the availability of a modern telephone system, internet transmission, and CNN—all these push toward further openness and the possibility of mutual influence among societies. The world does not require the immediate installation of democracy in all countries. This will be a very long process in any event. What the world needs are open domestic societies that are ready to receive foreign information and ar-gument about their national priorities.

ECONOMIC AND POLITICAL CONFLICT

Despite their virtues, economic interdependence and globalization (the movement of factors of production from one economy to another) have not produced peace in world politics.[64] Some have argued that the world economy was even more globalized in 1913 than it is today. France, Germany, and Britain traded extensively with one another. For-eign investment comprised a higher percentage of GDP than it is now. People could travel without passports from one country to another. Telecommunication was almost instantaneous. The telegraph arrived in the 1850s and telephones in the first decade of the twentieth century. There was no lack of communication between the antagonists who fought one another in World War I.[65]

How then can the world economy of the twenty-first century avoid similar outcomes? One cannot be sure of course that all conflict will be avoided. It is worth remembering, however, that the interdependence of 1913 was far different from the interdependence of 2000. The late nineteenth century was par excellence an imperial age. Countries either had colonies or were desperately seeking them. Africa, Asia, and the Middle East had already been divided up by Britain, France, Germany, and a few lesser states. Along with Austria, the same states fought over the spoils of the Ottoman Empire as Turkey gradually withdrew from Europe and North Africa. In North Africa, Germany and France were in conflict over these spoils. In the Balkans, Russia and Austria competed for the leftovers. Territorial annexation enhanced one's power. The largest territories would contain the greatest stock of resources and populations. The nations that acquired these would be the strongest powers. Germany, dissatisfied that it had not done as well in the imperial race as Great Britain, was ready to wage war to redress the territorial balance.

This is not the situation today. If openness and factor mobility continue, no country needs a larger territory. Access to the factors and markets of others substitutes for the past insistence on control of land.[66] In addition, a territorial fetish—reflected in the spoils of empire—animated much of the nineteenth-century economy. Foreign investment was high, but mainly concentrated in liquid instruments such as stocks and bonds that could be disposed of swiftly. Direct investment—a share of production—was low and tended to be channeled to one's territories overseas. Britain's productive investments were located not in Germany but in Australia, New Zealand, Canada, South Africa, and India. Interdependence was high within empires, but less so between them. The British Empire as a trading unit had much more independence than did Great Britain as an individual state. The empire provided markets, raw materials, and labor supplies for Britain's industry. As the nineteenth century drew on, Britain traded less with Europe and more with its colonies, dependencies, and South and North America.[67] British trade with Germany was not a deterrent to war, because Germany and Britain had other bases for their economic strengths.

The twenty-first century world by contrast finds major nations linked by foreign direct investments. These investments in production are relatively illiquid. They cannot be disposed of quickly. Japan sites an increasing proportion of its industry in the United States, China, and East Asia. The United States produces in Europe, China, and Latin America. European productive investments are coming to the United States in large amounts. Production facilities are lodged inside the very countries with whom power motivations might dictate conflict. The United States and Japan, Japan and China, Europe and America, America and China—these links forge bonds that are highly profitable and not easily dissolved. None is an imperial tie. The United States, Japan, and Europe are internationalizing their production and they are placing it within nations that in theory might become rivals. Today's horizontal economic links are much stronger than those between participants in World War I. These links do more than give potential rivals a strong incentive to resolve conflicts peacefully; they also give third parties with investments in each rival a strong incentive to intervene to prevent war.

REALISM RECONSIDERED

The theory of political realism claims that particular forms of domestic politics and economics do not prevent international conflict. It asserts rather that states are likely, perhaps even destined, to repeat conflict episodes in every era. In this theory states are independent units that do not rely on each other. Each country worries about its own survival. Thus states either balance against aggressors to maintain their position or succumb to aggression or annexation. Realist theory does not assert that states will balance against those who would change the system, only that they have an incentive to do so. "Balances of power have a tendency to form."[68]

What states actually do of course is a function of the relationships they maintain with other nations. If these links are both positive and strong (such as, for example, the relationship between the United States and Canada), war need not occur. Stronger ties mean greater peace. Economic links can establish one form of interdependence. Political ties—in the form of democratic institutions—can create another. The realists traditionally deny that there is any specialization or division of labor between nations.[69] Countries do not perform different functions within the international system. Nor, realists contend, was there a division of labor in past international history.

It is not enough, however, to say that states are "like units." States are actually quite unlike one another. Totalitarian autocracies operated differently and more aggressively than democratic states. Capitalist nations have maintained very different links with markets and sources of raw materials than statist or socialist economies. Capitalists have actually sought interdependence, while socialist economies have aimed at autonomy and self-sufficiency. Communist nations did not develop any significant division of labor internationally. Yet head and body nations may be in process of doing so. Establishing one's manufacturing production within the confines of another nation creates a substantial economic and political commitment that is not easy to break. Thus while the assertions of realism have not been confuted internationally, neither does the trend of events in the world economy support their conclusions. The virtualization process now taking place is creating a substantial differentiation of function among states.

The Conflict-As-Usual Thesis

Because present and future ties among nations are so important, the conflict-as-usual thesis can neither be accepted nor definitively rejected, but prospects for peaceful economic change are good. Countries are more open than they have ever been, economically, politically, and in terms of communications. Links on the Internet continue even between countries whose governments are opposed to one another. Communication ties knit together countries with a substantial stake in each others' well being. Factors of production flow easily in and out. The incentive to use force declines because there is abundant access to the resources and capital of other nations.

Yet countries will exist for a long time at different stages of industrial maturity. Wherever land containing agricultural or mineral resources is still the most important factor in the economic equation, countries will use military force against each other. In Eastern Europe on the borders of the erstwhile Soviet Union, in the Middle East, land is still very important. In these areas, with their unsettled political, cultural, and ethnic traditions, war appears (perhaps mistakenly) as a way of settling disputes. Borders are fluid; nationalities can adjust to territorial conquest through migration. If one can populate a territory with one's co-religionists, one can seek to govern it. (At least there is the temptation to try.) Hence Kosovo, Bosnia, Tajikistan, Azerbaijan, and Georgia have been locations of civil conflict. In the Middle East the prospects for peace and economic renewal have not allayed the territorial concerns of Arabs and Israelis. Nowhere in these regions do the mobile factors of production yet have primacy.

Even where virtual ties exist between nations, conflict will not entirely cease. If capital can flow, so can terrorists. If knowledge can move, so can arms. The very openness of modern societies makes them more vulnerable than closed autocracies. Yet democratic societies have always been vulnerable to their own people as well as foreigners. The key to ending such violence is inclusion within the democratic process. Of course, democratic procedures will not halt all violence. The crazed individual or militant group will always act in an antisocial way; but the fabric of modern nation-states will become stronger as they become more democratic. The commitment to openness ultimately strengthens the political order.

Some regions of the world continue nineteenth- and twentieth-century patterns of conflict. The Middle East and South Asia—where land still dominates the economic equation—manifest military rivalries like those of the cold war. These regions suffer the same kinds of conflicts that are presently being allayed in Northern Ireland and Central and South America. Continuing ethnic and national conflicts usually exact a price in curbed economic development. Other regions of the world progress more rapidly, as East Asia, Europe, and North America continue to do. This implied lesson may eventually strike home: there is no surer path to becoming an economic backwater than making war on your neighbor.

Rivalries among states will not disappear, but will increasingly take the form of competition for market share. There will be winners and losers. The ultimate question, however, is the means by which this competition is carried on.

Finally, the openness of the international economy also is its intrinsic strength. If the countries that do best are open and receptive to international migration, capital, and flows of factors of production, they are also vulnerable to episodic or systemic disruption. Only national and group self-restraint backed by the threat of retaliation can maintain such a delicate system. Will such disruptions occasionally occur? Very possibly, but the ease and flexibility of flows make the international economy resilient enough to transcend the disruptions' impact. World prosperity itself has become a bulwark against divisive national tendencies.

The whole trend of international politics in the past half century moves against the notion of perpetual conflict. The zone of peace and economic growth is increasing. The zone of war and internal conflict imposes economic stasis and retrogression on its members. Conflict as usual will continue in retrograde portions of international society, but it will increasingly be eliminated among advanced countries.

—— Part Two

Political and International Implications

chapter 5

Domestic Implications: The Market and the State

As described earlier, virtualization creates three kinds of states: fully virtual nations with little home production; intermediate nations that focus on services and in which an important part of production has been shifted overseas; and nations that concentrate on home manufacturing. In all three cases countries increasingly specialize and rely on one another. This chapter seeks to develop the domestic implications of these outcomes.[1]

Two primary indicators of virtualization—corporate outsourcing and downsizing—entail domestic consequences. In the employment sector workers and middle management may initially suffer as jobs are transferred abroad. Downsizing is nothing new; it has historically reduced employment in particular industries when routine work is either terminated by technological improvements or moved elsewhere. In the early nineteenth century British weavers, tinsmiths, and other craftsmen were thrown out of work as machines took their places. By mid century, however, the growth in demand for England's industrial goods had reemployed labor and increased real wages. Late twentieth-century America has undergone a similar transition. As a result of inflation and technological change, real wages declined from 1973 to 1992.[2] International competition has both delayed wage increases and reduced employment. Now real wages (wages discounted for inflation) are rising again.[3] Unemployment is lower than at any time since 1970. Wage earners and service workers are making up their losses.[4]

Individual income, however, still has not returned to previous levels. Many households need two breadwinners to make ends meet. Does this suggest that long-term unemployment or a possibly irreversible downturn is in progress?[5] Almost certainly not. Reemployment takes the form of higher-level service or industrial jobs. Programmers, office managers, skilled data processors, product designers, consultants and the like—will form the bulk of the new professionals. There will be relatively few hamburger flippers, janitors, and clerical personnel. As the Educational Testing Service points out in a recent study, office workers (both management and technical) will form the bulk of twenty-first century employment in the United States.[6] In addition, in the service sector good and elite jobs will greatly outnumber less skilled ones. As a percentage of total employment, less skilled jobs such as sales clerks, orderlies, janitors, and farm laborers have declined from 47 percent in 1959 to 36 percent in 1995. In the same period good and elite positions such as supervisors, craft workers, technicians, clerical workers, police, firefighters, managers, and professionals rose from 53 percent to 64 percent of employment. These trends will continue.[7] The American economy will create more service jobs at the high end of the spectrum. To gain these posts, individuals will require higher education. Workers without such credentials may be limited to lower-paid employment. The same is likely to be true in other countries.

Since 1992 the U.S. economy has added ten million new jobs. This is fewer than the twenty million reemployed in the Reagan recovery a decade earlier, but then, the Clinton boom did not start from the bottom of a severe recession, as Reagan's did in 1982. And the rapid Reagan upturn was based on a workforce of lower productivity. If each worker only contributed a small amount to output, the economy would need many more employees to sustain rising production. Due to productivity increases in the 1990s, however, fewer workers have been able to augment output. Still, although employment did not rise as quickly as in the Reagan recovery, overall it has reached very high levels. The percentage of unemployed in 1998 and early 1999 was lower than it had been since the Vietnam war. This time the new jobs were not created by a military crisis but by rising consumer demand for American goods. If this demand continues and corporate profits continue to increase, high employment is likely to be sustained.

Economies of Scope versus Economies of Scale

Traditionally and particularly from the 1930s to 1950s, industrial output was characterized by economies of scale. Standard products could be manufactured with decreasing unit costs as the volume of production increased.[8] Production needed to reach high output levels before costs could be reduced. In the 1990s in contrast, more sophisticated production methods have brought *economies of scope*.[9, 10] Economies of scope permit a business enterprise to produce different products on the same assembly line or quality circle without incurring higher costs.

Thus today, modern bakeries do not offer a single variety of spongy white bread. They produce rye, sourdough, olive, French and Italian, as well as traditional white bread in a single production process.[11] GMC offers trucks designed to individual buyers' specificatons—cab size, seats, cylinders, horsepower, number of wheels, flatbed capacity, and so on—with rapid production rates. Gateway Computers constructs a computer to order in terms of megahertz in the microprocessor, RAMs of memory, and gigabytes of hard drive. Levi-Strauss offers personally tailored jeans for women. Measurements are transmitted over the Internet to the factory, which delivers finished jeans to the customer within days.[12] In each case the company either anticipates or directly responds to the demands of particular consumers.

Such tailoring of production might be expected to yield high inefficiencies and greater cost. It is possible because advances in computer technology permit much closer tracking of individual orders throughout the manufacturing and distribution process. Instead of being devoted to bulk production and shipping, modern factories and warehouses concentrate on high volume fulfillment of individual orders. Different combinations of (relatively) standard components are used to produce varied products. Even if costs rise somewhat, the ratio of costs to higher-value output still sustains high productivity rates. In addition, the incorporation of higher technological content within the production process increases value. Custom manufacturing embodies a greater service (that is, intangible or knowledge) content. The shift to economies of scope means more attention to consumer wants and needs.

The measurement of industrial productivity has difficulties with economies of scope. If production is uniform, the only questions are how much output and how much labor cost. One can measure productivity by dividing the unit value of output by unit labor costs—which is precisely how government statisticians do it. The issue is not so simple when output is not uniform.[13]

Innovations make prices of a supposedly uniform product unreliable guides to quality: a computer produced in 1995 has far less memory and processing power than one made in 2000.[14]

If the quality of output rises, then price increases should not be counted simply as cost of living increases for the average citizen,[15] because the consumer's enhanced value may exceed the price increase. The mass custom manufacturing made possible by economies of scope is even harder to quantify than more traditional quality improvements, because each product coming off the assembly line may be distinct—designed for a particular customer. The government-formulated consumer price index therefore may be set too high.[16] Under its strict definitions, productivity output in unit terms ostensibly remains the same or declines, even as the quality of output, which is not measured, rises.[17] There is thus an unmeasured increase in real productivity. It is just this uncaptured increase that brought higher corporate profits in 1997–98, when inputs of capital and labor into the production process did not rise.[18] Alan Greenspan, Chairman of the U.S. Federal Reserve Board, observed that "it is difficult to avoid the conclusion that output per hour has to be rising at a pace significantly in excess of the officially published growth rate of nonfarm productivity."[19]

Under these circumstances the movement to high-level services (which itself makes possible differentiated and higher-valued output) need not decrease productivity, occasional studies to the contrary notwithstanding.[20] Higher-service employment based on economies of scope sustains productivity and may increase it.[21] Even the traditional numbers have begun to show better productivity increases.[22] As economies of scope begin to take precedence over economies of scale in many industrial countries, the result is not further declines in productivity but rather significant increases.

The Market and the State

We have examined two of the three major characteristics acquired by modern economies as they move toward virtual status. First, service production rises as compared with manufacturing, mining, and agriculture. Second, modern virtualized economies have become more open: this permits factor flows to move easily from one society to another. As a result, nations do not need to think of conquering others to gain access to their resources and markets.

The third characteristic is that impartial government regulation combines with market processes to produce favorable economic outcomes. To maintain economic success, countries need to draw a fine balance between the roles of market and state.

This point is especially important. Society works only if political and economic sectors cooperate. Jane Jacobs sees these relationships reflected in two vocations: the merchant and the guardian. For the merchant all values are economic. The guardian on the other hand seeks to protect social life according to political values, irrespective of trade. Despite their different functions, merchant and guardian need each other.[23] Without the legal protections of state guardians, a merchant cannot enforce contracts; but guardians are inherently territorial and predatory if left unchecked. "Guardians see the relations between the area they control and those controlled by others as intrinsically hostile."[24] The paradox is that to survive, even traders and merchants need guardians to enforce noneconomic values. In the words of Martin Wolf of the *Financial Times*, merchants require "well paid and carefully structured guardian institutions that understand what commerce needs, but are not themselves imbued with commercial values. Merchants need honest courts, not ones they can buy."[25]

Alone, each is insufficient. A state that cannot sustain a growing economy soon stagnates politically as well. This was the problem ultimately faced by the post–World War II Soviet Union. Rejecting capitalism, the Soviets gave power to guardians, soldiers, and bureaucrats. Despite an early stimulus to heavy industry, however, Russian communism did not foster commerce. In a vain attempt to extract "surplus value" Soviet Communists obliterated economic incentives, and the bureaucracy they ruled ultimately ground to a halt.

The same example shows what chaos results when there exist only merchants. When communism collapsed, economic motives assumed too great a role, and material values overwhelmed past guardian values that sustained Soviet society. "Economized" officials found it natural to sell their services. Corruption became rampant. A successful state therefore requires a balance between political and economic influences. An excess of the guardian mentality creates predatory behavior that undermines free markets. An excess of market dominion gives government policies a market price, and groups such as the mafia ascend and flourish.[26]

The virtualization process requires an effective regulatory state. Countries lodging their production overseas need their assets to be treated fairly and impartially and their property rights to be sustained on a worldwide basis.[27] This means that essentially Western commercial codes, legal systems, and relatively incorruptible political practices should be emulated in other regions of the world.[28]

Consequences for the State

The state itself must adopt a more focused if more modest role. As governments no longer can guarantee full employment for their populations, they increasingly rely on foreign factors of production to keep their populations at work. Governments need to attract foreign investment to the domestic state.[29] This raises the important question posed by Robert

Reich: "Who is us?"[30] Foreign technology and purchasing power inside another nation may seem alien, but they are of the greatest importance. If they are not us, they greatly affect our output and employment.[31]

Exchange rate changes may induce or deter foreign direct investment. When the dollar was high valued (as in the 1960s), the United States adopted a strategy of investing abroad, which made it unnecessary to export goods from expensive U.S. manufacturing locations. The Europeans returned the favor when the dollar declined and European currencies became relatively expensive in the 1970s. When the dollar declined from the peaks of 1985, both Japanese and Europeans invested heavily in the United States.

The political leaders of the virtual state must encourage domestic factors of production to seek out areas of the highest return, given prevailing exchange rates. The state and its domestic population can benefit from their corporations' overseas success through tax policies. Internally, governments must use monetary and fiscal policy to aim at stable currencies, low interest rates, low inflation, and a minimal government deficit. A stable democratic order will be far more likely to attract foreign capital and labor than a chaotic internal system. Flexible labor and welfare laws will be more likely to bring in foreign technology and investment than rigid welfare and employment requirements. As governments seek to institute more labor flexibility—in hiring, wages, and hours worked—some domestic workers may react unfavorably if benefits are reduced; but all workers do not oppose flexibility. Skilled and office workers have different interests from those who perform routine tasks on an assembly line. If foreign investment creates new jobs, workers of all kinds will benefit. In any event, virtualization calls for a restructuring of state and labor policies to meet international economic requirements. Governments will have to negotiate with foreign factors of production to persuade them to enter and produce within the domestic economy.

Consequences for Society

Virtualization places a premium on the attainment of middle-class goals and interests—good jobs, education, and a consumer existence. The more middle class the society, the more effective it is likely to be in the virtual world. Even India and China have large middle classes—in the range of 200 million each—and these groups are more important than their number in terms of influence, electorally and otherwise. In democratic nations middle-class citizens almost always register to vote, and they are more likely to go to the polls than farmer-tillers or industrial workers. The educated middle class is also the source from which individuals will be found to run the enterprises of tomorrow. If government does not recognize and assist them, it will encounter greater international economic difficulty.

For middle-class citizens the key requisite is education for their children and low inflation to preserve their living standards. Low inflation also protects the purchasing power of their retirement incomes. Government policy in many countries has been more effective in achieving the second than the first. A mix of education systems may be necessary to meet all the needs, since universal public education has not been an unqualified success. The government could subsidize private, nonsectarian education through a voucher system. It could sponsor new and innovative programs of training and certification, capitalizing on a strong liberal arts background. It could also improve the recruitment of teachers by offering higher salaries and rates of promotion.

This does not mean the middle and professional classes—shopkeepers, clerical workers, teachers, public servants, and managers—will or should prosper at the expense of the rest of society. No government can guarantee good jobs for all its valued citizens.[32] In the United States, for example, President Clinton received a great deal of support from middle-class African-American and Hispanic voters even when he was unable to generate enough jobs to employ them all. The less well-off members of the middle class retain a strong desire for economic independence. These citizens cling to middle-class values and views.[33] Even where both spouses must work to maintain income and to provide education for their children, such families still aspire to the good life, and they inculcate like values in their children.

The virtualization process transfers production overseas. In the United States, at least, this means greater economic uncertainty. Increasing numbers of middle-class Americans know that they will not have a lifetime job. Many accept that they will have to move to a different part of the country to find or keep a job. One employee may have to hold two jobs simultaneously to ensure minimum support.[34] This uncertainty represents a huge change from the 1950s or even the 1960s, when most Americans believed they would face few economic challenges.[35] Today people work harder. They also respond with greater alacrity to new opportunities and tend to seek the educational qualifications to do well in the white- or blue-collar workforce. The distinction between the two in any event is rapidly eroding.[36] As economies of scope replace economies of scale, service and creative functions become part of industrial outputs.[37]

In the past, citizens sought upward mobility and middle-class status for themselves and their families. The most debilitating prospect was to be forced into poverty with little prospect of rising from it. Recent U.S. Census data, however, suggest that this prospect is less worrisome than some once thought. About 20 percent of the U.S. population in recent years was located beneath the poverty line. Only 5.3 percent, however, remained in poverty for more than two years.[38] Higher education was one signal means of achieving upward mobility. Middle-class status remains as an objective for virtually everyone. What has been altered is that individuals recognize that they may have to move from home town or home university to achieve that goal. Geographic mobility has become necessary for vertical mobility. In time, many will also come to recognize that they may need to move to foreign countries to achieve their objectives. Like production, intelligent workforces may also become available for export.

The virtualization process creates states with limited governmental powers relative to the problems they confront. The entire history of political and electoral reform in modern nation-states rested on the hypothesis that extending the political influence of the average citizen would also control the economy that affects him. Further democratization was the answer to social problems. Yet what if, as democracy was installed, the scope of problems came to extend well beyond the state—

indeed, beyond the scope of the democratic process? Suppose that democratic decision making wanted to extend its range of jurisdiction to
other countries. What then?

In some ways this already has happened. Under the Helms-Burton
law the United States can punish foreign companies for dealing with
Cuba—an extraterritorial extension of American fiat. Equally, the European Union's competition commissioner can attempt to dictate terms
of U.S. and foreign company mergers or even of American company
mergers that might affect competition among corporations in Europe.
This contraverted process undoubtedly will continue to agitate relations
among states.

Since, however, the results of such mutual political interventions into
the affairs of other nations can never be decisive, the political citizenry
is not in command of its economic fate. It can vote a government out of
office, but installing a new one will not bring world economics and
globalization under its heel.[39] Governments still spend a great deal of
money but they do not control what is going on in other jurisdictions.
They can negotiate with foreign factors of production, but cannot simply determine outcomes.[40]

Does this mean that citizens will fail to support their own leaders?
Considerable discontent has surfaced in the past two decades in both
Europe and the United States as this process unfolded. As long as the
world economy is growing, however, there has been no strong disaffec-
tion among societies participating extensively in that growth. The stock
market reverse of 1987, the recession of 1990–91, the stock and currency collapses of 1998—these had political repercussions; but heads
did not roll in all countries. The character of political leadership did not
appreciably change. In fact, more centrist politicians have come to the
fore in most countries, eschewing the past alternations of left and right.
The virtualization process in addition has allowed political elites to es-
cape from some degree of responsibility. If economic outcomes are not
under their control, then reverses cannot be entirely their fault. Knowl-
edgeable electorates have not punished their parliaments or prime ministers extensively. Under these circumstances wholesale reform

proposals have not generated great domestic support. More typical have been strategies to "redefine government"—getting it to perform more purposefully and efficiently the tasks it has already been assigned.[41]

———————

The state and state policy thus have been weakened, relative to the market. It remains true, however, that the market and the state must work together to achieve favorable economic outcomes. To achieve virtualization, the state must facilitate the movement of its own factors of production and also offer a hospitable environment for foreign factors: capital, labor, technology, and information. It must develop a regulatory environment that administers commercial laws impartially and does not discriminate against the foreigner. The domestic state must enforce contracts and minimize corruption. Government servants and police have to be sufficiently well paid that they are not routinely tempted by bribes to bend the laws. If overambitious governments seek administrative control of foreign or domestic factors of production, they will ultimately fail. Governments maintain and police the structure in which markets operate—but they do not themselves determine market outcomes. The process of virtualization, however, engenders mobility among factors of production, allowing domestic factors to concentrate on what they do best. In the case of developed nations, service industries, creative capacity, and new technology will make the difference in long-term economic performance.[42]

chapter 6

Governance and the World Economy

As the preceding chapter explains, if the virtualization process is to work, the domestic state must protect international factors of production. Foreign capital must have legal safeguards if it is to invest in domestic production. An impartial government must enforce contracts between international and domestic traders and maintain the engagements of the economic system. Ideally, the political state should incorruptibly maintain the rights of poor as well as rich, foreigners as well as nationals. In such a state a wealthy person cannot buy nonenforcement of a claim against him—canceling a murder conviction, for instance, by bribing state officials. The government collects taxes from all citizens, and under progressive income tax statutes, proportionally more from the rich than the poor. The domestic state can thus meet the requirements of virtualization.

Domestic and International Enforcement

International enforcement, however, is more problematic than domestic regulation. How are international contracts to be enforced or corporations compensated if these contracts are broken? Companies may need insurance protection.[1] International reinsurance supplements the protections of national companies. Financial deterrence offers some restraint. If a domestic party breaks one contract, he may be likely to break others. Then foreigners will not deal with him, and capital leaves.[2] A local court can also order penalties against performance failure. International courts or arbitration procedures may find in favor of the plaintiff.

Yet how can awards be carried out internationally? World government does not yet exist, and thus awards cannot be strictly enforced. In the past, the British Fleet might intervene against countries defaulting on their obligations, as it did against both Turkey and Egypt in the nineteenth century.[3] By bombarding large coastal cities, the Royal Navy had a galvanic impact on defaulting governments. The American Commodore Matthew Perry forced Japan to establish trade and diplomatic relations with the United States by threatening a naval broadside on Tokyo. Today, however, such military intervention would be both crude and counterproductive. The International Monetary Fund can act more subtly: it can postpone delivery of monies already appropriated for an indigent party, as happened to Russia and Indonesia. It can insist on interest or exchange rate changes to qualify the country for future loans. It can offer or postpone debt relief.

Such tactics work, however, only if they have essentially united great power support. During the cold war these techniques were not always successful. Breakers of the rules still might hope to get help from one side of the bipolar world. After Iraq defaulted on Soviet loans for military assistance in the 1980s, Baghdad was still able to get more money from the United States. Until 1990, America wanted to use Iraq as a counterbalance against a Muslim fundamentalist Iran. (The United States ceased all aid, however, when Iraq invaded Kuwait.) After expropriating the real estate of Cuban exiles Fidel Castro was subjected to economic sanctions levied by the United States and some other countries. Yet this did not stop the Soviet Union from buying Cuba's sugar crop at above-market prices. When the great powers were divided, economic sanctions and incentives did not work—or, they worked only on one side of the fence.[4]

The Rationale for an Encompassing Coalition

In the future, decentralized enforcement will succeed only if the major powers accept a significant role. This means in practical terms that an informal grouping of great powers—an encompassing coalition—needs to energize the UN Security Council and to oversee general stability in world politics, giving international institutions a chance to operate. An encompassing coalition in world politics is necessary to maintain international compliance with and enforcement of those engagements.

The creation of such a coalition, however, generally confronts a public goods problem. Public goods are collective benefits that, once provided, can be enjoyed by all—such as clean air, sidewalks, police protection, or international enforcement mechanisms. When such goods are created, some participants may wait for others to pay for the good, hoping to benefit as free riders. In local communities, if people waited for their neighbors to build roads (a domestic public good), none would be constructed. Instead, a municipal public works department solves the problem. It taxes homeowners and obliges everyone to pay their share. Yet this solution is not available internationally. International organizations do not have sovereign taxing power over the nations of the world. The United States, for example, has remained hundreds of millions of dollars in arrears on its UN assessments. It has not yet paid its share of the public good provided by United Nations activities.

Like common roads, the security for the international system as a whole is also a public good. Those who pay for this good will receive its benefits, but so will those who do not contribute. Why then should anyone pay for it? Unless great powers gain from such provision, they will hesitate to act.[5]

One reason for cooperation is the great powers' overriding need for security for themselves. In international relations the great powers are large contributors toward the security of other nations, but they are also the greatest beneficiaries of worldwide stability and security.[6] In the absence of security, states must devote more resources to military preparations and less to domestic welfare. Nations will not move their production plants abroad unless trade routes are secure. They will not rely on the courts of another nation to enforce contracts unless there are good relations between the states concerned. Short of the definitive application of international law, there have been two well-known means of providing security on an international basis: (1) the balance of power, and (2) an encompassing coalition or concert of powers system. Each of these has different requirements, strengths, and weaknesses.

THE BALANCE OF POWER

The balance of power has only one requirement: that states act to prevent a single power from asserting preponderance over the system as a whole. States do not have to agree ideologically for a balance to function.[7] Yet the state system does not always meet the minimum standard. Countries frequently hesitate to enforce a balance of power against a misbehaving state.[8, 9] They do not always rearm or form counteralliances to restrain an expansionist power. Sometimes countries even find it in their interest to reach agreement with the aggressor, allowing balancing to fall by the wayside. Napoleon got all the great powers except England to support him for much of the period from 1800 to 1812. Hitler won cooperation from most other powers from 1933 to 1939.

It is not surprising that these lapses occurred. Under a balance of power system, a great power is the most likely source of imbalance. The other powers, therefore, must be prepared to rebuff one of their own number—a very strong requirement. The military demands of a balance of power system, therefore, are very onerous. Since each of the great powers could become the enemy, they do not and cannot fully trust one another.

A balance of power system attempted to govern world politics as early as the seventeenth century. The historical record of the balance of power is, however, a checkered one. Often the balance requires weaker nations to discipline the actions of an aggressive nation-state by military force; but too few states may join in the balancing coalition. Sometimes the powerful nation has persisted in the face of balancing actions. For example, Louis XIV made great gains for long periods even though several coalitions fought against him. Though the Triple Entente of Britain, France, and Russia balanced the Triple Alliance of Germany, Austria–Hungary, and Italy in 1914, it did not prevent war.

AN ENCOMPASSING COALITION OR CONCERT OF POWERS

An encompassing coalition or concert system requires more trust but less military capability than a balance of power. For the concert of powers to succeed, states must share common political objectives as well as the need to offset preponderance.[10, 11] Concert systems are directed against smaller disruptors on the fringes of the system. In the nineteenth century the Concert of Europe agreed ideologically to maintain legitimist (conservative) elites in power domestically, as well as agreeing on the need for peace and stability internationally. They successfully intervened in Spain and Naples from 1818 to 1820, and prevented the Belgian revolution from causing a dispute between Britain and France in the 1830s. They also dampened the pretensions of Egypt's Mehemet Ali in his revolt against the Ottoman Empire in 1839 to 1841. The revolutions of 1848, however, undercut ideological agreement, splitting the concert into liberal and conservative camps. When Russia undertook to protect Ottoman Christians in 1853, the two sides clashed in the Crimean War. This failure ultimately unleashed four aggressive wars between 1859 and 1871. The concert could no longer agree or compel obedience.

Today the situation is very different. At the cusp of the twenty-first century, most great powers also share some fundamental ideological objectives, including the desire to maintain an open world economy and to promote international economic growth and a measure of domestic liberalization. They agree on the need to maintain the basic structure of international peace. These ideological agreements have given the great powers a stake in the international system, enabling them to cooperate to provide the public good of security for themselves and other nations.

Douglass North shows that shared ideology is also critical to providing the public good of a functioning marketplace. In North's homey example, an individual has to be willing to pay for an orange rather than steal it. In deciding to pay for the orange he makes a short-term sacrifice (refusing to steal), but he gains the respect of his peers and obtains the long-term benefit that a market system provides.[12] In the same manner, the cost of cooperating in an international order can be counter-balanced by the benefits of ideological agreement. Trust increases when all share certain fundamental ideals. As legitimacy rises, the advantage of free riding declines. This is why American and NATO action in Bosnia in 1994 was generally internationally supported (and indeed regarded as overdue). It is also why American intervention in Vietnam did not receive general international support. The Russians supported North Vietnam in the bipolar contest, and many other nations disapproved of U.S. efforts to install a quasi-colonial regime in the south.

Today an informal international concert or encompassing coalition exists among the great powers. The end of the cold war has at least temporarily put an end to rigid ideological divisions among major states. While not all nations have accepted democratic procedures, most countries want to use and support the international trading system, shifting their production as economic incentives beckon from country to country. Even China wishes to join an essentially Western-oriented international economy and has accepted the need to restructure or sell off major parts of its state industry to the Chinese public. Liberalizing domestic coalitions are in power in many countries of Latin America, Southeast Asia, and some in Africa. The great powers now want to join the international economy, not divorce themselves from it, as Russia did under the Soviet regime.

The Advantages of an Encompassing Coalition

An encompassing coalition offers an important advantage over a balance of power system. In concert form, it represents an overbalance of power directed against opponents. As long as the great powers are agreed within its structure, the coalition will likely prevail over all challengers. Conquerors such as Napoleon, Kaiser Wilhelm II, or Hitler never confronted a dominant coalition already in place. Balancing took place too late to prevent major wars.

An encompassing coalition offers better results. Consider for a moment the political effect of a strong economic and political coalition linking the United States, key European nations, and Japan. Such a core group would possess nearly three-fourths of the world's combined GDP.[13] In military terms it would be stronger still.[14] What would be the effect of such a group on a possibly recalcitrant China or Russia? There is a point at which power shifts accumulate rather than dissipate power. If well over one-half of world power has already been amassed, its possession acts to draw other nations in, not repel them. We then have an overbalance of power. If Russia and China then join, there is a further centripetal effect on India, Pakistan, Brazil, and ultimately even Iran. Success breeds greater success.[15]

The Economic Advantage of an Overbalance of Power

Not only is this overbalance of power stable (given the reality and validity of the economic and political assumptions underlying it), such a coalition is also a relatively cost-effective regulative institution. Unlike a balance of power, an encompassing coalition is not primarily concerned with defeating one or more members of its own club; it seeks to discipline weaker powers such as Iraq, Serbia, Iran, or Libya. An encompassing coalition presumes the costs and benefits, favors continued adherence by members of its group, and uses its forces to prevent or limit local conflicts. Thus its members do not require inflated military capabilities. There is no need for military expenditures akin to those of the cold war period. In a period of increasing virtualization the great power members of an encompassing coalition can largely devote their resources to internal development and international trade, relying on centripetal forces to draw other nations in. International stability becomes easier to maintain.

The Feasibility of an Encompassing Coalition

As we have seen, virtual nations need the protection that a united group of great powers can offer. There is no certainty, however, they will receive it. An encompassing coalition depends on a "mixed system" of international relations that embodies elements of both cooperation and conflict. Each major state has differences as well as areas of common interests with every other great power. Russia has both cooperative and antagonistic relations with China. In Siberia, Russia fears Chinese expansion; but Moscow welcomes Chinese help in offsetting American preponderance. The United States and China have disagreements as well as cooperative links. Both favor an expansion of the world trading system but differ radically on the treatement of Taiwan. When "mixed relations" obtain, domestic populations may not understand the occasional need to achieve limited agreements with uncooperative foreign countries. An overarching reason for the cold war was that both Russian and American decision makers required largely unalloyed cooperation from the other side. They each insisted on linking arms control with cooperation in Africa or the Middle East. When one party failed to give cooperation across the board, the other decided that all cooperation was impossible. In the United States, public opinion wanted either to like or hate Russia. Americans did not understand that the rapprochement between great powers can never be total.

Today, however, America could greatly assist in strengthening the encompassing coalition if it sought to capture whatever cooperation is feasible. This means tolerating complex relationships with other countries. In the past, if other nations did not do what Americans wanted, they tended to be labeled opponents, particularly if they were not fully democratic by U.S. standards. Both China and Russia have suffered from this predisposition of American politics.

The need to accept a mixed system of international relations, however, does not suggest that all issues can necessarily be compromised. Nazi Germany's bellicose and inhuman behavior demanded a tough and military response. In the twenty-first century, however, judgments must take into account the developmental stage that other nations have reached. Emerging countries may eventually become rich and democratic. Developed nations may overcome past tendencies to be militarily aggressive. Today's Germany and Japan do not offer threats to the international system; in fact both are among the most cooperative modern nations. This is because their fates are linked to an open international economy.[16] Neither Japan nor Germany wants military conflict to force an end to economic exchange. These nations have also reached out to Russia and China to bring them closer to the encompassing coalition.

Still, it is possible that an encompassing coalition will break down because of a collapse of agreement or the emergence of military rivalries among the great powers. The European concert broke down in the second half of the nineteenth century when Germany challenged France, and Russia sought to undermine the Austrian position in the Balkans. Traditional rivalries have existed between Russia and key European nations, and between Japan and China. Today, however, these old differences have been influenced by the attitude and policy of the United States. America is not only the world's strongest military power, it is also a moderator among other nations. It seeks no European or Asian territory for itself and thus can be friendly to both sides in regional disputes. Neither Japan nor China, Russia nor Germany wishes the United States to withdraw from Europe and Asia. Power and geographic considerations continue to place the United States at the center of an encompassing coalition.

The Economic Underpinning of the Encompassing Coalition

A successful world economy knits together the policies of major states. Trade in goods is critical because none of the present great powers has within its confines all it needs for civilized life. Some nations must import food; some manufactured goods; and others raw materials and oil. Virtualization tends to strengthen the links among major markets. As we have seen, these links give the great powers an ever-increasing stake in enforcing the obligations inherent in the world economic system.

International financial markets are the means by which countries transfer assets and production abroad. Portfolio investment in another country's stock market represents an important claim on its assets. Direct investment in production (the virtualization process), represents an even more serious and long-term commitment to the country involved.

As developed countries have increasingly concentrated on the production of international services and relied on others for physical goods, the world economy helps to bring together the great powers whose cooperation makes that economy work politically and internationally. The result may be a worldwide economic system of extraordinary stability and depth.

Part Three

States in
the Virtual Age

chapter 7

The Virtual States: Hong Kong, Singapore, and Taiwan

Hong Kong, Singapore, and to a lesser extent Taiwan are major virtual states. Along with a few other small nations in Europe (principally Switzerland and the Netherlands) they have pioneered a new method of international economic relations focusing on services at home and production abroad. They have been influenced by Japan but have gone beyond Tokyo in transferring manufacturing overseas to reduce labor costs.[1] Over time this has enabled them to influence or even decide what gets produced in other nations. Hong Kong's base of production has become Guangdong province in South China. Singapore also produces in China but has located additional capacity in Johore—across the Strait in Malaysia and in the Riau archipelago (Indonesia). Taiwan has kept part of its production at home but has been responsible for a large portion of foreign direct investment in China, channeled through Hong Kong. Taiwan has also invested in Indonesia and Thailand. It has upgraded its home production of semiconductors, and is making that production capability available to a range of other countries and industries.

Taiwan's new manufacturing capability is supported by industrial alliances—agreements between companies that enable foreign firms to use Taiwanese facilities to produce their semiconductors. Industrial alliances to manufacture a particular product may create difficulties if the partner-firm is also a competitor in other areas. Taiwan's new foundries, however, do not pose this problem, since they have no proprietary products of their own.[2]

The basic strategy of Hong Kong, Singapore, and Taiwan has been to employ Chinese firms to produce goods for them. They thereby avoid building new production capabilities at home, such as buying land, constructing buildings, installing machinery, and hiring new labor. This also reduces the duplication of production facilities worldwide.

In practical terms the three economies have evolved a new strategy of economic prowess: adopting the downsizing of firms as a national strategy and transferring their excess production elsewhere.[3] All three have also upgraded their research and development capacities so that they can design and market products for manufacture abroad. Their infrastructures—educational facilities, communications, ports, highways, air links, and financial environments for capital inflows—have been modernized. High-tech services rise in value compared to manufacturing in all three economies, but particularly in Hong Kong.

Yet these three economies have not significantly increased their productivity. Their growth has been mostly attributable to higher investment and capital inputs, not to greater output per unit of input. Unlike Japan, the United States, and key European economies, Hong Kong, Singapore, and Taiwan have not yet made labor or capital much more productive.[4] If these three economies are to avoid downturn as capital inputs reach diminishing marginal returns,[5] they will have to invest more in education and research and development. The same goes for China's economy, which has seen few productivity improvements.

Despite the Far Eastern financial crisis and the drastic downturn in stock and currency markets, the future of these dynamic Southeast Asian tigers remains bright.[6] Brookings Institution experts calculate that total factor productivity is now beginning to increase in Singapore and Taiwan.[7] The three economies were not weak on "fundamentals" before the financial crisis. Their banking systems had not heedlessly extended credit or become vulnerable to incoming "hot money" flows. They suffered because of the contagion effect of capital outflows and the

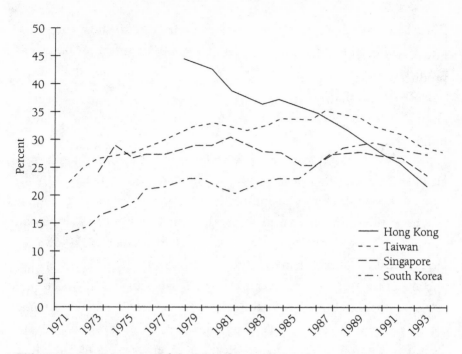

FIGURE 7.1   Percentage of the labor force employed in manufacturing for selected East Asian countries, 1971–1994.
SOURCE: *ILO Yearbook of Labour Statistics* and the *Statistical Yearbook of the Republic of China.*

depreciation of currencies in Thailand, Malaysia, and especially Indonesia. International investors assumed that they would have to devalue in response and attacked reigning currency values in all three states. Only Hong Kong successfully held the line. Without this unforeseeable attack, the nations would have moved from strength to strength.[8] Most observers agree that they will revive and that for some time high capital inputs will continue to produce large returns in output. In addition, further research and development will eventually increase the productivity of those inputs. As the productivity of high-tech services grows, the rewards of producing elsewhere through industrial alliances and mergers with other firms should also rise.

Retaining some high-end production capability at home, the three virtual nations have sought to assist other countries in financing and marketing their production. While the three countries moved their more labor-intensive production overseas, they did far more than this: they established a consulting role in the economic future of other nations. The knowledge they have offered is worth more than their tangible exports of the past.[9]

Hong Kong

As a Special Administrative Region of China, Hong Kong is highly attuned to economic forces operating there. In many ways Hong Kong is China's window on the world for both capital and goods. This is an enormous change from its historic role as a bastion of British power in the Far East, acquired as it was by Great Britain in the opium wars before any of the other European great powers had gained treaty ports and extraterritorial rights in mainland China. Hong Kong was the original commercial entrance to China. Later, however, it lost its special advantages over Canton or Shanghai. Typical British enterprises had an office or even their headquarters in Hong Kong, but the real business was done in Shanghai or Nanjing. In the later nineteenth century Hong Kong thus had more political than economic significance. After World War I even this role was overshadowed by the construction of the giant British naval base at Singapore.

After World War II Hong Kong underwent a radical transformation. When the Communists took over China in 1949, the resulting boycott of mainland China forced a Hong Kong previously dependent on Chinese reexports to develop a manufacturing industry of its own. More than a million refugees from the mainland brought energy and capital to this task.[10] The colony began to specialize in light industry—textiles, toys, and watches.

It was not the industrial structure of Hong Kong that made the difference, however. None of Hong Kong's products was at the cutting edge of industrial innovation. When Hong Kong gradually moved its producing factories to Guangdong province and effectively divested itself of manufacturing industry in the 1980s and 1990s, this was a novel but logical evolution. Low labor costs and an energetic workforce on the mainland (that could be managed by former mainlanders now living in Hong Kong) served as an economic magnet for Hong Kong entrepreneurs.

After the embargo on trade with China was lifted by the United States and Western nations in the 1970s, however, the Hong Kong entrepôt became the entry point for 60 to 80 percent of all foreign direct investment going into China. Taiwan, the United States, Japan, Europe, and Southeast Asian nations used Hong Kong's financial acumen in making their investments on the mainland. More than any other locale, Hong Kong became the judge of China's credit worthiness and of the financial soundness of China's government as well as of its public and private enterprises. Hong Kong's financial competence on China became akin to the monopoly on economic intelligence that Britain maintained on the world's borrowers during the nineteenth century. Hong Kong today retains this edge.

There is also another sense in which Hong Kong is unique. It is the source of reexport of Chinese goods to the outside world. Hong Kong harbor has now exceeded Rotterdam as the world's busiest container port. Perhaps more important, Hong Kong's financial and marketing tutelage has enabled China to become an exporting power of the first magnitude, with an annual trade surplus of more than $40 billion with the United States. When mainland reform began after 1978, Hong Kong's influence became decisive on China's economic course. Channeling more than $76 billion of foreign investment into China, Hong Kong took industries that were inefficiently producing for local consumption and turned them into export machines.

This total is no more than 5 percent of China's GDP, but this foreign investment produces two-thirds of Chinese exports—providing for most of China's foreign exchange. China puts a considerable proportion of this back to work in Hong Kong itself, contributing to the strengthened Hong Kong dollar.[11] Hong Kong therefore has been largely responsible for the boom in the coastal provinces that today account for over 50 percent of China's GDP. If a significant amount of money or people were to leave Hong Kong, China's boom would be checked and its export drive directly affected.

In time, of course, Shanghai will learn the skills of the commercial trade. Other container ports will emerge in southern China, but no Chinese city is likely to duplicate Hong Kong's financial intelligence. Nor is it likely that mainland cities will earn the same trust among Western and Japanese investors and manufacturers. Hong Kong capitalists can promise to deliver a quality product made in China, and they can be held accountable in the impartial Hong Kong court. This is not true on the mainland, where *guanxi* (politics) influences and sometimes determines economic decisions. China's prosperity therefore is linked to Hong Kong's intermediary role. Hong Kong weathered the economic buffeting of the 1997–98 financial crisis. Despite the check to economic growth, the Hong Kong dollar was not devalued, and as long as Beijing supported the renminbi (China's external unit of account), Hong Kong's financial competitiveness would be sustained.

China's treatment of Hong Kong, moreover, will also determine the success of the later reintergration of Taiwan into the mainland. The more democratic Hong Kong can become under Chinese tutelage, the more willing pro-independence Taiwanese will be to accept Chinese sovereignty over Taipei.

Hong Kong remains as the paramount virtual state with political and economic influence radiating deep within mainland China. It serves as the major conduit of foreign direct investment into China, and like Britain in the nineteenth century, it selects and evaluates Chinese industrial prospects. Hong Kong will provide economic training to a new generation of Chinese leaders and achieve new heights as the world's most prominent service economy.

Singapore

Modern Singapore is an economic powerhouse with the best-educated population in the world. Until recently a factory for the world, it has adapted to rising labor costs by shifting its manufacturing to Malaysia, Indonesia, and China, thereby moving toward virtual status.

In the eighteenth century Singapore was a neglected backwater ruled by the Sultan of Johore. It had little geographic or economic importance, because the main shipping lane between Europe and East Asia lay to the south, in the Sunda Strait, which separates Sumatra and Java. In 1824, through the efforts of Sir Stamford Raffles, Singapore was ceded to the British East India Company, and in 1867 it became a Crown Colony under direct rule from London. Under colonial rule Singapore emerged as a major commercial entrepôt for the entire region. With the opening of the Suez Canal in 1869, the Straits of Malacca replaced the Sunda Strait as the main link to Europe, and Singapore's trade benefited commensurately. In the twentieth century the British developed the tin and rubber industries of Malaya, with Singapore as the regional hub. The oil of the Dutch East Indies also made Singapore a center for the processing and reexport of petrochemical products. Britain built a major naval base on Singapore after World War I, part of a chain of bases stretching from Gibraltar and Malta through the Mediterranean Sea to Bombay, Calcutta, and the Far East. During this period Singapore was a commercial and not a manufacturing center.

After 1959 Singapore moved gradually toward independence from Britain under Lee Kuan Yew and the Peoples Action Party (PAP). Singapore had always had a special relationship with Indonesia, serving as a free trade port for the processing and sale of Jakarta's raw materials. When the British withdrew, they sought to include Singapore as part of the newly created Malaysia, and Singapore briefly developed an import-replacement industry whose products it could sell to Kuala Lumpur. When that union broke down in 1965, Singapore turned to face a wider world, and PAP developed a strategy of export-led growth in manufacturing. Initially it confined its efforts to capital-intensive industries such as chemicals and petroleum. While these industries grew rapidly, they did not solve the chronic unemployment problem. Only after Singapore began to solicit foreign direct investment in new manufacturing and electronics industries did employment rise. The island state then began to produce for Japan, the United States, and Western European countries. Foreign plants received incentives to export and Singapore's growth rate accelerated to nearly 10 percent per year. By the early 1990s Singapore had attained the status of a developed country and a per capita income of close to $25,000.

After 1990 the island nation strengthened its gains from manufacturing with new service industries. It moved part of its new production overseas to Malaysia, Indonesia, and China. Older home manufacturing stabilized at about 29 percent of GDP. Services rose from 40 percent of GDP to 56 percent. Singapore stressed the industries of the mind at a time when its students attained the highest worldwide test scores in both mathematics and science.[12] In the future Singapore's diversified strategy helped to lead the East Asian comeback from the financial crisis.

Taiwan

Taiwan has followed a strategy of export-led industrialization based on small firms. The role of the state was critical in funneling investment into favored industry, but unlike Korea, Taiwan did not favor large-scale conglomerates (the *chaebol*). After a period of government direction it has moved more to private investment and smaller enterprises. Under the Japanese occupation Taiwan was treated better than Korea and already had a small sector of light industry in the 1940s. When the Kuomintang took over the reins in 1947–53, they were determined not to repeat the mistakes they had made in ruling China. They avoided printing money, initiated land reform, and maintained high interest rates both to control inflation and to increase the savings rate. U.S. economic assistance in the early years smoothed the transition from Japanese rule. Initially Taiwan pursued an import-substitution strategy, developing a high-cost light industrial structure in textiles, plastics, glass, and plywood. These products could not be exported, however, owing to the overvalued New Taiwan (NT) dollar. Bureaucrats resisted lowering its value because they feared inflation.

The import-substitution policy did not last long. In 1958, faced with stagnant growth, Taiwan shifted to an export-led growth strategy. The government lowered the value of the NT dollar from 25/$1.00 to 36/$1.00 (U.S.). After the successful outcome of the Taiwan Straits crisis in 1958–59, the Kuomintang cut military spending and moved to accelerate the economy instead.

Labor-intensive manufacturing, largely for export, fueled the economy for the next thirty years. Export industries attained higher productivity than those engaged in domestic manufacture. Enterprises grew, though not to the large-scale Korean level. In 1988 the government freed industry to invest and produce in China, causing a dynamic shift that sent huge new investments to the mainland. By 1998 Taiwan had invested more than $35 billion in China and had become after Hong Kong the second leading investor there.

In May 1997 the Taiwan government put new limits on such ventures in China for political reasons. It limited investments to $50 million each and ruled out investment in mainland infrastructure: roads, power plants, communication and telephone systems, port facilities. Given the opposition of Taiwan's industry, however, this prohibition seemed unlikely to endure as other countries moved in to take Chinese business. At a certain point, moreover, the economic link between China and Taiwan becomes too important for either to sacrifice. In 1998 China took 16 percent of Taiwan's exports. More and more of Taiwan's production is sited on the mainland. In the longer term, Xiamen, the Chinese port just across the strait from Taiwan, should become another link in the chain uniting the two economies. Five thousand Taiwanese businessmen have already taken up residence there. With labor costs on the mainland only one-fifth of those on the island, Taiwan's investment in China gives substantial returns. As production costs rise in Kaohsiung and Taipei, the mainland will become even more preferred. *The Economist* concluded in 1998:

> Taiwan Inc. is becoming a virtual company. A small headquarters in Taipei now supports vast manufacturing and distribution facilities around the world. Profits are made abroad and increasingly reinvested abroad as well. Over the past eight years, Taiwanese compa-

nies have invested $80 billion outside the country and 300,000 of
their best people have followed to manage these investments.[13]

Foreign Direct Investment, Diversification, and the Rise of International Services

The main significance of the three Asian tigers is their pioneering development of two forms of economic relationships with other countries.
First, they have encouraged substantial foreign direct investment that
has made possible an export strategy in high-tech products. Second,
while producing for export at home, they have also diversified their
production plants, locating a larger proportion of them in other nations,
particularly in China and Malaysia, where costs are low. In this respect
Singapore, Hong Kong, and Taiwan have become advanced countries,
investing in the production of still-developing nations nearby. In each
case the proportion of GDP earned by high-level services has risen.

These nations are in the vanguard of the virtual state movement, and
Western and developed countries have emulated the trend they initiated. Many of these larger nations have also sought to diversify their
production bases. Downsizing of their manufacturing plants has
brought greater profitability and productivity. Whereas manufacturing
at its peak in the 1960s and 1970s represented about 35 percent of GDP
of these countries, most of them now have reduced it to around 20 percent. Their foreign revenue increasingly comes from financial services,
income on foreign investment, shipping, insurance, telecommunications, and software. England, Holland, and the United States have
moved most strongly in this direction, with Germany not far behind.

In the never-ending quest for higher shareholder value, the companies of these nations have become consulting as well as producing
mechanisms. Traditional manufacturing concerns such as IBM and Motorola derive a greater share of their profits from services and royalties
rather than computers and chips. General Electric exemplifies this evolution. Not long ago Jack Welch, GE's CEO, announced that GE eventually would earn 80 percent of its revenues from services. A subsidiary,

GE Capital, is now the largest American investment bank in Europe, ahead of Morgan Stanley and Goldman Sachs. GE Capital has moved to accumulate smaller and peripheral European firms whose acquisition would not create disturbances in the local media or business community. Its strategy has been to take on state-of-the-art firms whose shortages of capital have prevented them from expanding in local or regional markets and to make them into bigger players in international services. Many European service enterprises do not want to be taken over by a neighboring European country but consider investment from the United States more acceptable.[14]

Rapidly expanding investment in services accompanies a more familiar investment in manufacturing abroad: industrial alliances, foreign corporate acquisitions, and production overseas. U.S. midwestern auto and truck suppliers are diversifying well beyond the *maquiladoro* plants along the Rio Grande to set up new production lines throughout Mexico. As Mexico gears up for a huge upgrading of its infrastructure, its demand for large construction equipment rises—and the United States has helped to meet that need. The result is that U.S.–Mexico trade now exceeds that between Japan and the United States.

Other nations and regions slated to receive Western manufacturing investment are China, India, Eastern Europe, and Russia. Turkey is a preferred location for investment because of its links with the former Asiatic republics of the USSR. After its standoff with the energy company Enron, the Indian government has accepted new investment in a series of industries, including automobiles. Japan is rushing in to challenge past U.S. dominance in foreign direct investment in India. Whether the BJP government in India will continue to be hospitable to foreign direct investment, however, has yet to be tested. Meanwhile, Revlon has decided to move its Asian cosmetics unit from Japan to China. Its Shanghai factory will export 30 percent of its output.

What is striking about this surge of investment into new realms is that it has not awaited the completion of needed commercial and legal reforms in the countries concerned. Companies that want to play a greater role in the economic future of Eastern Europe need to get there soon. Once shunned as a regulatory nightmare, India could become one of the most rapidly growing economies of the twenty-first century. China will remain the most favored location for foreign direct investment. Thus the paths pioneered by small virtual states are attracting imitators from the ranks of developed countries.

The innovations made by the three Asian tigers, Hong Kong, Singapore, and Taiwan are not unique. The three virtual states represent a trend in manufacturing industry on a worldwide basis: the movement toward high-level services "is not a negative phenomenon but is the natural consequence of the industrial dynamism in an already developed economy."[15] The movement of plants overseas did not derive simply from the impact of globalization. It was rather the reflection of a gradual change in factor price ratios (between physical capital and information) that over time has made intangibles grow in value relative to more tangible assets (such as machinery and physical plants). What the three tigers have done is to chart new means for reclaiming value as manufacturing declines. Their answer is to improve research and development capacities so as to be able to advise other nations on how and what to produce. They have initiated a trend that is now becoming worldwide in scope.

chapter 8

Japan

After its defeat in World War II, Japan was forced by the Allied states to embrace democratic government and adopt a peaceful international policy. Since then, however, Tokyo has chosen its own course. The reason Japan has become pivotal in the world economy is not only its stellar economic performance but the way it achieved success. In many respects Japan has extended its internal decision-making processes to international relations. Consensus, patience, consultation, and elaborate shows of politeness and deference have characterized Japanese dealings with the outside world. Along with Western Germany, Japan pioneered the role of a trading state—a state that abjures military expansion and territorial aggrandizement—and founded its position on commerce with other nations. After it was forced to give up its Pacific empire Japan adopted a new strategy: it prospered by seeking access rather than control of the resources and markets of other nations. Unlike all previous world powers that defined success in spatial terms (the breadth and width of territorial extent), Japan was the first country that sought success in time. In this sense Japan discovered an entirely new strategy of international advancement, one that brought it far greater achievements as a "small nation" than did its previous empire building.

Today Japan is critical for another reason. It is in a position to reequilibrate the world economy and prevent an economic recession that could affect many countries. If it acts forcefully to stimulate its economy (which in turn would increase demand for the wares of other nations), it can recirculate capital to countries in trouble in East Asia and elsewhere. If on the other hand Japan continues to export goods on the basis of an undervalued yen, it will run East Asian economies into the ground and spread recession. For the first time since World War II Japan needs to sell its products at home—stimulating domestic demand and producing for the Japanese people. The choice Japan makes will determine its long-term influence in both economic and political relationships on a worldwide basis.

——————

Japan's emphasis on international cooperation after World War II has masked a strong and still chauvinistic attitude toward foreign affairs. Inside Japan, as Chie Nakane contends, social conflict has had to be confined within a "frame society," in which group struggle was contained by the iron hand of the state.[1] Japanese historical experience in part explains this result. Isolated from the Asian mainland and yet subject to invasion, Japanese history oscillated between social consensus when the threat of foreign intervention loomed and discord when it passed. As democracy emerged, however, politics became subject to veto groups. Shumpei Kumon points out that "there is a deep-rooted belief that as long as a unanimous and spontaneous decision is reached in a 'democratic' organization, the organization should be allowed to do whatever it wants."[2] This belief, however, is set against the *wa* principle: a principle of harmony that demands "egoistic" action by subgroups be subjected to restraint for the good of the whole.[3] Yet the contentious unity of the Japanese social order is not buttressed by agreement on universal moral or philosophic norms that link Japan with other nations.[4] The country's mores are rules about how Japanese should behave toward each other, not toward citizens of other nations. This marks an important difference from European history and philosophy. Western philosophy developed in ecumenical European culture, in which competing states were not isolated from one another. As rulers of erstwhile Roman provinces, European kings emerged from an overarching framework in which no nationality or territory enjoyed precedence over others. Thus eighteenth-century European political theory never elevated the role of one state or nation above others. Rights and duties were universal, not national.

Among the Japanese, however, Nippon enjoys moral priority. Regardless of individual rights, yielding to other states can never be fully justified. Yet Japan cannot always triumph, and it has much to learn from the outside world. Since Japan cannot rule the world but still needs to protect its own cultural integrity, it has suffered from the absence of an international government to adjudicate and control relations among powers in the way that the Japanese government contains conflict domestically. Under conditions of international uncertainty, Japan has had to feel its way gingerly in its relations with other states, many of which do not accept Japanese principles.

This was not a major problem as long as Japan could rely completely on the United States for protection and guidance. This dependence, however, could not continue after the end of the cold war. Japan's own higher standing and the decline in America's hegemonic position combined to force on it a more autonomous stance. Japan is now an associate of the United States, no longer a pupil. It benefits greatly from the extension of American power to East Asia and from the U.S. protection of trade routes for Japanese goods and imports of oil. Yet Japan also competes with America for markets in East Asia and around the world[5] and must chart its own long-term relations with China, Russia, Europe, and the rest of the world.

Recently Japan has encountered an entirely new kind of economic competition. As long as industry and manufacturing were the standards of excellence in economics, Japan prospered. It still excels in these important sectors;[6] but while "manufacturing matters," it matters much less than it once did.[7] Achievement is now measured not by manufacturing productivity increases but by excellence in creative and information services: product design, fundamental research, and intelligent software. As Japan was mastering hardware, the world was beginning to shift to software as the standard for economic excellence. As Japan triumphed in tangibles, the world shifted to intangibles. It is Japan's failure to excel in both elements of economic strategy—manufacturing and services—that creates problems today. If Japan had shifted to a services strategy, the financial crisis besetting Asia would have been overcome earlier.

The Japanese "bubble economy" of the late 1980s has of course given way. Stock values fell more than 50 percent, the property market collapsed, and the banking system remains insolvent. Japan has not yet matched its mastery of industrial processes with superiority in banking or finance. In fact the very strengths of administrative guidance as applied to industry by the Ministry of International Trade and Industry have turned out to be weaknesses when deployed by the Ministry of Finance in monetary affairs.

The Bank of Japan and the Ministry of Finance consciously decided to deflate the Japanese stock market and prick the property bubble in 1989. They raised interest rates, leading to a collapse of the stock market from 38,000 on the Nikkei Index to less than half that. The banks had lent a great deal to firms and investors whose holdings included vast amounts of urban property. When interest rates temporarily rose, banks could not collect from debtors whose property holdings had crumbled in value. Today nonperforming loans total as much as $1 trillion, and many of Japan's largest banks are in trouble, even though interest rates have fallen back to very low levels. Japan now faces a banking crisis seven to eight times as great as the savings and loan debacle in the United States in the early 1990s.

The crisis has gone on so long partly because the government has not acted promptly either to close down insolvent banks and sell off nonperforming property assets or to stimulate the economy. Economic growth with resulting inflation and a rise in property values would obviously bring some banks back to profitability. Yet despite great pressures from foreigners, including the United States, the Japanese government has not yet devised a successful stimulus strategy.[8] A windfall from temporary tax cuts would almost certainly be saved by the consuming public. Public works expenditures appear to offer a short-term stimulus in rural regions of the country but do not represent a national solution. Consumption vouchers helped to increase spending but did not solve the problem. Government printing of yen and further deficits clearly were needed. Meanwhile, owing to the crisis, the Japanese yen has oscillated and fallen in value, undercutting export competitors in East Asia who are already under heavy pressure. The fall in the yen has taken business from Korea, Taiwan, and Singapore in shipbuilding, semiconductors, and consumer electronics. Japan continues to act as a manufacturing exporter seeking an export surplus with an undervalued currency, when it needs to move to an import surplus and capital exports based on a more highly valued yen.[9]

Virtualization has nonetheless had an influence. Japan's service sector has grown, and agriculture and mining have declined. Manufacturing has decreased as somewhat more than 10 percent of Japanese production has been transferred abroad. Yet even the Japanese policy of building export platforms in East Asia has made for greater long-term instability. These export platforms still export to North America, not Japan. They disguise the Japanese surplus with the United States as an Asian surplus. Except for Brunei and Indonesia, from which it imports oil, and China (textiles, toys), Japan has a balance of trade surplus with every Asian nation[10] (see Table 8.1).

Unfortunately Japan continues to increase its export surplus and permit devaluation of its currency, which increases the surplus even more. The domestic stimulus strategy currently being followed will lead to a depreciation of the yen. Japan can always invest its returns abroad, creating indebtedness in East Asian countries; but since the problem created by the Asian financial crisis was too much indebtedness in key economies, this would not facilitate a long-term solution.

Complicating the problem is the nature of Japanese production networks in Asia, which essentially export *kereitsu* (interfirm market-sharing) arrangements to Asian trade. Kozo Yamamura points out that Japanese production in Asian countries consists mainly of assembly plants for components manufactured in Japan, increasing the Japanese surplus. This means that the output of Japanese factories in Taiwan, for example, will not be exported back to Japan to compete with Japanese component producers there. The predictions of product cycle theories

TABLE 8.1   Japanese Trade Balances with Asian Countries (yen), 1997

Hong Kong		Singapore		Thailand	
Exports	*Imports*	*Exports*	*Imports*	*Exports*	*Imports*
3.3mil	272 thou	2.4 mil	710 thou	1.7 mil	1.1 mil
Malaysia		Philippines		South Korea	
Exports	*Imports*	*Exports*	*Imports*	*Exports*	*Imports*
1.7 mil	1.3 mil	1.0 mil	506 thou	3.1 mil	1.7 mil
Taiwan		Cambodia		Asian Newly Industrializing Economies	
Exports	*Imports*	*Exports*	*Imports*	*Exports*	*Imports*
3.3 mil	1.5 mil	7.0 thou	1.5 thou	12.2 mil	4.2 mil
China		Indonesia		Brunei	
Exports	*Imports*	*Exports*	*Imports*	*Exports*	*Imports*
2.6 mil	5.0 mil	1.2 mil	1.7 mil	18 thou	169 thou

SOURCE: JETRO, 1998

are not borne out.[11] Due to *kereitsu* market restrictions in Japan, this production will be sent to North America. Yamamura warns:

> It is indisputable . . . that Japanese multi-national enterprises have built production networks in Asia in the automobile, auto parts, electronics, machinery and other important industries and that these networks continue to be expanded and strengthened. Unless a specific policy is adopted, we will see in Asia in the coming decades what we have already witnessed in Japan: extreme or substantial difficulties for non-Japanese foreign firms wishing to enter markets dominated by *kereitsu* networks.[12]

In this respect Japan is strengthening purely manufacturing ties with other nations when it might be developing high-level services. Japan restricts its foreign direct investment production overseas to assembly plants dependent on Japanese suppliers. Little high technology is transferred to Asian nations.

A Long-Term Solution

In devising longer-term strategies Japan might usefully contemplate British practice before World War I and U.S. policy in the 1960s and 1970s. In the third quarter of the nineteenth century, Britons lent and invested large sums in European and Latin American nations, the United States, and the empire. Having done so, they had to allow these nations to pay back their debts. The borrowers could do this only by running an export surplus in the British market. By 1910, all of the countries Britain had lent to or invested in—Germany, the United States, Australia, New Zealand, Canada, South Africa, and Argentina—had won surpluses in the British home market. Thus there was no European or world financial crisis. Debtors were able to discharge their obligations.

Britain did not lose its overall balance of payments surplus. Even though its trade balance was negative, its balance of payments was still in surplus. England maintained that surplus through exports of "invisibles" such as financial services, shipping, insurance, and income on foreign investment. Britain had moved to a mature creditor strategy. Had World War I not intervened, Great Britain would have gone from strength to strength and might even have dominated the twentieth century as it did the nineteenth.

The United States in the 1960s and 1970s similarly found ways to allow indebted countries to repay their debts to America. The United States deliberately opened its markets to Japan, Korea, and the European states to allow them to sell freely in North America. Even though the United States maintained a balance of trade surplus until 1970, it recirculated the surplus through foreign and military aid and investment abroad.

If the tottering structure of international indebtedness is to stabilize, Japan today needs to move in a similar direction. East Asians are not the only debtors to Japan. The largest debtor is the United States of America, whose balance of trade deficit with Japan typically runs from $40 to $50 billion a year. The American deficit with China is approaching Japanese proportions. Overall, the United States has about $1.4 trillion more in obligations than it has in assets abroad. Each year the deficit continues, another $150 to $200 billion is added to the total that the United States owes foreign governments and citizens. At some point the supply of dollars held abroad may exceed demand. What happens when investors get tired of holding the dollar and come to believe that they would be better off in yen or the new Euro? Lester Thurow observes:

> When a run against the dollar starts, there are enormous amounts of money that can, and will, move into appreciating currencies. Sixty percent of official reserves and 50 percent of private reserves are currently held in dollars. Those funds will certainly move, but they will be a small fraction of the total funds avalanching down the slope. Financial speculators will pile on the downward trends in the dollar and the amounts moving will be many times the world's dollar holdings. . . . Those whose debts are denominated in the appreciating currencies (most likely yen and marks) will find the real value of their debts explodes—evaluated in their own currency or dollars. Many will be unable to repay their yen- or mark-denominated loans. Financial institutions in Japan and Germany will take big losses as foreigners default on their loans.[13]

If such scenarios are to be avoided, both Japan and the United States need to act to allow debts to be repaid on a worldwide basis. Japan in particular needs to find ways of allowing East Asian countries and the United States to regain surpluses in the Japanese market, lessening the debt overhang. In the East Asian case this means allowing Asian goods to find their way into the Japanese market. Singapore, Taiwan, and Korea are not sloppy economies. Highly educated nations, they make goods with the highest degree of precision. In the U.S. case, the export of high-level services to Japan could begin to cut the American trade deficit. Yet these goods and services have still not found their way into the Japanese market.

The Japanese People Benefit from Internationalization

There is a harmony of interest between what foreigners need from Japan and what the Japanese need from their government. Japan is run for the benefit of producers and workers. High and lifetime employment for workers has been important to Japanese industry, and until now, the Japanese strategy has been to favor the domestic producer and worker over the Japanese consumer. This has caused high prices for food, housing, transportation, and consumer goods within Japan, with few benefits in social security or retirement plans for ordinary citizens. Given the inadequacy of social welfare programs, the Japanese people have had to save for an uncertain future. This is why Japanese savings are so high.

With abundant domestic savings, interest rates could be very low for Japanese industry. These low rates have allowed industry to obtain capital at bargain-basement prices, enabling higher-than-average employment rates. Overseas, Japanese industry has been able to sacrifice profits for market share. The low cost of Japanese capital meant that exporters did not have to generate quick profits to pay back their loans. Financial links between Japanese banks and industry in any event made repayment less pressing.

Since interest rates were lowered to float business enterprise, savers suffered. One of the paradoxes of the modern international economy is that the Japanese save large amounts on the basis of negligible real interest rates while Americans save much less, even though the premium they earn is much higher. If Japanese depositors holding postal savings accounts (which earn less than 2 percent a year) were suddenly allowed to invest abroad, capital could leave in a flood, and a number of Japanese banks would collapse. There is already evidence that Japanese savers are stocking up on foreign currency holdings. The "Big Bang" (or financial opening) initiated but not completed by Prime Minister Hashimoto remained unfinished business on the agenda of Prime Minister Keizo

Obuchi. In another indication that it does not favor consumers, the Japanese government in 1997 raised the consumption tax from 3 percent to 5 percent, ostensibly to provide money for welfare payments to the rising number of the Japanese elderly. This increase, however, led to a tax rebellion and to attempts to scale back or abolish the tax altogether. If the Japanese government were to reduce or lift the consumption tax, consumption would undoubtedly increase, and repeal of the tax is one means of reflating the depressed Japanese economy.[14]

For a society so tilted toward business and labor and away from the consuming public, it was not surprising that Japan's leaders should emphasize selling abroad rather than at home.[15] If domestic demand were the engine of economic expansion and markets were unregulated, consumer sovereignty would decide which companies would prevail. Some companies would founder. The economist Yasusake Murakami has suggested that unfettered capitalist competition in Japan would result in "domestic dumping."[16] He believed it was better to "dump" goods abroad, where foreign companies would be the targets of Japanese competition. While the present system unquestionably prevents cutthroat competition in Japan, this analysis doesn't fully include the interests of Japanese consumers, who have been asked to buy Japanese goods at very high prices and have seldom enjoyed the alternative of excellent lower-cost foreign products. Japanese entrepreneurs who sought to buy Japanese goods abroad at low prices for the purpose of reimporting them into Japan have been sanctioned by the government. As the economy enters its eighth year of stagnation, food, housing, transportation, and consumer goods remain very expensive in Japan.

A domestic stimulus strategy would strike a blow for domestic consumption and a reduction of savings.[17] In addition to stimulating the economy, the government could also institute social security programs that would make saving for retirement less necessary. Greater consumer buying power would not only bring imports, but more important, it would stimulate demand for the products of Japan's small and medium-sized enterprises that have been bypassed in Japan's exporting strategy. If open markets and rising consumption stimulated economic growth, foreign capital would enter Japan seeking new investment opportunities. At

TABLE 8.2   Japanese Growth Rates

Year	Percent
1991	3.8
1992	1.0
1993	0.3
1994	0.6
1995	1.5
1996	3.9
1997	0.9
1998	−2.8

Average growth for the 1990s = 1.1 percent

SOURCE: Economic Planning Agency.

first the influx of foreign goods might actually lower prices, but an expanding economy abetted by low interest rates could soon bring a much needed reflation. Higher Japanese prices would also make Japanese goods less competitive internationally, reducing Japan's chronic foreign trade surplus. As domestic prices rose, foreign capital would return to the depressed property-market sector. This could support the yen, which otherwise might fall as a result of inflationary pressures. Japanese economic growth has responded to fiscal stimulus as well as monetary tightening. In 1995–96 the government reduced taxes and growth responded, only to plunge with consumption tax increases in the years following. Japanese growth rates indicate the effect of the changes (Table 8.2).

These growth rates will not increase appreciably without significant foreign investment. This calls for a further opening of the Japanese economic system: it must open itself not only to goods and services but also to investment. If Japan achieves full economic openness, economists Ronald McKinnon and Kenichi Ohno predict that interest rates in Japan cannot remain low relative to the rest of the world unless the yen stays undervalued.[18] The 4 or 5 percent difference between Japanese and Western interest rates will be eventually eliminated as yen appreciates to the purchasing power parity level of about 120–125 yen to the U.S. dollar.[19] This represents a considerable fall from the dollar highs near 150 yen reached in 1998, and it seems to be happening. As a result, barring government obstruction Japanese imports will rise and exports will decline. A greater proportion of the Japanese production of goods and services will be offered to the Japanese people.

In time Japanese shareholders should also benefit. American corporations have typically aimed to increase "shareholder value" in terms of stock price and dividends. Japanese corporations pay few if any dividends, and company boards of directors do not aim to increase earnings per share. These policies have helped keep stock prices in Japan far below those of 1989. It is a paradox that one of the most successful countries in world economic politics has not turned corporate gains into investor benefit. By Western standards, even the most successful Japanese firms have shown only moderate profits. If individual Japanese are to invest in Japanese firms, they must be convinced that this choice is preferable to investing in Western stocks or mutual funds. To date this has not been true.[20] Shareholder value must become an objective of Japanese firms if, with the Big Bang, Japanese investors are not to send their funds overseas and imperil Japanese banks and insurance companies.[21] In one way or another consumer and investor sovereignty will make itself felt in the Japanese market.

Japanese and American Strategies

Despite recent stirrings of revolt at traditional management secrecy, Japanese stockholders remain pliant servants of the corporate bond.[22] They give management unlimited latitude to chart strategy. Few Japanese corporate leaders have shown a desire to increase earnings per share or to augment the stock price. The languishing Nikkei Index is simply the aggregate measure of its component companies' inattention to stock price. Since they frequently aim at market share, not profitability, few Japanese companies are notably profitable. Very few have downsized or reduced their management overhead. They have been loath to lay off workers. Their relations with component suppliers continue as before, even though suppliers might be expected to bear a greater share of the joint costs. Unlike U.S. firms, many Japanese companies still operate on economies of scale rather than economies of scope. As we saw in chapter 1, it appears that production runs have to be longer in Japan than in the United States to attain minimum profitability.[23]

We have already seen that Japanese savings accounts return on average less than 2 percent per year. As the banking crisis abates, with insolvent banks closed down[24] and nonperforming loans sold off, savers will eventually be given the opportunity to invest abroad, and earn far higher returns. The Big Bang will ultimately open up Japan for incoming as well as outgoing capital.[25] Failed property loans will be bought up by foreign capital at 10 cents on the dollar. At the same time, Japanese savers, once they are able to invest in Western mutual funds and insurance companies, will force new and salutary lessons on Japanese industry. Managers will increasingly have to shift to shareholder value as a criterion of economic performance. This will finally give Japan an impetus to move toward virtual status. If firms need to become more profitable to please stockholders, they will have to downsize. This will shift production to cheaper and more efficient locations (many of them abroad), and the ratio between services and manufacturing will rise.

Virtual or head nation status for Japan will mean progressively conceding body nation manufacturing to other countries. China, East Asia (including ASEAN), and South Asia will benefit as Japan limits and divests itself of production capability. This concession will help the region's stability, however, only if Japan further agrees to reimport its production from foreign locales. Without such reimportation, Japanese consumers will continue to suffer from high-cost production based in Japan.[26] Foreign countries will still have huge trade imbalances, and Japanese producers will not greatly increase Japanese sales. The profits of Japanese firms will remain too low to justify significant price increases on stock exchanges in Japan, New York, and London. Japanese investors instead will buy into foreign firms. The threat of seeing their investment funds dry up is the best assurance that Japanese firms will abandon domestic economic closure and embrace virtual status.

A Mature Creditor Strategy

As the Japanese government gradually moves to benefit the economic interests of the Japanese consuming public, a mature creditor strategy commends itself. Japan already has several trillions of U.S. dollars invested abroad and a $10 trillion pool of domestic savings. It will accumulate even more as its current export drive proceeds. It can take the income from foreign investments bought with these funds and improve the lives of the Japanese people. Over time it can focus less on exports and move to an import surplus. Consumption will naturally rise in consequence, benefiting all Japanese. The result will also reduce the debt overhang facing countries that owe money to Japan. Such a mature creditor strategy will help stabilize the international financial system and would also permit Japan to move toward virtual status. As more of Japanese production is relocated abroad, the Japanese public would expect to benefit by having some of that production imported into the Japanese market. This would create a foreign trade benefit for the country in which the Japanese production was situated, again reequilibrating the system.

As Japan diminishes its home manufacturing plant and moves to higher-level services, it will pass the economic baton to new manufacturing nations rising in East Asia, Latin America, and elsewhere. Like Britain and America in years past, Japan will move up the economic ladder to higher-level functions embodying a greater knowledge content. In so doing, it will allow the United States to further diminish its indebtedness by selling high-level services in Japan. Since 1970 the United States has run a balance of trade deficit. In recent years it has sought to compensate for the trade deficit with a services surplus. This surplus more than doubled in the 1990s, going from $43 billion in 1991 to $88 billion in 1997 and making the American balance on current account (including international services) much more favorable than the balance on visible trade (exports minus imports).[27] American financial services will become even more valuable to Japan as the numerous elderly seek higher returns for their retirement portfolios by investing in the United States.

If the older population grows as forecast, Japan may even become more dependent on foreign investment and capital inflows.[28] This is because as the population ages, the Japanese savings rate should decline. The International Monetary Fund forecasts a decline in savings from 21 percent of GDP to 10 percent over the next several decades. Every percentage point change in the ratio of elderly to working-age population is expected to reduce aggregate savings by 0.4 percent.[29] The fewer younger workers will increasingly be unable to pay for the social and retirement benefits of their older colleagues. The burden will then fall on the Japanese government, whose capital budget is already deeply in debt. Ultimately Japan will have to borrow abroad, probably in large amounts, to finance social services for the elderly. At this stage, when Japan's export machine can no longer provide for every financial contingency, it will have reached mature creditor status. The value of the yen will have risen, and imports will flow into Japanese markets.

As it moved to mature creditor status, Japan would already have helped stabilize partner economies and benefited from their help in return. It would become a locomotive providing markets for others rather than an export Titanic, dragging Far Eastern nations down in its wake. One hopeful sign of this movement is the Japanese role in bailing out Thailand and Indonesia during the financial crisis. Japan's move to stabilize the markets of countries indebted to it is a welcome new role for Japan in the international economy.

Japan and The United States Compared

Both the United States and Japan have adopted trading stances toward the outside world. Each has sought to improve its political position by enhancing its economic strength. The U.S. strategy has been to move increasingly to international services while locating production abroad. It has relied on control of flows rather than domestic stocks of goods to achieve economic benefit. The Japanese export strategy has been to restrict flows entering Japan. It has mastered half the revolution: it encourages flows outward, not flows inward. Until it manages to perform the latter Japan will lack the capital, technology, and ultimately, the skilled manpower fully to participate in future economic transformations. Without free capital flows into Japan, the yen will remain a parochial rather than a fully international currency, and investment in Japan will not reflect market values. The problem will grow if, as some experts predict, Japan runs short of capital to modernize its infrastructure and quality of life in the twenty-first century.[30] There are limits to the Japanese population's ability (and willingness) to make sacrifices. They will want greater benefits than they have received in the past and will not be eager to accept new tax burdens. Other nations must help finance Japan's further modernization.

The United States will play a large role in this refinancing. The strange and unbalanced marriage between the United States and Japan defies historic precedent. Never have the two leading powers in the world system been so intricately involved in each other's domestic economies. Never has this intertwining presented such momentous issues. When a Japanese prime minister threatens to sell U.S. Treasury bonds, the market shivers. The term *interdependence* is too pallid to convey the intensity and depth of the U.S.–Japan relationship. If one country goes down, it will surely drag the other with it. Recognizing that the American economy may be surfeited with foreign goods, Japan seeks to reduce its dependence on the American market. Yet as Japan moves to sell its products in East Asia and China, the United States remains by far its primary market. Japan's new focus on East Asia and China also leaves it more dependent on American military protection, as Chinese naval and nuclear power intrudes into the South China Sea.

The trade imbalance between the two countries remains a point of friction. While all states can be exporters, they cannot all attain surpluses in merchandise trade simultaneously; for every surplus on current account there is a correlative deficit elsewhere in the system. For some years the United States has been a net importer of merchandise trade partly because it has sought to be a "system stabilizer," allowing others to develop by selling in the U.S. market while America invests abroad to provide funds for the industry of developing countries. Sometimes this has raised problems for the American economy, and the United States now needs others to share the stabilizing task.

Regardless of past difficulties, Japan and the United States will resolve their frictions and Japan will move in the long run to produce more of its goods abroad while responding more attentively to the needs of its own domestic market. Domestic production will increase relative to exports. Japanese manufacturing in China, Indonesia, India, and other large countries will be directed to those domestic markets, not exported to the United States. Some Japanese goods manufactured elsewhere, including Europe and North America, will be imported to Japan. Initially, factories producing these goods will be assembly plants. With time, however, and for both political and economic-technical reasons, these industries will increasingly buy local components, not those produced by *kereitsu* in Japan. Domestic content legislation will ensure this outcome in Europe and North America, to say nothing of politically sensitive India and China.

In the United States and Europe, moreover, Japan will want to invest in local technology regardless of the political necessity to do so. Given Japanese prices and a stronger yen, Japan will prefer production abroad to expensive production at home. In time the rewards from foreign investment may come to rival those of exporting. This could lead Japan to become a financial power rather than remain a trading state.

The United States will see a parallel evolution, exporting services that embody a high knowledge content to East Asia, China, the Middle East, Latin America, and even Europe. As America moves to greater reliance on "invisibles," however, it will still need Japanese investment to help compensate for the deficient American savings rate. Short of capital for its own industry, a capital-exporting America will continue to rely on funds from Tokyo.

Japan, the United States, and the Future of World Politics

Besides their economic incentives to cooperate, the imperatives of world politics will keep Japan and the United States together. Japan was the first country to pioneer a nonterritorial strategy: instead of seeking to expand militarily abroad, it has sought to expand economically at home. Its success taught both the Soviet Union and the United States that spending great sums of money in a territorial and military competition was wasteful and anachronistic. Although some believe that armed conflict could eventually break out between Washington and Tokyo, the prospect is extremely unlikely.[31] This does not mean that great power conflicts will vanish. If Japan and the United States have learned to settle their disputes, it is less clear that other countries have drawn all the correct conclusions. The futures of both Russia and China remain uncertain.

Japan and the United States will be the leaders of the twenty-first century international system.[32] As we saw in chapter 6, that system requires political governance if the world economy is to function. Japan and the United States are now creating an encompassing coalition of great powers in which China is integrated into Asia and Russia is stitched into Europe. With the assistance of the European Union—still more an economic than a political grouping—Japan and the United States have managed world relations so that a political-military balance exists on each continent. Russia cannot expand westward because of the enlarged NATO and the European Union and the United States; it cannot expand eastward because of both China and Japan. China is equally hemmed in by Japan in the north and by the U.S. Seventh Fleet in the south.

At the same time, both China and Russia are being woven into a web of cooperative relationships. An expansive China would face a balancing coalition of the United States, Russia, and Japan. An expansive Russia would confront Europe, the United States, China, and Japan. The United States, however, has a built-in advantage in these coalitions. It is not a regional power in either Europe or the Far East and seeks no territorial gain in either realm. Thus it is trusted by Asians and Europeans in ways that regional powers are not. While Japan currently seeks no additional territory (except the return of four islands from Russia), its past expansion in China and Southeast Asia has not been forgotten.

Russia still harbors designs to retake its "near abroad" in what used to be the USSR. China still seeks territory in the South China Sea. The United States on the other hand is a disinterested nonregional power seeking stability, not gain.

America's position renders the twenty-first-century system more stable than its late nineteenth-century counterpart. In the 1890s Britain wanted stability and would have been eager to conciliate Germany, but its own territorial expansion made this difficult. As the major beneficiary of past territorial and imperial growth, England was hardly a neutral arbiter and balancer. In the twenty-first century U.S. power will be more heeded in Europe and Asia because it has no empire to defend. When it opposes the expansion of others, it can hardly be accused of hypocrisy. Even if it is not all-powerful, the United States remains the pivotal nation—the central interlocutor of world politics.

————

The twenty-first century will be an epoch of flows, not stocks. Although Japan and the United States are the leaders of the international economic system, Japanese flows have proceeded outward and not inward. The Japanese population has not yet received the full benefit of Japan's outward economic success. Its citizens have not yet been enabled fully to participate in the rapidly expanding international economy. Even Japanese businesses lack the expertise that major informational and service imports can impart.

Japan's desire to operate in one direction—moving into the open economies of others while keeping its home market substantially closed and tightly regulated, is a major cause of its current stagnation. Like the former Soviet Union, a nation cut off from "best practice" standards in industry or services, Japan's partial isolation from international flows has cost it needed flexibility. It has continued to focus on visible, merchandise trade when the future lies in invisibles. Knowledge and creativity—intangible products—are the tools of twenty-first century economics.

In *The End of the Nation State* Kenichi Ohmae notes that Japan lagged behind in the knowledge industries of the future.[33] Japan's strategy of seeking to benefit from the open goods and capital markets of other countries while keeping its own largely closed has become more difficult in light of the Asian financial crisis. Still, while other countries have moved to software and high-level services, Japan is seeking to retain its manufacturing capability as a more or less fixed proportion of GDP. While other countries benefit from flows of factors entering their economies, Japan has generally stood aside, a stance only recently starting to change with the new opening in Japanese politics.[34] In this sense Japan harks back to a prior industrial age, in which countries relied on fixed rather than mobile factors of production—a world of stocks rather than flows. To keep abreast of international market trends, Japan must seek to master the flow of intangibles as it moves to become a mature creditor power.[35]

chapter 9

The
United States

Among major developed countries, the United States has progressed most rapidly toward virtual status. Seventy percent of its GDP now resides in the service sector and less than 20 percent in manufacturing. About 20 percent of U.S. production has moved overseas. Service industries are growing more rapidly than manufacturing both as a percentage of employment and as a percent of valued added.

For some analysts the increasing move to services represents a setback to U.S. economic performance. At the Berkeley Roundtable in the 1980s Stephen Cohen and John Zysman argued that "manufacturing matters" and that decline in manufacturing output tended to reduce productivity and employment.[1] Although manufacturing certainly has declined as a percentage of total employment, the number of American jobs has vastly increased. Not only this, the percentage of good jobs is rising. The relative decline in manufacturing has not apparently slowed growth or productivity in the U.S. economy.[2]

Even if the decline of manufacturing meant a decline in employment, American efforts to maintain a fixed base of manufacturing at home would certainly have been counterproductive. Foreign competition would have led to corporate losses and a restriction on growth. Production and sales in emerging economies account for an increasing share of American markets. They will continue to do so.[3]

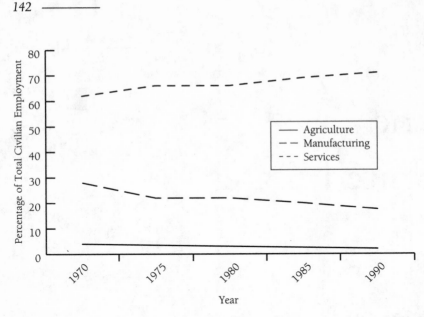

FIGURE 9.1   Employment in the United States, by economic sector, 1970–1990.
SOURCE: Bureau of Labor Statistics, 1992.

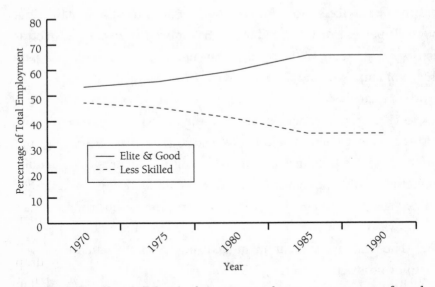

FIGURE 9.2   The skill level of American jobs as a percentage of total employment, 1959–1995.
SOURCE: Anthony P. Carnevale and Stephen J. Rose, "Education for What? The New Office Economy" (Princeton, NJ: Educational Testing Service, 1998).

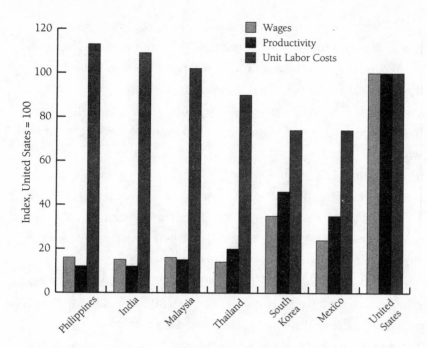

FIGURE 9.3 Wages, productivity, and unit labor costs for selected Asian countries and Mexico in 1990, as compared with the United States. Because productivity can vary, countries with the lowest wages do not necessarily have the lowest labor costs.

SOURCE: Stephen Goulb, "Comparative and Absolute Advantage in the Asia-Pacific Region," Federal Reserve Bank of San Francisco Working Paper, 1995.

U.S. Decline?

U.S. economic performance over the past two decades, however, has not satisfied observers. American productivity has grown less rapidly than that of other countries, at least until recently.[4] The United States dollar has plummeted in value from 360 yen in 1971 to 120 in 1998, a drop of two-thirds. The mark and the franc have also risen against the dollar. The American dollar (along with gold) had been the main reserve currency until the 1970s; now the mark, the yen, and the new euro have emerged to assume part of its role. American real wages declined from the 1970s to 1992, are only now beginning to rise, and have not yet attained earlier peaks. U.S. government indebtedness increased rapidly during the Reagan administration and now totals over $5 trillion. Owing to higher economic growth and the 1993 tax increases, however, the federal government showed a surplus in 1998. The trade balance turned negative after 1970 and has remained at over $100 billion for the past seven years. For 1998 it rose to $164.3 billion.[5] Household savings rates have hit bottom as U.S. investment has increased, requiring more borrowing abroad.[6]

Some have linked these changes with American hegemonic decline, forecasting a diminished U.S. role in foreign policy and international economic decisions. Few in 1990 predicted an American economic resurgence.[7] Japanese observers believed in 1990 that Japanese growth would increase at the rate of 4 percent per year, while the United States would reach no more than 2.5 percent.[8] Japan would become a relentless economic challenger to America. On the military side, not many understood that the end of the Soviet Union and its territorial retreat would bring a temporary collapse of the Russian economy as well. Further, virtually no one predicted that the forces of democracy and economic liberalization would open closed economies in Latin America, the Far East, and Eastern Europe, and recast China's attitude toward participation in world trade and investment.[9] In other words, few understood that the world would change in ways uniquely suited to American strengths.

The American Strategy

Despite occasional lapses, the United States has followed a distinctive economic and political strategy since World War II. In general terms it sought to compensate for deficient investment and savings with productivity improvements, keeping prices down and profits up. This strategy was most effective up to 1973. Through the 1950s and 1960s manufacturing and overall productivity both grew at rates of 2–3 percent per year. The decade of the 1970s changed this picture dramatically. Low-cost exports began to flood the American market, and the traditional U.S. balance-of-trade surplus disappeared. Inflation mounted. Oil prices quadrupled and then doubled again (though they have now been reduced by a factor of four). Until the oil price increases of the 1970s, the U.S. inflation rate was much lower than the interest rate.

It took very high interest rates—reaching 20 percent—to contain inflation at the beginning of the 1980s. In the first half of the 1980s high interest rates pushed up the value of the dollar, weakening American exports, and the balance of trade deteriorated still further. Inflation, however, was brought under control by a combination of high interest rates and reduced government spending and today is less than 2 percent. Initially, however, the U.S. government deficit increased as the military budget spiraled upward while the Reagan administration cut taxes. To counter the invasion of foreign products that followed the rise of the dollar, U.S. investment in new technology increased, but America had to borrow abroad to finance it. By 1997 indebtedness to foreigners had risen to $1.2 trillion while U.S. government debt had mounted to $5.3 trillion.[10]

At the end of the 1980s and the first half of the 1990s, however, American industry geared up to meet foreign competition. The average corporation cut the size of its workforce.[11] These workers, however, produced the same or increased output. Thus, the productivity of the manufacturing sector increased even if it lagged in service industries. Computers, printers, fax machines, voice recognition software and other technologies added greatly to the quality and reliability of American services and manufacturing. At first, however, these devices did not increase output or diminish clerical staff. The same number of secretaries and administrative assistants continued to be employed in office work.

This has now changed in two ways. Purely clerical personnel have been reduced, and the remaining office staff perform upgraded functions. This has led to an increase in productivity. Even in the official statistics, U.S. nonfarm (including service) productivity increased in the third quarter of 1997 by a hefty 4.1 percent and is now running on a yearly basis around 2 percent.[12] In his June 1998 testimony before the U.S. Congress's Joint Economic Committee, Alan Greenspan underscored the "increase in output per hour," observing: "Signs of a major technological transformation of the economy are all around us."[13]

America's increased competitiveness, however, has not improved the trade imbalance. Despite a favorable balance of trade on services, the deficit in merchandise trade is still very large.[14] The emergence of a (domestic) fiscal surplus should have led to smaller trade deficits over time. Yet it has not, because in 1998 the U.S. household savings rate hit an all time low of 0.2 percent per year. Together, low savings and high private consumption draw goods from overseas. Low revenues and high government expenditure further compound the problem. One solution might have been to cut U.S. consumption (perhaps with a value added tax) to bring the whole equation back into balance. Even without this remedy, however, the United States has still been able to secure a dependable flow of foreign funds to finance investment. The trade deficit has not reduced the acceptability of the U.S. dollar.

The basic shift in U.S. economic and political strategy since the Second World War has been American acceptance of an open international economy with full mobility of factors of production.[15] As the United States came to favor capital mobility, it acknowledged that it could not determine the value of the dollar, which would be influenced by flows in and out of the American economy. U.S. or foreign capital might enter or leave the United States. Of course American corporations make a significant profit on their overseas operations; but U.S. policy also has rested on persuading foreign capital, technology, and industrious labor to enter the United States.[16]

As late as the 1950s and 1960s American firms could content themselves with selling in the U.S. market. Since the 1970s, however, companies have had to sell abroad as well as fight to keep markets in the United States. To maintain competitivness, U.S. policy makers need to dampen inflation, contain or eliminate the government deficit, and keep the currency stable. Under purchasing power parity assumptions the prices of U.S. goods and property have remained quite low, drawing foreign capital into the U.S. market. Significant foreign production now takes place on American soil.[17]

Policy makers recognized that additional flows of foreign money would come into the United States if Treasury bonds improved in value. This in turn would take place if (as in fact happened) the U.S. reduced or eliminated the government deficit. Interest rates would fall and bond and stock prices improve. Robert Rubin, then head of the National Economic Council, helped convince President Clinton in 1993 to move toward a balanced budget. As the *New York Times Magazine* noted, "this would stimulate the economy, which in turn would boost tax revenues, inducing a 'virtuous cycle' and a sustained recovery."[18] The bond-market strategy worked, stock prices recovered, and the United States has enjoyed a remarkable run of prosperity with low inflation since 1993. President Clinton's economic strategy (abetted by Greenspan and Rubin) has been very successful.

Besides seeking the benefits derived from international flows, U.S. strategy has been aimed at "consumer sovereignty" to allow individual Americans to invest and spend in the most attractive markets, foreign or domestic. Business schools teach the presumptive leaders of American industry that they should seek "shareholder value" as their corporate goal. This means high profits, significant dividends, and a rising stock price. U.S. economic policy has aimed at making goods in the United States less expensive than those abroad. Low tariffs and free mobility of capital bring a profusion of foreign goods to the United States on extremely favorable terms. As a result, consumers have a great range of choice.

While high employment has been a government objective since the Full Employment Act of 1946, unfettered consumption in fact has received greater emphasis. The government has maintained employment by diversifying production out of industrial and into service occupations. Initially the displaced manufacturing worker found that his new job paid less than his old one. Increasingly, however, the disparity has been made up by the increase in real wages since 1992. In time the differential between old and new jobs will be entirely eliminated as more highly educated workers are recruited to perform high-level service tasks.

As we have seen, globalization and technological change have revolutionized business procedures and produced corporate downsizing and

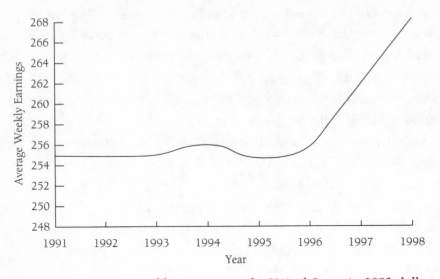

FIGURE 9.4   Average weekly earnings in the United States in 1982 dollars, 1991–1998. SOURCE: U.S. Bureau of Labor Statistics.

outsourcing of jobs and components to other countries. At the same time businesses have oriented themselves to seek shareholder value. In the 1970s, however, corporate managers did not fully understand this idea. Peter Ackerman, formerly a strategist at Drexel Burnham Lambert, points out that stocks were then selling at 60 percent of the replacement value of their underlying assets.[19] Conglomerates were the preferred vehicle of corporate organization, businesses having decided that a disparate collection of firm-assets in different sectors would smooth out peaks and troughs in the business cycle. Management aimed at greater sales rather than earnings per share, and was compensated accordingly. Even institutional shareholders did not vote against management.

Conglomerates required huge management staffs to oversee diverse operations in different sectors. The resulting overhead often ate up profits. Businesses could not expand because equity capital was very expensive and bank debt unduly restrictive. In the early 1980s high yield bonds entered the picture. These were technically risky instruments, immediately dubbed "junk bonds," that allowed smaller and newer companies access to capital on favorable terms. Financial institutions started to buy these bonds in substantial amounts. Even though some firms defaulted on their obligations, the higher yields more than compensated investors for their risk. Using such bonds, outside investors could shake up a somnolent management and win control of a firm, rewarding shareholders handsomely. As Ackerman observes, when T. Boone Pickens bid for Gulf Oil in 1984, no one believed he could succeed. Yet he was able to offer shareholders 50 percent more for their stock. Gulf's directors rebuffed him but quickly put the corporation up for sale. In the end, Chevron bought Gulf and the shareholders reaped a 100 percent profit.

From then on, any company that did not aim at shareholder value was in trouble. Corporations responded with internal restructuring: downsizing and selling secondary businesses. Profits increased as a percentage of the asset base. Unneeded management was pruned. Technological innovations allowed companies to trim their inventory-to-sales ratios. They could outsource production abroad and still keep control of all the data at home. Their progress was monitored by large pension and mutual funds, which were quite willing to sell their holdings if management did not provide a satisfactory return to shareholders. Pension funds intervened with boards of directors to make sure that management took their views seriously. Finally, not all profits were returned to the shareholders. Creative managements retained funds to invest in improving their product.

As John Edmunds of Arthur D. Little contends, the quest for shareholder value was ultimately guided by the needs of middle-class households, the pension and mutual funds' customers. Their objective was a greater return on savings.[20] Corporate managers, pressed by shareholders, tried harder to deliver higher and higher returns. Edmunds observes:

> The organization that has been able to deliver high returns is the virtual corporation, which cuts loose any fixed costs or obsolete lines of business that might drag down the rate of return. The virtual state is a friendly place for it to have its headquarters. The virtual corporation and its investors earn a high rate of return, while traditional land-based activities like agriculture offer lower, more erratic, returns.[21]

Does this shift portend a long-term U.S. economic resurgence? It is too early to tell. One talisman of change, however, is that American corporations are leaner than their Japanese counterparts and readier to offer returns to shareholders. As one example, consider the role that middlemen (the often reviled distributors that link manufacturers with retailers) are now coming to play in the production process. Middlemen, without offering a proprietary product, are becoming informal manufacturers for a variety of high-tech companies, assembling components into systems for the end user. Ingram, the world's largest wholesale distributor of computers, has become such a manufacturing giant for many other firms, including Compaq, IBM, Hewlett-Packard, Apple, and Acer. This means that the original equipment manufacturer (OEM) does not have to maintain inventory. They make the wholesalers do it. This is extraordinarily important, because the value of a personal computer falls by 1 percent a week.[22] As a partial solution, major firms forced suppliers to keep the inventory. OEMs would ship to Ingram or Vanstar half-built PCs with the motherboard, floppy disk drive, processor chip, and some memory already installed. The middleman would then complete the installation of circuit boards, memory chips, and disk drives, snapping on the OEM logo as the last step.[23] As Jim McDonnell, an IBM vice president observed, "We own all of the intellectual property; we farm out all of the direct labor. We don't need to screw the motherboard into the metal box and attach the ribbon cable."[24] In the supercompetitive computer market, saving on costs is earning profits for the shareholder. By becoming virtual manufacturers the computer companies do just that—they pass on the costs and the inventory to others.

The United States as a Well-Rounded Economic Power

The worldwide financial crisis of 1997–98 demonstrated clearly that honest and open political regulation is needed for a vibrant economic market.[25] If a nation is to attract investors over the long term, it has to offer them a reasonably incorruptible system of regulation that ensures against manipulation, insider trading, or financial cronyism. Transactions must be open to inspection by the public. Balance statements must reflect real values, not contrived estimates of earnings per share. If markets become suspicious of industrial or banking claims, capital leaves. Moody's bond ratings are critical international measures of honesty and fair dealing as well as financial performance. When Moody's downgrades a bank, a financial institution, or government bonds, capital will flow elsewhere. The $40 or $50 trillion of investment capital circulating in the world economy can eviscerate any national market.

One central bank is powerless to offset market decisions. Confidence is the key, and political and economic openness is necessary to sustain it.[26] Once lost, only the combined intervention of many central banks, the IMF, and the Bank for International Settlements can restore confidence. In the aftermath of the Asian financial crisis, the American economy gained adherents because its political-economic system was competent to handle the regulation of financial transactions. In the past, capital poured into the United States for security in times of international military crisis. Today it comes for economic advantage. Returns are not only substantial but more reliable than in many other countries, because transparency and an impartial regulatory system guarantee their safety.

Foreign investors in Japanese stocks, by contrast, could not avoid fears of government or other manipulation. Were NTT shares correctly valued when the government sought buyers? Brokers frequently compensated favored clients for their losses. Banks became insolvent, but the government failed to shut them down. The investing public was denied much critical information. Investors did not know the real situation of the companies and banks whose shares they purchased or whose assets they depended on. In the past, Sumitomo traders did not acknowledge huge losses in copper shares. Financial institutions were sometimes beholden to the *yakuza*—criminal elements. The American financial and currency markets, which do not tolerate such practices, drew away capital from manipulated markets in other countries.

The Virtual State and America's Political Centrality

What is America's political entrée in world markets? In theory, host nations should welcome foreign direct investment from the United States because it employs workers, conveys new technology, and contributes to the manufacturing base of developing societies. Yet many countries, from Brazil and Mexico to India, Guinea, and Tanzania, refused such investment in the past. Bent on a strategy of import-substituting industrialization in the 1970s, they wanted to build national factories that could compete with foreign imports. Foreign manufacturers on their soil would have interfered with this strategy. While Brazil, African countries, and Mexico have recently changed their views, India remains very sensitive toward American investment. Japan is only now permitting foreign direct investment.

In part the reaction against U.S. investment has declined because it comes on competitive terms from Japan and Europe as well as the United States. Asian body nations can play head nations against one another and win greater benefits. Yet the United States has a particular entrée. Asian and Latin American nations realize that U.S. production can be sold in American markets as well as locally. American production thus contributes to their exports. Beyond this, however, East Asians (more than Latin Americans) have sought to diversify their economies beyond their immediate region, and the United States as a nonregional power provides an alternative to local dominance by China or Japan.

American foreign direct investment typically returns to Asian countries emigré expertise that has been formed in the United States. It also creates the possibility of training in the United States for key Asian personnel. In addition, the virtual nature of U.S. investment means that the foreign input is not intrusive. After an initial training period, communication with U.S. managers is mainly by internet and fax. U.S. manufacturers also frequently work at arm's length through Hong Kong intermediaries to find the appropriate sites (in terms of communications infrastructure and labor costs) for their plants. These may be as easily found in Mauritius as in inner China. Then the Hong Kong intermediaries become responsible for the quality and timing of output.

Except in Latin America, U.S. foreign direct investment brings a non-regional presence. Since China and Japan are already competing for manufacturing capacity in East Asia, U.S. production is more neutral. In East Europe and Russia, American industry offers European countries an alternative to the domination of German manufacturing. And in each case, unlike Japanese capital, American manufacturing raises the possibility of exports to the home country market, rebalancing trade accounts.

The Role of the Dollar

Purveyors of reserve currencies (such as the pound sterling in the nineteenth century and the U.S. dollar today) have to provide liquidity to other countries. Unless debtor nations can get access to holdings of reserve currencies, they cannot use them as a medium of exchange. Great Britain performed this function by investing abroad and running a trade deficit with many countries in the last quarter of the nineteenth century. The United States put its currency in the hands of others by overall deficits on current account since 1958, and deficits on the trade account since 1970. Even when it did not run a trade deficit, America's economic and military investments abroad placed currency in the hands of foreign countries. The yen cannot compete with the U.S. dollar as a reserve currency, because Japan's habitual trade surpluses create a shortage of yen liquidity. Foreigners do not earn enough yen to use that currency as a major medium of exchange. If the new euro is to become a reserve currency, Europe will have to run either a trade or a capital deficit to place the euro in the hands of foreign buyers. This could happen if the euro is high valued, allowing others to earn it through export surpluses in the European market. It could also happen if Europe invests heavily overseas.

In the American case, treasury bills and notes at relatively high interest were sold to foreign states and individuals. Thus U.S. government bonds performed the same function as supplies of American dollars. Yet European or Japanese bonds do not circulate widely in other countries. Europe has a surplus in its foreign balance of trade, and (except for the United States) it has not yet invested heavily in the rest of the world. Neither the yen nor the euro therefore is likely for some time to rival the dollar as a medium of international exchange.[27]

Rejecting Triumphalism

Still, the American economy confronts many problems. Inequality of incomes is increasing rather than declining. While growth has been relatively high and inflation low, this combination will not persist for all time. Labor shortages will eventually bid up wages, and the Fed will increase interest rates. Stock prices cannot be maintained at their current high levels while profitability lags. Correction is in the air. Savings rates have fallen and individuals have increased their consumption as inflated stock prices have contributed a strong but perhaps fleeting sense of well-being.[28] The success of U.S. industry is increasingly coming to depend on reducing costs: inventory, production, and plant and equipment. Many observers have remarked on overcapacity in key industries, such as autos, textiles, steel, and civilian aircraft. The countries and corporations that succeed will be those that find ways of reducing or merging this capacity.

In addition, some U.S. companies confront a major shortage of credit. Those with low bond ratings (Moody's BBB or lower) need to be able to issue high yield bonds. Yet they have had to pay very high premiums, because prudent investors have moved to U.S. treasuries. Monthly high yield bond financing has been reduced by a factor of seven over the past several years. Without access to credit, businesses cannot invest, and this problem in turn could push the United States into recession if it is not remedied.[29]

In the longer term, easier credit and greater virtualization of U.S. industry is the leading solution. The first provides access to cash; the second increases investment returns. The United States has excellent positions in services and intellectual property and is poised to become one of the major head nations of the virtual world.

chapter 10

Europe and Russia

Throughout Europe's history, Russia threatened to dominate the continent militarily. Contemporary Europe, in contrast, wields vast economic power over Russia. European Union countries are fast developing high-tech services and are locating their manufacturing production more in Eastern Europe, the United States, Asia, and Latin America. Russia lags in both production and services. Despite the Soviet attempt between the 1930s and the 1970s to develop a powerful heavy industry, for the most part Russia has remained a producer of natural resources: minerals, natural gas, and petroleum. The nation cannot yet manufacture consumer goods, and leftover Soviet industry constitutes an unreclaimed rust belt. Until tax collection begins to approximate government expenditure, Russian planners cannot even begin to think of new industrial strategies or attract foreign capital to invest in them. Russia today therefore remains limited to selling the products of land.

Russia's relations with Europe have always been ambivalent. Many historians have drawn the geographic boundary of Europe at the Vistula, excluding Russia entirely.[1] Typically, observers have envisioned the relationship between Russia and Europe developing in one of two ways: Russia might become a participant in European development through modernization and the growth of ties to Western countries; alternatively, it might hold aloof, seeking the power to control European states. For most of modern history Western Europeans have feared the latter

outcome—but Russians have themselves faced recurrent European in-
vasions, led successively by Napoleon, Kaiser Wilhelm II, and Adolf
Hitler. Their ambivalence toward the West is understandable. Now the
end of the cold war should permit better Russo-European links as the
economic pull of Europe transcends the waning Russian threat.

Europe as a Magnet

Europe itself has been riven since the sixteenth century into disputing
regional or national blocs: Catholic v. Protestant; Hapsburg v. French;
British v. French; French v. German; British v. German. When parts of
Europe united, it was usually against some other part. At no time prior
to 1990 have rivalries abated except in the immediate aftermath of war.
If Russia is considered part of Europe, then the cold war was primarily
a struggle between Europe's western and eastern halves.

The year 1990 saw for the first time the possibility of all-European cooperation. This startling outcome is the result of continental integration
sponsored by the European Union in the absence of the Soviet threat.
The advent of economic and political integration in Europe has revised
previous canons of state practice. From the 1950s through the 1980s
European integration merely solidified the Western camp against the
Soviet bloc. Integration added strength to NATO and fostered economic
cohesion among Western members. Since the end of the cold war, on
the other hand, Western European unity has pulled eastern countries
into its orbit. Possibly in time it will do the same with Russia. For one
of the few times in history the gradual accretion of economic and political power by one bloc has not caused balance-of-power effects against
it. The integration of Europe has operated centripetally to concentrate
rather than divide power.

This effect has been possible principally because Europe has not become a political or military superstate.[2] Rather, the European continent
remains a confederation of separate nations bent on improving their
economic welfare. Europe is neither an integrated nuclear power nor,
despite the Western European Union, a military power. The military

strength resides in NATO, a trans-Atlantic entity. The European Common Security and Foreign Policy propounded at Maastricht in 1992 is an organizational title without political content. Under these circumstances nations seek membership to win concrete benefits and help shape Europe's ultimate role. Eleven nations presently share a common currency (the euro) and the European Central Bank. Meanwhile Poland, Hungary, the Czech Republic, Estonia, and Slovenia want to be included in the enlarging EU, even though they do not yet qualify for membership in the European Monetary Union.[3]

The number of states acceding to the European Union has snowballed since 1957 when the original six (Germany, France, Italy, Belgium, the Netherlands, and Luxembourg) created the European Common Market. After de Gaulle's veto was overcome, Britain, Ireland, and Denmark joined the community in 1973. Spain, Portugal, and Greece made twelve. With Austria, Finland, and Sweden joining in 1994, the twelve became fifteen. Among Western nations only Norway and Switzerland still abstain. Those on the threshold of admission include the five aforementioned nations plus Slovakia, Latvia and Lithuania, Romania, Bulgaria, and Cyprus for a total of twenty-six. Other former Soviet countries, particularly the Ukraine, may eventually want to join. Russia itself may ultimately seek admission to a single European market, even if it does not formally gain membership in European institutions.

The surprising thing about European enlargement is how easily it occurred. As central countries joined, there were always peripheral members waiting in the wings. At no point after the end of the cold war did outsiders hesitate, fearful of creating a European superstate. This was not solely because Europe was a union of democratic nations. It was also because unification proceeded from the bottom up. Nations were admitted only when they could meet stringent requirements: stable democratic institutions, low inflation, small government deficits as a proportion of GDP, and basic standards of welfare for the population as a whole.

European institutions tackled the small and technical issues first—trade, capital movements, agricultural policy, common occupational standards, weights and measures—postponing the larger questions of a common foreign policy for the last stages of the union. The European Parliament, composed of members popularly elected by each member state, could take a critical view of the technocrats in the Commission or the government representatives in the Council of Ministers. There was no ministerial responsibility to the Parliament, however, and except for budgetary matters, neither the Commission nor Council of Ministers had to win majority approval from Parliament.[4] As a result, there was no single dominant European executive who might frighten outsiders as Hitler and Napoleon had done in the past. European executives still had to work out policy matters with member states and their officials.

Potential new members were reassured by Europe's political disunity and drawn by the economic pull of the single market. Within the common external tariff zone, member nations could protect their inefficient agriculture and also negotiate with outsiders about which foreign industrial products would be admitted and when. Until recently, Japanese cars were essentially excluded from the markets of France and Italy and only minimally tolerated in Germany. Only in England, where assembly plants had been set up, did they have free access. Even there, Japanese autos made in the UK could not circulate to other member countries unless they contained a high percentage of local (i.e., European) content. Members of the European Union could thus invoke protection against outsiders while enjoying a growing internal market for themselves.

Nations weighing participation in the EU calculated the particular costs and benefits. On the one hand, EU members did not want to be dominated economically and possibly militarily by Germany. On the other hand, the European Union tied Germany to an integrated arrangement, binding it to Western allies. Lesser EU member states could now bring capital and foreign direct investment into the German market. France and Italy could participate in the success of German capitalism by buying into German firms and into the Frankfurt stock market. Moreover, if some countries could not meet the standard of German competition right away, they would be allowed a transition period to get their economies in order. In the 1970s and 1980s, the EU gave Spain, Portugal, and Greece such leeway. Poland, Hungary, the Czech Republic, Slovenia, and Estonia will be allotted a similar grace period. EU funds compensated members with backward economic zones and high unemployment. Poland presented a special problem due to its agricultural exports, which did not fit into the protected market created by the Common Agricultural Policy. Yet because of its continuing costs, the CAP would have to be changed eventually in any event, so Poland could not be denied admission for that reason.

The integration of Eastern Europe into the EU was made easier because manufacturing capabilities could be located there. As Germany, France, and particularly England moved increasingly toward high-level services, Western production could move east, to Eastern Europe and perhaps eventually to the Ukraine and Russia. New automobile production capabilities were set up in Poland and the Czech Republic.[5] Pharmaceutical companies went east, to Hungary and Russia. Battery capacity was designated for Macedonia. The Greek subsidiary of Heineken has considered transferring production to the Skopska Brewery in Skopje, Macedonia. Hugo Boss moved part of its production out of Germany and into Eastern Europe. In some cases companies sought cheaper production sites and lower labor costs. Increasingly, however, European and American corporations flush with cash are seeking new markets, siting their production within growing consumer markets whose tariffs might rise.

The movement of European capital into Eastern Europe has so far not extended to Russia. Although markets in cities such as Moscow and St. Petersburg beckoned to Western and European businesses, the Russian economy as a whole has advanced only in fits and starts. Before the recent debt crisis arose, the financier George Soros committed large sums to the development of Russia. The Heritage Fund initially moved billions of dollars of Western money to Russian companies. Western and IMF investment then ceased, awaiting an improvement in Moscow's finances.

Russia and Europe

The prospect of closer association with European institutions, as well as the Group of Eight and the Paris Club, gave Moscow an incentive to modernize economic policy in a western direction. Modernization, however, presented many problems for the emergent Russian state. How would Russian pensioners, workers, and the military be paid as inflation rose? Printing money (which caused still greater inflation) could only be a stop-gap measure. The government could cut deficits by trimming subsidies, but this would be highly unpopular, especially since Russian industry and mining were still uncompetitive. Increasing tax collections was critical, but Russian taxes were already confiscatory, and most businesses, including Gazprom (the world's largest producer of natural gas), managed to avoid paying them. Privatizing—selling the old and archaic state industries—produced windfalls for a few oligarchs but did not put gold in state coffers. And consumer industries did not produce goods people wanted. They could scarcely pay the going tax rate.

Nor could Russian leaders look to the external world for solutions. If they raised revenue tariffs, they would face outcries from Western trading partners and from ordinary Russians who wanted high-quality foreign goods. European and Japanese loans were only a short-term fix, because the state could not find hard currency to pay them back. Another expedient, remittances from Russians living abroad, required not only that Russians could find remunerative employment elsewhere but that the state could somehow capture part of their gains. Until the tax crisis was solved, economic activity in Russia would grind slowly to a halt.

Russia of course was fully aware of the standards it would have to meet to join Europe and other Western institutions. These included a stable currency, successful democratic institutions, an end to internal conflict, and peaceful ties with neighbors. Most of these requirements would not be met in the short run. To some degree, they conflicted with nationalist ambitions to bring former republics of the Soviet Union back into the Russian fold. Some Russian leaders yearned for past glories when victorious Russian armies dictated terms to defeated enemies in Paris or Berlin. These traditional attitudes delayed Russia's adjustment to Europe.

The expansion of NATO to include the Czech Republic, Poland, and Hungary dealt another blow to Russian pride. Great Russian nationalists had assumed that the Soviet Union could eventually be reconstituted, together with Russia's traditional protectorate over Eastern Europe. As NATO moved nearer the Russian frontier, however, this prospect receded. Although the Russian populace seemed indifferent to regaining the Soviet empire, in policy circles NATO enlargement raised hackles. If Russia was not an enemy, why did NATO need to expand, or even continue to exist? It did not help that Western diplomats claimed that NATO was not "aimed" at anyone. The Russians were aware of course that their own domestic instability caused uncertainty among their neighbors. The Russian invasion of Chechnya is what first started the Poles thinking about joining NATO, and talk of restoring the Soviet empire did not allay Eastern European anxiety.

Still, threat and counterthreat did not increase Russian or European security. Unless Russia could be drawn into Europe, neither party would rest easy. In certain respects the expansion of NATO placed a gently restraining hand on the traditional rivalries among Eastern European states. As it has done to a degree in Bosnia, NATO's existence has promoted regional pacification. Slovakia and Hungary could not threaten one another if they wanted to join either NATO or the European Union, nor could Romania and Hungary. In the economic field similar pressures prevailed. The more Eastern nations were tied up into prevailing economic "clubs" in world politics, the greater the funds they might expect to receive. A modicum of good behavior was the minimum standard for participation in elite councils that offered international support. And Russia particularly wanted to be linked to Europe.

The Top Club

Russia wants to join Europe in part because Europe now occupies the pivotal role in the international structure of overlapping clubs. The European Monetary Union has the most exacting admission standards of any international institution, and is thus the most exclusive of all international clubs (even though some non-European states better fulfill the EMU's criteria). Its standards set the highest benchmark for economic achievement of countries worldwide.

What does this mean in practical terms? Europe's economies still have not solved problems of rigidities in the labor market, their social programs still need to be reformed, and chronic unemployment remains too high. European technology lags behind the finest achievements of American and Japanese industries.

Europe's supremacy is not so much economic or technological but normative. Its attractive force makes others wish to be associated with it. Of course Russia cannot formally join the EU, because it is not fully a European nation, but it may seek a close relationship. Geographically, the United States cannot be a member, but the establishment of the euro requires far greater European-American coordination to moderate currency fluctuations. As the European economy becomes both more exclusive and more attractive, a free trade zone linking Europe and North America is not out of the question. The requirements imposed on the central members of EMU (the inner core of Europe) may well ultimately extend even to China, directly or indirectly. Will China resent their imposition? Perhaps. Beijing may recognize, however, that such standards are unavoidable if one wants to become a member of the top club in world politics. It is perhaps a paradox that the continent that once ruled the world through the physical mechanisms of imperialism is now coming to set world standards in normative terms. Europe enjoys a form of symbolic and institutional primacy, even though its hegemonic political form has vanished.

Is Political Unity Necessary?

As recently as the 1980s it was fashionable to assert that Europe had become sclerotic economically and ineffective politically. The huge sums of foreign investment that have come into Europe belie the image of stagnation. The potential rivalry between a strong euro and the American dollar undercuts the claims of European economic weakness. Many countries will likely hold euros as a percentage of their reserves, lessening the dollar's importance.

Concerning Europe's political progress, some commentators say the EU should have adopted a single foreign and defense policy. They criticize Britain and France for resisting Chancellor Kohl's proposals for political unity.[6] Such views are shortsighted. The European Union is a powerful attractive force in economics, and political unity might well negate the attraction. In economic terms an established core of centralized and open markets—in trade and finance—draws outsiders in. Neighboring countries want to participate in and benefit from the growing market. Despite the effects of worldwide globalization, propinquity is still important. Countries that are geographically near a high-income economy benefit more (in terms of per-capita income) than those further away.[7] Just as the success of the Canadian-American Free Trade Area made NAFTA possible, the economic success of Western Europe most immediately benefits the East.

In politics and international relations, however, the reverse tends to occur. Rather than seeking further centralization, political forces typically oppose strong and concentrated power. The balance of power generally operates centrifugally, diffusing power more evenly throughout the system.[8] In the European case the gravitational force of economics has dominated the divisive force of politics. This is a signal that political unity is not necessary for the European Union to exert a major pull on international relations, both within and outside Europe. It is precisely because Europe has no single political center that it can attract outsiders. Some of these outsiders will become official members of EU; others, while remaining outside, will be friendly to European purposes.

The European Economy

The European economy is an open international economy that seeks and accepts foreign investment. European states and industries also invest heavily abroad. The share of manufacturing is declining for all European states as they move to capture returns in high-level services. Switzerland, Holland, and England have shifted strongly to services, France somewhat less so, Germany still less. Virtualization is well advanced in most European nations.

The external European tariff does not create a "fortress Europe," but if it did, foreign direct investment would move into the integrated market and produce goods there, substituting for foreign exports. In this sense Europe, like the United States, China, and East Asia (excluding Japan), has greatly benefited from inward flows of capital, goods, people, and technology. It does not seek one-way flows: European investment abroad is offset by foreign flows to England, France, and Germany. In monetary terms the London foreign exchange market is larger than New York's, and Frankfurt, the seat of the European Central Bank, is a growing financial center. Insurance, transport, tourism, and financial services of all kinds are rising in value, as is income from foreign investment.

Except in the United Kingdom, unemployment in Europe tends to be higher than in the United States. Social services, generous vacations, and the inability to dismiss workers have made European companies reluctant to hire new staff. Most of the expansion in these companies' labor forces has taken place outside of Germany, France, and Benelux—in the United States, Latin America, East Asia, Eastern and southern Europe. Germany has invested heavily in research and high-technology products both within and outside the Federal Republic.

For example, Daimler-Benz is now testing a new "hydrogen car," powered by fuel cells that generate hydrogen from methanol. It has formed an alliance with Ford to carry the project further. The exhaust product is mostly nonpolluting water vapor. The cost, however, is still many times that of an automobile powered by conventional gasoline engines. Airbus Industries, a European consortium, is making plans for a 550-seat passenger airliner, to exceed the capacity of Boeing's 747. In chemicals and pharmaceuticals, but not yet biotechnology, Europe has great strength.

Europe has also become a financial power by keeping the value of its currencies high. The Swiss franc, the German mark, and even the British pound have maintained or increased their parities with the U.S. dollar. As compared to a lower-valued dollar, high-value currency countries have kept competitive by reducing the amount of inflation in their economies through higher interest rates. Therefore Germany can sell abroad, because (with the exception of the United States) its inflation is lower than that of most other nations. It compensates for high currency values with stable domestic prices.

Even European industry, however, has reinsured its markets and reduced its costs by producing in North America and elsewhere. BMW and Mercedes-Benz both have factories in the United States. Michelin has moved tire production to the American south. As long as U.S. inflation rates stay low, Europe's relatively high-valued currencies make it difficult for European goods to compete on a pure export basis. As inflation abates in many countries, more and more European production will be moved abroad. If current labor market conditions continue, German companies will add jobs overseas and in the East, but not at home. Redundant European workers will then seek to find jobs in services or conceivably move elsewhere. Within Europe itself, the growth of high-level services in insurance, finance, transport, and marketing will continue to attract new employment.

Preventing Tension Between Russia and Europe

A potential for longer-term tension exists between the economic enlargement of Europe and the political-military enlargement of Russia. Russia is competing with Europe and the United States for the allegiance of the oil republics of Kazakhstan, Kyrgyzstan, and Azerbaijan. It has developed military links with Tajikistan and Turkmenistan and has occasionally intervened in Georgia. While the United States has sought to help the Ukraine solve many nuclear and economic problems, Russia criticizes Ukraine's rule in the Crimea. The United States is seeking a link with Uzbekistan as a mediator in Afghanistan. Moscow's ties with Iran are designed to ease its dependence on previous oil-rich Islamic republics of the former Soviet Union. Russian nationalists would like to bring much of the Commonwealth of Independent States (members of the old Soviet Union) back into the Russian fold. The nationalist faction, frustrated during Yeltsin's presidency, may gain strength when he departs.

Any attempt at political or military enlargement will bring Russia into conflict with Europe and the United States. An expansionist Russia will never be admitted to Western alliance and political councils, whereas a Russia that renounces expansion should be admitted. The expansion of NATO guards against Russian military aggression and therefore serves one important purpose, but it does little to bring Russia into Western arrangements. Despite the NATO contract with Russia in the Founding Act, Russia has not been granted membership in the North Atlantic Council. Instead the new Permanent Joint Council (which Russia has been allowed to join) will meet separately from the North Atlantic Council. The latter will presumably take the major decisions. Unlike Russia, the new members of NATO (Poland, the Czech Republic, and Hungary) will be represented on both councils and thus will enjoy a higher status than their neighbors. Even if Russia objects, NATO can still act to defend them. NATO expansion therefore has not yet succeeded in drawing the Russians into better relations with their neighbors. Other means must be found of doing so.

Russia and an Encompassing Coalition

In the longer term, Europe will draw Russia further into Western economic and political councils. The United States will help by enlisting Russia in a new and encompassing Concert of Powers in world politics. Opposed partial coalitions of great powers have always raised tensions and sometimes caused wars.

An encompassing coalition that contains the major great powers is more likely to succeed in diminishing hostility. As we have seen, it is the international equivalent of domestic enforcement of market institutions. Without a political umbrella over interactions between great powers, maintaining reliable economic relations can be difficult.[9] During the cold war it was not surprising that the international economy was confined to the Western and democratic half of the world. The Soviet and Chinese blocs did not participate, nor did reliable connections with them exist.

Economic ties among major states—reinforcing great power political links—are even more important today than they were previously. The twenty-first-century globalized economy will be much more intrusive than the European economy of the late nineteenth century. Countries then invested abroad, but they did not typically produce abroad.[10] They therefore did not intrude into the foreign domestic political system as much as they do today. In the contemporary world economic and political transparency, like democracy, is a growing precondition for international investment. If countries are not yet democratic, international investors and producers want to see a domestic "liberalizing coalition" in power[11] that is moving the economy toward openness. Such coalitions existed in Argentina, Brazil, and Taiwan prior to full democratization. They paved the way for better international behavior by the still autocratic regime. Domestic liberalization, however, is not enough. Internationally, investors are more willing to raise capital for emerging markets when an international coalition of great powers presides over results in these areas. As applied in Eastern Europe, this principle suggests that investors will not go into Bosnia or Serbia until NATO declares that it has accomplished its mission. If and when China joins the World Trade Organization, the present stream of foreign investment into China will likely become a torrent. When countries receive validation by clubs associated with an encompassing coalition, inward investment flows will increase.

Russia and Europe: The Trend Away from Land

The greatest long-term danger in relations between Russia and Europe is that Moscow will remain wedded to land as the major factor of production. Russia has not yet entirely outgrown the Stalinist fetish with territory. In the short term, oil, natural gas, and minerals may help to regenerate the flow of Russian exports to Western markets. The downside is that Russian nationalists still hanker after more territory on their borders with Eastern Europe and in the Far East. Russia may also be tempted to move south toward Iran, reincorporating Azerbaijan and the oil resources on both sides of the Caspian Sea.

The longer the Russians emphasize the products of land, however, the longer they will delay a new pattern of industrial and high-technological growth. South Korea faced a similar transition some decades ago. Seoul was an agricultural exporter in 1959 but quickly moved to industrial goods and to exports of high-technology products. Like Japan, South Korea did not rely on its raw materials or minerals, but instead used its highly proficient labor force to imitate foreign technology. Japanese investment provided the initial technical component for Korean industry. Russia needs a similar strategy. Without German and American investment, Russian products will lag behind those of developed economies.

In Russia neither banks nor new industries have been able to stand on their own feet. In their absence, land and its products are still the most highly valued assets in Russia—including diamonds and gold in addition to oil and natural gas. After the Russian economy is reorganized, light manufacturing may become possible. Service trades will also grow rapidly. As this occurs, Russians will start to invest abroad as well as at home, as they have begun to do in Cyprus, European countries, and the United States. Their own foreign direct investment will tie them increasingly to economic opportunities in the outside world. Ultimately, land will become less important to Russia's future, just as it has in the case of South Korea.

As Moscow moves to high-technological industries and services and away from land-based production, Russia and Europe will move closer together. Despite the distortions of the EU's Common Agricultural Policy, Europe has divorced itself from reliance on land. Industrial (specific) capital and finance capital now form Europe's major economic base. As Europe continues to invest an increasing fraction of its GDP in the production capability of other nations, Russia will eventually receive and benefit from this flow of funds, just as Poland does today. Thus the long-term problem in European-Russian relations will be to bridge the economic differences between an economy based on capital and one that has been based on land. The more rapidly Russia shifts into industrial and finance capital, the less it will diverge from Europe and Western nations. This in turn will help to remedy Russia's traditional inclination to go to war to acquire more land.

chapter 11

China and Emerging Nations

The less developed world must make major adjustments to the world economy. Moving from raw material and agricultural production, emerging nations must now change over to quality manufacturing for the international market. They must, in short, overcome their land fetish. In the next generation or two, economic factors alone will not prevent wars on the periphery of the international system. Land will remain a primary factor of production in many areas.

Even where a country no longer relies mainly on land, differences among countries and regions may continue to generate conflict. Countries seeking land may clash with those based on alternative factors of production unless the international community intervenes. In the past, agricultural and nomadic peoples have sometimes sought to conquer the riches of cities, largely without success.[1] Territorial empires have vainly striven to capture the wealth of commerce.[2] Conversely, trading countries seeking to gain access to the resources of other nations have not always resisted the temptation of military expansion.

Russia remains a pivotal country because it straddles Europe and Asia. To socialize Russia to the Western world economy and political system may not be impossible. At the end of World War II, Japan and Germany were induced to embrace the Western system of democracy and capitalism. Since the cold war ended, the fundamental question has been whether Russia and China can be enlisted as well. If they join a

Western democratic coalition, then the system will remain stable at the core, regardless of what happens on the periphery. If they do not, new bipolar or tripolar balance of power arrangements will emerge, and tension will rise, diverting production from civilian needs. A hemispheric American system linked with Europe could be opposed by either Russia or China. As the weaker party, Russia would likely join with Europe and America, perhaps tipping the balance against East Asia. Such conflicts would last until the underlying economic bases of the different regions had adjusted to one another.

The forces of land and capital have sometimes been opposed. Whatever the intrinsic interdependencies between states based on different factors of production, landed powers have been tempted simply to take over sources of industrial or finance capital in nearby countries. Imperial Germany, believing in the efficiency of territorial expansion, hesitated to rely on trade to provide reliable markets or sources of supply. Like Great Britain, it wanted an empire of its own—either in Europe or overseas. Earlier, commercial empires such as those of the Dutch or Portuguese also sought new advantages from bringing exotic products of land—gold, silver, sugar, and spices—to Europe. Trading empires became territorial ones. In any event, the military projection of empire continued in century after century.

Differences within the factor of capital, or conflicts between capital and labor, did not usually engender similar conflicts. Despite Lenin's pronouncement in *Imperialism: The Highest Stage of Capitalism* (1916), the First World War was not a conflict between two groups of finance-capitalists (England–France v. Germany–Austria). Germany wanted land, not capital: Berlin was still seeking a territorial empire similar to England's.[3] The same was true in 1939. Key raw materials and oil were at the top of the German and Japanese agendas of expansion. The two World Wars were essentially territorial conflicts. The question is whether such wars can occur again.

Countries differentially situated in respect to other factors of production need not make war. States endowed with abundant capital do not have to conquer labor, which they can easily acquire through immigration. Countries with an abundant and highly trained labor supply can attract foreign investment from capital-rich countries. This is precisely what contemporary China is doing. No one seeks to invade China, nor would Beijing expect to be able to conquer sources of capital. Rather, Beijing persuades investment to come to the Chinese market through economic incentives. China now receives more foreign direct investment than any other nation.

Africa of course presents a different problem. There, labor abundance does not yet attract enough foreign investment. The labor is undereducated and lacks technical training. Yet this does not lead a labor-abundant continent such as Africa to seek to invade capital-abundant Europe. Rather, African labor seeks to migrate to Europe, thereby making use of the latter's capital-intensive industrial sector. And Africa's own development offers the longer-term prospect of greater capital goods as well as agricultural production.

Among nations with abundant capital, the most propitious linkage is between industrial (specific) capital and finance (mobile) capital. Industrial capital furnishes the production plant. Finance capital sets the standards of what should be produced. Finance capital ultimately evolves into high-level services such as product design, marketing, insurance, transport, and of course, financing. There is an inherent synergy between the two types of capital. In the future, China may become the production plant for the world, but China's industries would only attain completeness when mated to research, development, product design, marketing, and financing provided by other nations. Japan, Europe, and the United States would remain indispensable partners in Chinese industrial development. For many years Chinese financial institutions in Shanghai and elsewhere will not perform the functions of finance capital on their own.[4]

Still, Beijing may strive for omnicompetence—that is, abundance in every sphere of production. It will surely fail. Even if economic theory technically permitted it,[5] no nation has ever attained factor abundance across the board; and even if one country could do so, the logic of comparative advantage still argues for trade and exchange. To take a few examples: industrial England was not abundant in land. The nineteenth-century United States, well endowed with land, was short on capital and labor. The two countries thus had the makings of a natural alliance: American exports of food in exchange for British migrants and capital. Contemporary Japan possesses abundant sources of capital, but little land and only a limited (though highly trained) labor supply. It imports the products of land from other countries and exports goods made by its abundant specific capital factors. Countries have tended to compensate for their deficiencies by associations with others. Sometimes, one partner might seek to annex the other through military action, as early modern Spain sought to take over the low countries; but that was when land could be readily captured and occupied. Today a mobilized population will resist assimilation by a foreign state.

Still, Beijing may seek both territorial expansion into the South China Sea and industrial competitiveness in high technology industries. If so, it faces a major collision with Japan, the United States, and the rising Southeast Asian nations. Some Chinese continue to think in imperial terms. They proclaim China's rights to hegemony over traditional peoples to the south, including Burmese and Vietnamese as well as those inhabiting the offshore island territories. In the South China Sea, China covets the oil reserves of the Spratly Islands and may seek to encroach on areas claimed by the Philippines and Vietnam. It seems difficult, however, to imagine peaceful Chinese oil production and shipment from floating oil-drilling platforms without the sanction of international law. Nothing is more vulnerable than an isolated oil rig. Only the negotiated division of North Sea oil parcels between Britain and Norway permitted production and distribution of that oil in Europe. China cannot produce from the Spratly fields without international consent.

China is unlikely to revive past territorial demands. It is also possible that China's version of capitalism will be more open than Japan's. Japan and South Korea have pursued a state-driven strategy of industrial development[6] that fused industrial policy with a program of excluding foreign imports and capital. Under *keiretsu* and *chaebol* protections, foreigners could not buy into Japanese or Korean production, and had difficulty setting up dealer networks to sell imported products.

The pattern in Southeast Asia is quite different. While Singapore, Taiwan, and Thailand have well-developed industrial policies, they are much more open to foreign investment and exports than Japan has been. China is now a leading recipient of foreign direct investment. Though Beijing prefers joint ventures and joint production arrangements, it is not entirely averse to industrial imports, as its purchases of airplanes, autos, and computers clearly demonstrate. The Chinese model allows others to benefit from Chinese growth. The Japanese model previously barred such participation, though the current financial crisis has opened the door to outsiders.

The Chinese Economy

The Chinese economy is an amalgam of state-controlled and private industry, of prosperous coastal provinces and poverty-stricken inland regions. It has departed from the Soviet model of an entirely state-run economy. The private sector now creates more than 50 percent of Chinese GDP.

Even before the Communists took control, Russia never had a strong private sector. Its nineteenth-century development was largely state-sponsored and controlled. In the 1890s, when Count Sergei Witte set up state textile factories and railways, Russia had few independent entrepreneurs. When the USSR collectivized Soviet agriculture after 1927, it held agricultural prices down and invested the surplus in industry, thereby ruining incentives for production on the collective farms. As a result, Soviet agricultural production went into deficit, limiting further transfers.

China, on the other hand, broke up the agricultural communes and gave long-term leases of land to the Chinese peasantry in the 1980s. This brought an upsurge in agricultural production, whose surplus could be invested in industry. In another deviation from the Russian pattern, the Chinese economy experimented with special economic zones in the coastal towns, giving leeway for private investment.

Today, China presides over an economy that proffers the "iron rice bowl" to Chinese citizens. Subsidized food, housing, and state-supported industry help to keep unemployment within manageable limits. As in Russia, however, state industry is not competitive. Subsidies need to be trimmed; much of the state economic apparatus should be sold off. Some of it can be unloaded to foreign investors, but most must either be disbanded or purchased by Chinese capitalists and workers. This will create unemployment. China could, however, use its previous subsidies to state industry for unemployment benefits for displaced workers.[7] Beijing also wants a transitional period of protection for these industries against external competition. This will raise hurdles for Chinese admission to the World Trade Organization. Beijing has a large trade surplus with the United States and a small one with Japan, and Western nations will need to be assured that they can sell in China on competitive terms. If China is admitted to the WTO, it will have access to most-favored-nation treatment on a worldwide basis. Thus there is a basis for a deal in which China reduces its protection of inefficient Chinese state industry in return for admission to WTO. As of 1999, the Chinese application to join, however, was on hold owing to the financial crisis. China does not want to open up until international economic conditions are more favorable.

State-owned industries (SOEs) have not yet benefited from productivity growth in the private export industries sustained by foreign direct investment. Nor has their share of manufacturing exports been maintained. Township and village enterprises (TVEs)—the private sector in China—have grown much more rapidly than their state equivalents. Because exports from TVEs and foreign-owned production have risen rapidly, China now maintains an overall surplus on current account, permitting Chinese investment abroad. While foreign direct investment has been responsible for the transfer of technology to China, the investment inflow into China is only somewhat larger than the investment outflow.[8] The returns from both types of flows (China's foreign exports and Chinese foreign investment) have been higher than that from the domestic production of state enterprises. The export sector therefore has become crucial to Chinese development.

If it continues at or near 10 percent a year in real terms, China's economic growth will allow it to surpass the United States as the world's leading economy by the year 2030. Japan will remain considerably behind the United States as its growth rate slows. The key question will then be whether the international system can socialize its strongest member to shoulder previously unrecognized world responsibilities. This was the problem that faced Europe after 1920 when the United States withdrew from the system and from 1929 to 1931 did not act as an international stabilizer. After 1945, however, partly because of the cold war, the pressures on the United States brought forth a much more cooperative response. In seeking to stabilize the Western half of the bipolar system, the United States was doing no more than serving its own interest.

After the year 2000 China will increasingly be asked to act as a system stabilizer, but without an apparent foe. Some of China's strategists will not see the need for "good international behavior." Possessing the world's largest economy, some Chinese leaders may be tempted to seek military hegemony. This could not succeed, and indeed would only range the rest of the world against China. Chinese aggression against Russia in the Far East would not add strength; it would only consume it. Chinese aggression against Japan or Taiwan would risk alienating bountiful sources of capital that the Chinese need. Chinese aggression against the United States could not possibly be successful and would terminate export-led growth for the Chinese economy. A drive for hegemony would only repeat the Japanese error of 1937–45.

The lesson of the new international economy should be that countries that have already achieved economic hegemony do not need to assert it militarily. They can use their economic instruments to influence others. Thus the largest economies in recent international history have been defensive rather than offensive states. Great Britain did not seek to dominate the European continent after 1870 but rather to use liberal policies to keep Europe open economically and move toward democracy politically. Britain did not succeed, but London did not initiate World War I to compensate for that failure. It played the role of defender, not aggressor.

The same was true of the United States after 1920. America either absented itself from the system or sought to cooperate with others.[9] Confronting the choice between imperial expansion, isolation, or cooperation, the United States chose the third option. It could use economic techniques to bring cooperation among members of its alliance camp. It reverted to military techniques only where economic ones failed, notably with regard to the Soviet Union. These precedents will be taken seriously by China. The choice it makes will not only be based on precedents, however. If by that time an encompassing coalition of major powers has emerged among the United States, Japan, Russia, and key European states, it will be harder for China to go against the group. Then power pressures will act in favor of joining rather than opposing the previous coalition. As we have seen in chapter 6, the agglomeration of power in the hands of a large coalition of great powers will ultimately attract rather than repel additional members. If this happens, an encompassing coalition for the world would begin to act as Europe has done within its own continent.

If China decides to follow an economic tack, its strategy is still uncertain. America sought through APEC (the Asia-Pacific Economic Community) to prevent other nations from following the exclusivist Japanese strategy. Japan has taught the East Asian tigers to export industrial products to the United States, but some of these countries have been unwilling to concede an equivalent openness to European and American goods. They have followed the Japanese capitalist developmental state approach. Via export platforms in East Asia, Japan has sought to disguise the Japanese surplus with the United States as an Asian surplus. Goods once exported to the United States from Japan are now assembled in East Asia and labeled as Taiwanese or Malaysian exports. The imbalance in the world trading system continues. Japan's portion of it is only technically reduced.

While the new American policy to oppose this redirection is formally aimed at the Asian tigers, its indirect and most important target is China. China should not be led to believe that it can develop in the same mode as Japan, selling low-priced but high-technology exports to the American market. The U.S. market is saturated with such exports; new developers will have to find new markets to sustain their growth.[10] For Japan this means creating markets for East Asian products within Japan, just as Britain offered the market of last resort for nations that had borrowed heavily on the London exchange at the turn of the century. Japan has invested heavily in East and Southeast Asia and now has to let indebted nations export to Tokyo in order to finance those investments and repay the loans. As a major recipient of Japanese capital, China will have to sell more in Japan than it markets in the United States if heavy imbalances are not to accumulate.

It seems unlikely that China will opt for a one-sided development path like that of Japan. China needs foreign capital and technology. It cannot raise capital solely from local banking and government sources (as Japan and Korea both did), but must tap the Hong Kong and Shanghai exchanges as well as foreign direct investment.[11] In addition, as other nations move to become virtual states, China will represent the low-cost production facility for many countries. China fits like a glove into existing outsourcing tendencies in Japan, the United States, Europe, Hong Kong, and Singapore.

Such a model compensates for China's past isolation from high-technology economies in the rest of the world. Without help, Chinese firms do not know what to produce for the sophisticated European or American consumer. They are not fully aware of the requisite designs or the need to factor in energy savings, avoidance of chlorofluorocarbons, compactness, and microchips. As one example, the Chinese textile and fashion industry depends on the designs and marketing of the finished garments in New York, Milan, Paris, Tokyo, and London. For the next generation or so, Chinese capitalism will be incomplete: a body governed by ganglia but without a fully developed central nervous system. It will work best in association with other nations.

The Emerging Nations

As long as the developing world earns its living from the products of land, there will be wars among its members. The carving out of new states from old empires puts a premium on the location of borders. Nationalism asserts itself, but then the old empire may try to regain lost territories. This issue reverberates in Serbia, whose leaders have not yet conceded the secession of some of the erstwhile union republics and want to hold onto Kosovo. At some point the process of nationalist subdivision will come to an end with more than 200 nation-states in world politics. Islands will assert sovereignty. The old territorial empires—French, Spanish, Dutch, British, and American—will lose their remaining dependencies.

The developing world will remain the poorest part of humankind, but it will begin to grow more rapidly in the twenty-first century. In many regions, particularly in Africa and South Asia, governments have stood in the way of per-capita economic growth. In Africa governments extorted low prices from farmers in order to finance their generally unsuccessful import-substituting industrialization programs based on high tariffs. Under this discredited policy farmers left the countryside, swelling the ranks of the urban poor and accentuating food shortages. Many of these states now have structural adjustment programs in place, returning free markets to agriculture and stimulating local production to meet home and export demand. Food deficits remain in the Sudan, Ethiopia, and Somalia. Yet Ghana, Senegal, Tanzania, Uganda, and the Sahelian group now manage to support themselves. Currencies have been devalued and a form of floating exchange rates installed through currency exchange bureaus. Foreign investment is now welcomed as currency risks decline and democracy and property rights spread. It remains to be seen, of course, whether new African governments can attain fiscal credibility and pursue the stable monetary policies necessary to attract foreign capital and direct investment. The long-term picture, however, is brighter than it has been.

India needs foreign investment as well as caps on inefficient state industry for market forces to be unleashed. The prospect, however, is uncertain. India has already reduced the protective tariffs that sustained its uncompetitive import-substitution industry; but economic sanctions following its nuclear weapons tests may keep foreign capital away. India now needs to build an export industry as efficient as the great software complex in Bangalore and the textile and movie industries in Bombay. As the government's off-and-on approach to Enron's massive investment in power generation shows, however, sanctions and curbs on foreign direct investment still bedevil India's relations with the outside world.

The developing world has at least three different camps: the newly industrializing countries (NICs), the oil countries of the Middle East, and the non-oil agriculturalists. The latter two are firmly based on the products of land. Only the NICs have made the transition to industry and services. While Africa and South Asia are moving toward specialty agriculture and some industrial development, they are far from attaining the productive strengths of the new China. On the other hand, nations such as the Philippines are beginning to grow more rapidly, and Vietnam will likely emerge as an export platform for Japanese and American industry. In some of these contexts economic liberalization will begin before political authoritarianism ends.

In the Middle East the situation is more uncertain. Israel has the educated workforce and technical expertise to transform itself into a virtual state, but it must achieve peace with its neighbors so that it may divert its resources from military to civilian production. Iraq, Iran, Libya, and the Sudan will remain as military threats to the oil balance in the Middle East, challenging Saudi Arabia and the Gulf producers. The issue of territory will remain paramount in their calculations. The Gulf sheikdoms are still quasi-feudal principalities, vulnerable to military assault and probably to an invader's dictation after a successful war. Nationalism there does not yet have popular roots or constitute an effective deterrent to attack.

Latin America contains some of the most advanced young capitalist economies: Mexico, Brazil, Argentina, and Chile, as well as an economic backwater, Cuba. As NAFTA and other free trade pacts such as Mercosur are extended to new countries, structural adjustment will open previously closed markets to outside competition. Overvalued currencies will be devalued and foreign investment welcomed. Productive export platforms will be created in a host of new nations.

Drug and criminal economies of course will compete with legitimate markets. In some countries there may even be a fusion of guerrilla and drug cartels to oppose the regime in power. They may not topple elected governments, but they can corrupt popular regimes to accede to their way of doing business. If drugs were partially decriminalized in the developed nations, or even if drug prices fell, the return from such activities would decline, strengthening legitimate alternatives.

China and the Developing World as Factors in International Politics

Both China and erstwhile Third World nations have been outliers in international politics. The Third World once wanted to be "decoupled" from the First. China was isolated for fourteen years during the Cultural Revolution. In the early 1960s China also strove to lead the Third World in a movement of nonaligned nations against an international system dominated by the Soviet Union and the United States. The collapse of the Soviet Union and the end of communism as a political force has brought such schemes to a halt. Gradually one part of the developing world after another has enlisted in the essentially Western system of economic relations. The NICs proved that they could resemble Japan as sturdy Asian members of a world economic and trading system. New trading units, such as NAFTA, ASEAN, APEC, and other regional arrangements, have brought erstwhile Third World states to the threshold of rapid economic development, based on increasingly open economies. The extension of the European Union into Eastern Europe and perhaps to the Baltic nations increases the probability that backward countries on the fringes of the old Soviet Union will eventually benefit from Western capitalism and foreign direct investment. Despite financial crises in 1997 and 1998, Southeast Asia will remain a rapidly developing segment of the world economy. China's close ties with Hong

Kong and Singapore, to say nothing about the stimulus of Japan, will encourage Beijing to make a similar plunge.

Economic attraction also has political effects. As Russia moves toward Europe, China will move toward Japan and the United States. Perhaps for the first time, new rapidly developing countries will want to be linked with capitalist progenitors. They will seek to gain economic connections with other states that German, Japanese, and Russian capitalists had not forged in 1913. "Late developers" do not reap all the benefits; they gain only if they are associated with sources of capital and technical knowledge in other parts of the world.

Resolving the Financial Crisis

The financial crisis that exploded in Thailand in July 1997 rapidly communicated itself to the rest of East Asia, Russia, and Latin America. Banking systems in Indonesia, Malaysia, and even Hong Kong had always been capital-short by Western and Japanese standards. No single nation could withstand speculative outflows of capital. The problem was that to regain Western capital and confidence, small nations had to adopt IMF "shock therapy" to qualify for bailouts. They had to raise interest rates—hoping to attract foreign capital—which would force the domestic economy into recession. High interest rates would support local currency values, making it easier to repay loans in hard currency, but they would also undercut exports, making a rebound in foreign trade difficult or impossible.

No doubt the IMF reasoned that shock therapy was justified if it brought a rapid influx of foreign funds. If it didn't, however, high interest rates would make reflation more difficult.[12] Ideally, rapid foreign inflows would reduce rates quickly, and exports could be resumed on the basis of lower currency values. Yet IMF, Japanese, and U.S. assistance was neither quick nor substantial enough to buoy investor confidence. Foreign monies initially stayed away and Asia, Russia, and Latin America were left with austerity programs that only made things worse. In time, however, investor confidence returned—except in Russia—and funds began to reflate East Asian economies. Russia having failed, the United States, the Inter-American Development Bank, and the IMF turned their sights on Brazil, with larger resources in tow. Unemployment and high government deficits, however, made President Cardoso's task a difficult one. Only the establishment of an international stabilization fund seemed likely to prevent crisis the next time.[13]

———————

China and the emerging nations confront great opportunities to become major manufacturing nations in world politics, producing goods for Western and developed industries. They do not possess economic capabilities to go it alone, however. As late developers, they will not only need capital from virtual states but also industrial designs, technology, and marketing competence. A network of production interdependence can cement cooperative relationships with the developed world.

—— Part Four

The New System of International Politics and Economics

chapter 12

The Increasing Intangibility of Value in the World Economy

Modern states have witnessed a gradual transmutation of value. Whereas tangible goods were once the most prized assets, intangible goods are now rapidly increasing in value. This is true both in international trade and domestic life. Years ago, most of the world's productive effort was devoted to creating food, clothing, and shelter. With agricultural and industrial development in the eighteenth and nineteenth century, crop yields increased, steam power grew, and textiles were produced rapidly and in quantity.[1] The twentieth-century world turned to automobiles, refrigerators, and electric power. Smaller but powerful transistor-electronics, computers, and communication devices followed. By the late twentieth century the microchip and the microprocessor had added dramatic new value and performance to many products.

These developments show an accelerating emphasis on the intangible activities that make new products possible. The rise in complex products and options has further brought about an increase in the importance of the intangibles of ideas and knowledge. As Alan Greenspan has observed:

> Some individuals place more value on and are willing to pay more
> for style y rather than style x, whereas others prefer x. Producing
> both styles x and y, enhances overall consumer well-being. Fifty

years ago, only x was feasible. This striving to expand the options
for satisfying the particular needs of individuals inevitably results
in a shift toward value created through the exploitation of ideas and
concepts—or more generally information—from the more straight-
forward utilization of physical resources and manual labor.[2]

Such invisibles or intangibles are incorporated into modern life in
two ways. First, creative services make tangible products, from
Porsches to tribladed razors, more attractive. Product differentiation of
physical goods increases the range of consumer choice. Besides the effect of ideas in increasing options among products, tangible products
have an intangible component: to be successful they must capture the
imagination, increase loyalty to the brand name, and pave the way for
future creations. Advertising and public relations lie at the heart of
brand-name success, a truth illustrated when a brand comes under sus-
picion. Tylenol (Johnson & Johnson), embarrassed when poisoned
tablets were sold in Tylenol packages, repaired its fortunes by offering
new caplets and tamper-proof packaging. Jack-in-the-Box had to prove
to the public that its hamburgers were safe, just as a few years earlier
Ocean Spray needed to demonstrate the purity of its cranberries. Intel
had to replace flawed Pentium chips (even where new chips may not
have been necessary) to reclaim the integrity of its market image. Beyond the costs of recalling or improving the physical product, advertising and public relations "image manipulators" who repair reputations
are paid an extremely high return.

Second, many products are themselves intangible. Increasingly both
individuals and business concerns seek meaning and profit from intangible services. Individual well-being, defined in terms of personal success, in turn requires services that improve individual outlook and
capability. People want to develop their inner potential in every possible direction. Religious practice, psychiatry, psychological therapy, aer-
obics, weight reduction, body shaping, stress reduction, meditation,
beautification, and cosmetic surgery are all employed to increase personal effectiveness and fulfillment—sometimes as substitutes for

human commitment and companionship in an atomistic world. Financial, legal, and tax planning are essential to give people a larger income stream over a longer period of time. When people relax, they want to go somewhere else. Tourism offers a vital outlet, a flood of different messages, antidotes to the concerns of the routine moment. Skiing, ballooning, skydiving, snorkeling, or scuba diving usually require people to travel. A new climate or ecology is not next door. And sometimes the fun is just getting there. To learn more about the world, the twenty-first-century individual craves new experiences, travel that teaches.

Travel as an intangible service permeates the business sector also. Despite online means of communicating, foreign and domestic travel has never been a higher priority for the average business executive or salaryman. For executives who depend on trust in their dealings with associates, distant communication is not sufficiently reliable and informative. To know how another executive will respond to different situations depends on spending time with him or her in a variety of social as well as business situations. Hollywood executives and agents may excel in the art of telephonic persuasion; but when a deal must be concluded, people have to be together.

In business services the greatest value-added increment now comes generally from the design and marketing of the new product and less often from its production. The creative originators of new movies or TV series are rewarded handsomely, along with the actors who create the roles. The idea or "concept" is everything, with creators of story lines and screenplays receiving commensurate rewards. Outside consultants earn large returns making suggestions about what should be produced and how it should be put together and financed. The producer who brings the elements of the deal together, or the magnate who sees the serendipity to be derived from joining two firms in a new production unit, is the ultimate beneficiary of the transaction. Financiers take risks but enjoy a huge benefit if their idea, creative extravaganza, or merger catches on. Disney and other multimedia purveyors seek to offer a total concept, in which ancillary products—hotels, tourism, and education services—are bundled into one new creative product.

In rich societies service incomes are rising along with the service share of GDP; but services are also rapidly growing in international trade, adding strength to national balances on current account. Recent data indicate that services are growing more rapidly than merchandise trade to about $1 trillion per year in 1992.[3] In the ten years from 1982 to 1992, total trade in services grew by 9.5 percent per year, while total merchandise trade increased by only 7.1 percent. Both, however, increased more rapidly than domestic GDP.[4] The United States, as we have seen, has a deficit in merchandise trade, but an increasing surplus in services.

International Services

Intangibles have always been important to particular nations, but they have risen in value for all countries in the past thirty years. Historically, the British relied on a surplus in "invisibles" to make up for their deficit in "visible" trade. The last year in which the British had a surplus of merchandise (that is, visible) trade was 1822. From then until 1914 they had a deficit in merchandise trade, but a surplus on their balance of payments. Intangible exports—insurance, shipping, financial services plus income on foreign investment receipts—made up the difference.

The City of London, through its discount and acceptance houses, was able to determine which countries and which agencies or entrepreneurs within foreign countries would get credit on favorable terms. Since many foreign countries maintained large balances in the Bank of England and cleared their trade accounts through London, English bankers had unparalleled access to information about foreign clients and debtors. They knew how much money a particular tea plantation in Darjeeling could afford to borrow, and they knew which Australian railway bonds deserved the lowest rate of interest. Typically, British financial institutions assumed the unpaid bills owed to exporters and paid their cash value minus a "discount." They then collected (and pocketed) the balance from importers. The higher the credit rating of the exporter and the more reliable the importer, the lower the discount charged. In this way British financial houses gained an overview of economic operations throughout the globe.

In addition, most debts were cleared in British pounds sterling, which were literally as good as gold. Because the pound had a fixed relation to gold, it represented a standard of value that the whole world accepted, while other currencies, such as the ruble, the dinar, and the Italian lira, were more questionable. British interest rates could therefore be set lower because the demand for British currency exceeded that for any other currency, including the American dollar. Since other countries held their reserves in London and foreigners were constantly repaying loans (and interest charges) to Britain, the imperial city was awash with cash and could easily lend and invest large sums abroad. In 1914 British foreign investment was more than twice that of any other country. The successful activities of British banks and financial houses added strength to British shipping and insurance firms, which again dwarfed those of the rest of the world. British earnings on these activities more than covered the foreign trade deficit. "Invisibles" were Britain's real source of wealth.

The rest of the world was unable to imitate British gains in financial and other services. For Germany, the United States, and Russia merchandise commerce was the main avenue of economic progress. Outside of Great Britain a favorable balance of visible trade was the measure of success. While industrial goods were pouring out of continental factories, European agriculture and natural resources remained very important. As late as the 1930s every major textbook on international relations took pains to measure each great power's production of iron and steel, coal, oil, minerals, grain, and other foodstuffs. A successful power needed vast reserves of agriculture and raw materials if it was to go to war.[5, 6] No book spoke of achieving national mastery of intangible units of value.

After World War II, however, again invisibles became important, and not for just a few countries.[7] American, Japanese, and European firms vied for preeminence in services: consulting, computer-assisted design, marketing, financial and legal services, accounting, advertising, and public relations. Financial services became the key "intangible." A few brokerage, underwriting, and merchant banking firms such as Nomura, Merrill Lynch, Goldman Sachs, Morgan Stanley, Salomon brothers, and ING-Barings together dominated many financial markets. For a time Drexel Burnham Lambert purveyed new issues of high-premium, high-risk (junk) bonds that were used to gain control of underperforming companies. Financial wizards devised new "derivative" instruments that fluctuated wildly with interest rates and later caught gullible municipalities napping. Lured to Wall Street, mathematical "rocket scientists" devised program trading routines that accentuated rises and falls of the stock market. Hedge fund manipulators sought huge returns through leveraged investments around the globe. Bond and currency specialists made large fortunes in day-to-day trading or saw their luck run out. Takeover artists such as Kohlberg, Kravis, Roberts found ways to amass vast pools of money by buying out a firm (taking it private) and then selling all or portions of it again on the public market. The Reagan era of the 1980s was characterized by the gains and losses that resulted. Mergers were even larger in the 1990s.

Worldwide competition and downsizing accelerated the trend to mergers and industrial alliances in the 1990s. Given excess supply in many industries, including steel, textiles, aerospace, automotive, consumer electronics, and discount merchandising, firms had to radically restructure and cut costs. This meant not only paring workers and occasionally shifting to robotics but also increasing production per worker. Great increases in U.S. productivity in the late 1980s and 1990s made American firms much more competitive on a worldwide basis. Downsizing also fostered industrial alliances. Many firms sought to use the productive facilities of other companies rather than to increase plant and equipment at home. Ford and Mazda developed an effective relationship for designing, producing, and marketing new cars on a cooperative basis.

Sometimes the connection went even further. New "manufacturers" arose with no production lines at all. The corporation consisted of a group of engineering designers, marketeers, and financial experts (all rendering intangible services) wedded to a production line leased from someone else's plant. Sometimes one "virtual corporation" could share these same offices with the management of a firm that did something entirely different. In such a case the entire production of the virtual corporation consisted of services. This outcome represented the ultimate downsizing and cutting of production costs. Such firms were far more competitive than the giant industrial combines created in the late nineteenth century that vertically integrated many stages of production. The modern biotechnology corporation is an offshoot of this type, with its central core simply devoted to research into new products. Once the products are devised, they can be produced under contract in other pharmaceutical manufacturers' factories. Costs and payrolls can thus be kept to a minimum. This is the reason that the small biotechnology firms of the U.S. West Coast can more than keep up with their giant rivals. Large size may even become a handicap.

Nor are these advantages in new services captured by developed countries alone. "Back office" data processing in data entry and transaction processing (e.g., insurance claims) are often done in developing countries; but so are more sophisticated activities such as software development, systems analysis, and database management. Israel is a prime designer of software for U.S. computer firms. Bangalore, India, manufactures software for Texas Instruments, Motorola, Apple Computer, Digital Equipment (DEC), Sun Microsystems, and Intel. The gains made by highly trained but low-cost service professionals in some developing countries led the World Bank to conclude: "Trade statistics show that many developing countries have a revealed comparative advantage in services even if tourism is excluded."[8] With technological progress, service centers may be efficiently located anywhere on the globe.

———————

The world has witnessed a revolutionary economic progression from emphasis on land (agriculture and natural resources) to specific capital (industrial plant and equipment), to labor, mobile capital, and information. With this shift there has been a comparable increased return from each higher stage in the production process. The produce of land—commodities—continue to be valuable and could become more so; but they are less valuable than manufactured goods. In recent years, furthermore, services have not only become far more important as a proportion of GDP but far more highly valued than in previous eras. It is true that janitors, office messengers, short-order cooks, security guards, day-care givers, and temporary office workers are not highly paid. Yet even these services have become more highly valued as they have become more professionalized. They are now frequently performed by service corporations at higher rates of compensation. At the other end of the service continuum, highly trained individuals earn a fabulous return in designing and marketing new products in manufactured goods, multimedia, music, legal, and financial services.

It is not yet clear that intangibles now claim a higher reward than manufactured goods. What is true is that their value is increasing more rapidly than manufactured products, and far more rapidly than the commodities produced by land.

The military implications of this revolution in the relative value of different factors of production are extremely significant. It is already evident that states have difficulty seizing effective control of manufacturing establishments (which may be destroyed in the process). It is even more clear that they do not capture intangible services or direct them effectively. Even if Germany had defeated Britain in World War I, it would not have won control of the British financial empire, which was perhaps even more important and extensive than its territorial equivalent. Expertise cannot be forcibly seized, it must be recruited or patiently learned and cultivated. As services become the most important part of GDP for all developed countries, it is less and less obvious that an aggressor could master them through conquest. The decentralization of factories also makes warfare less successful. A nation seizing another country will not gain an integrated self-sufficient economy. Most modern corporations operate in different locales. Even seizing their headquarters does not guarantee that an invader can compel obedience from subsidiaries.

If the trend toward intangibles continues, human capital will be an even more important ingredient in the productive process than it is at the moment. Everyone recognizes that manual workers need much greater skills to compete on an assembly line designed for economies of scope than one that merely achieves economies of scale. Yet the main educational challenge is not that faced by production workers; for a country to succeed in the international economy, it must develop new and creative ideas in every field. Post-high-school vocational training does not solve this preeminent problem. Some degree of college education is necessary for almost every high-level service worker. For those at the helm of new service corporations—such as Microsoft or EDS— an extremely flexible educational environment is necessary, one that provides a challenge to all those who enter.

In addition, the corporation and legal systems must continue to re-shape themselves to employ the creative ideas that emerge from a first-rate system of higher education. Ideas mean nothing if the path from concept to physical or intellectual embodiment is too long and cum-bersome. The virtualizing state needs patents, financing, and production lines to turn the concept into reality. The utility of human capital depends on institutions that support and give substance to the educational process. Commercial laws must help start-up companies that will embody the creativity of highly qualified individuals. The political and legal realm must foster progress in economics and science. In the future the countries that excel will have the greatest access to human capital. Their systems will also be designed to exploit that capital to the maximum degree.

chapter 13

The State
and the World

The Rise of Virtual States

In the past two generations, virtual states and countries strongly influenced by virtualization have made unparalleled gains. Starting with efficient production and trading advantages, these states have begun to invest and produce abroad in large amounts. At home they have moved into high-level services—research, product design, financing, and marketing. The recipients of their skills and funds—China, India, Mexico, Brazil, and Eastern Europe—are becoming major producing locations. Such developing body nations will in time become head nations as well. The move to services is becoming pervasive. All major industrial powers are enhancing service production and moving away from manufacturing. The shift in shares of GDP from manufacturing to services has been remarkable. For many developed countries, services have risen since 1960 from less than 50 percent to 70 percent of GDP, while manufacturing has declined from 35 percent or 40 percent of GDP to less than 20 percent.

The Rise of the United States and the Asian Crisis

Less noticed, but still of great significance, has been the rise of the United States as an economic and political player on the world stage. It was customary at the end of the 1980s to forecast a continuing decline of the U.S. role in the international economy and political arena. Paul Kennedy, Lester Thurow, Paul Krugman, and others urged Americans to lessen previous expectations of U.S. performance. Even if American military forces remained strong, the U.S. economic position would deteriorate. The trade balance seemed impossible to correct, American industry would remain bloated and inefficient, and America's international political importance would shrink.

Such forecasts underestimated both the U.S. ability to reorganize itself industrially and the strength of its democratic regulatory system. Critics thereby entirely missed U.S. superiority in financial markets, which rests on both openness and impartiality. As we have seen, bond ratings are critical measures of honesty and fair dealing as well as financial performance. Confidence is the key, and U.S. financial management has inspired credibility.[1]

The United States gained therefore not only through the success of its cutting-edge industries but because the American political-economic system was competent to handle financial policy. In the past, capital poured into the United States in times of international crisis. Today it comes for reasons of economic advantage. Returns were more secure in the United States than virtually anywhere else because transparency and the U.S. regulatory system guaranteed their safety. Even the U.S. trade deficit had the advantage of creating liquidity for other countries and peoples, allowing them to obtain a store of value with which to purchase goods and assets.[2]

The financial crisis in Asia, Russia, and Latin America also underscored the importance of impartial commercial institutions. Though unforeseen, the crisis had been brewing for years. Thailand's troubles did not emerge because of an inherent weakness in the Thai economy but because of the uncertain position of the Thai banking system and the loans dictated by political cronyism. The weak Thai government did not seem able to resolve the crisis without outside pressure and help. The general problem in Asia, however, was too-low interest rates sustained by a very high rate of foreign investment, particularly in U.S. dollars. The

World Bank estimated that foreign investment in the Asia-Pacific region was at $25 billion in 1990. By 1996 this had skyrocketed to $110 billion.

The crisis emerged in part because Asian capital markets were undeveloped. Hence industrial expansion became more and more dependent on foreign investment. As the return on investment in Europe, America, and Japan appeared to stabilize in the early 1990s, East Asia seemed the one place investors could satisfy their demand for ever higher yields. Asia took more money than it could profitably absorb. Foreign investment initially went into large infrastructure and construction projects, but later funneled into the real estate market. New buildings were used as collateral for further loans. Since the loans were in foreign currency, repayment required exports to foreign lands. The stronger U.S. dollar accommodated such exports, but the much lower yen made Japanese competition in U.S. markets even more formidable. In 1996 more semiconductors were produced than the market needed. This glut affected producers in Korea, Taiwan, and other countries. As their exports dwindled, these countries' currencies came under devaluation pressure that governments at first tried to resist. Fearing devaluation, holders of local currency quickly shifted into dollars, putting on more pressure. This shift to dollars ultimately forced devaluation of the currency.

Once devaluation occurred in one country or region, it spread to other nations. After one or two devaluations, other nations appeared overvalued, and their currencies were attacked by speculators. Only Hong Kong and China (with very large reserves) were able to fight off devaluation, using high short-term interest rates. Nonperforming real estate and construction loans put banking systems in jeopardy. In developed countries these banks would have been quickly closed down, their remaining assets distributed to creditors. In some Asian nations, however, the government tried to support insolvent financial institutions or let them function without restructuring. The result was financial disaster, and foreign capital began a massive exodus. Interest rates rose and economic growth stagnated.

The difficulty was particularly great in countries such as Korea, which followed a politically-inspired industrial policy. In these cases the state would not let its favored industries languish. As Alan Greenspan noted, "policy loans in too many instances foster misuse of resources, unprofitable expansions, losses and eventually loan defaults."[3] Having delayed financial restructuring, many banks in Asia faced a lack of liquidity or outright collapse. They needed an infusion of temporary loans to facilitate adjustment. The World Bank, Japan, the IMF, Europe, the United States, and other countries put together temporary loan packages for the various parties: Malaysia, Thailand, Indonesia, the Philippines, Korea, and others that totaled more than $100 billion. These loans gave the countries time to recalibrate their banking systems and put loan portfolios in order, avoiding default. The IMF and United States refloated Brazil. Without such stringent medicine, needed foreign capital would not return.

The lesson of the Asian crisis and its extension to Russia and Latin America is that countries need independent and neutral political mechanisms to police banks and markets. Economic success is not measured simply by industrial expansion. This expansion must be based on creditworthy risks, not political bargains. When investors find political manipulation masking financial losses or potential losses, they will leave. Increasingly they will return to the U.S. market, further underscoring the integrity of American standards in financial regulation, accounting, and auditing.

A major reason for America's increasing international economic importance is that the balance in the U.S. economy—between economic and industrial success on the one hand and effective regulation and transparency on the other—is virtually unmatched elsewhere. This is why the sources of capital available to the United States remain unparalleled. It is mastery of international flows that today guarantees possession of needed stocks. The United States has proved its ability to weather both political and economic shocks.

U.S. economic performance, however, has not yet returned to standards of yesteryear. In the 1960s growth rates proceeded at nearly 4 percent per year. Real incomes were growing rapidly. Today household income has increased by more than 10 percent over 1970, but real wages have not yet regained their previous levels.[4] Productivity has risen more rapidly in the 1990s than it did between 1973 and 1980, but it has not matched the highs of the 1969–73 period.[5] Still, the U.S. economy has attained high employment without inflation, and either productivity or economic growth measures are probably considerably higher than those recorded in the official statistics.[6]

Political Agreement and Economic Stability

American economic health, however, does not fully solve the problems of a depressed world economy. Other great powers must agree to help bail out the economies of faltering countries. If there is no functioning concert of powers—an encompassing coalition—there will be no sustained international economic advance. As in the 1930s (when no concert of powers existed), countries in trouble will have to take care of themselves—to institute exchange controls and tariffs to protect their domestic economies.[7] This could mean a return to closed markets and economic autarchy. In 1931 the Austrian Kredit-Anstalt faced default, but foreign lenders did not come to its aid. Austria then underwent financial collapse. Soon afterward the contagion moved to Germany. Seeking to retain capital, Berlin levied high interest rates, but these did not regain funds or confidence, and the crisis moved to England and France. The United Kingdom was forced to devalue the pound sterling and leave the gold standard. The international financial system shortly collapsed and capital flows ceased.

Political agreement among major economic powers formed the underpinning of the international economy after 1945. The Western and developed half of the world saw rapid economic growth sustained by agreement among the United States, Britain, France, Germany, and Japan.[8] No such development occurred in the Soviet bloc. Since 1990 the remaining Communist countries (North Korea, Vietnam, China, and Cuba) have benefited where they could participate in the Western economic system. China has done increasingly well since it opened its economy in 1978; Vietnam has begun to progress. The others remain in the doldrums.

Nor does the "rescue of Asia" depend on a single hegemonic player. As Barry Eichengreen shows, international economic agreement was necessary even in the late nineteenth and early twentieth century, when Britain was ostensibly the hegemonic leader.[9] Today it is even more essential for great powers to concur. This is not only because the United States no longer holds a great advantage in sources of capital, but also because investors want to know that other economic players—Japan, Europe, East Asia—will support the necessary restructuring.[10]

War and Economics: Stocks and Flows

War has retained a place in international history because it enables one country to seize resources from another. If some nations did not believe the benefits of war exceeded the costs, war would seldom occur. Invasion is a threat to a country because it takes away land, a valuable asset. Countries agree to conclude peace when a new equilibrium is reached in their relative control of disputed territory. If a country cannot control territory (and reap its benefits), it withdraws. Thus, irrespective of cause, war is fought on the assumption that the more land one power takes, the weaker its enemy will become. Successful offensives gain control of the territory in which the opposing army operates, snuffing out the enemy's logistics and cutting his lines of communication. Once his base of power has been occupied, he has no further sources of support. Since states are territorial entities, they cannot exist without land.

This does not mean that hatred does not cause wars. Primordial antagonism between peoples will often generate conflict. Thus, Serb and Muslim, Arab and Israeli, Indian and Pakistani may fight. Cultural and religious differences can frequently explode into warfare. Success in war, however, depends on military and techno-economic factors. The amount of hatred does not necessarily predict victory against an opponent; a warring side must defeat its opponent militarily.[11] The ultimate measure of success is still the control of territory. The point is that war is the continuing mode in societies in which land continues to be the major factor of production.

Yet land is less important than it once was on a worldwide basis. Struggles in Eastern Europe, the Middle East, and South Asia are a reflection of historical atavism. And even where land remains important, it is harder to seize and hold. Other peoples' territories are hard to govern unless the intervention is supported and legitimized by the entire international community. Ex parte intervention by one power does not reliably determine political outcomes in another state.[12] The system rebels against extinguishing the existence of an independent country.[13] And even where great powers sanction collective intervention, as in Bosnia, they have not countenanced gains to the occupying powers that incur major costs. These circumstances strongly encourage nations to seek gains by exploiting their own national capacities. Perhaps surprisingly, countries can succeed with only a little land. Indeed, some of the most potent advances in the past two generations have been made by smaller states in East Asia or Europe. Achievements no longer require a country to be of the size of Russia, China, Canada, Brazil, the United States, or Australia.

Although wars are fought for resources, attackers do not always seek to occupy a country and control its population. In the past, nomadic horsemen plundered the agriculture and industry of a nearby country for booty—slaves and gold—that they could use at home. This style of war was a form of industry—it enabled a country to acquire resources in the form of new stocks of value.[14]

Such resources were highly important because all economies are based on stocks. Adam Smith believed that the nation with the greatest access to stocks would be the richest. Unlike his mercantilist colleagues, he did not seek to minimize imports—these were important additions to the national stock of consumer goods.[15] Stocks could be obtained in three ways: by producing them, by seizing them from some other country, or by trading for them. War, then, could be a substitute for production. In certain periods and in rudimentary economies it was a very successful substitute.

The historical development of the modern world economy, however, shows that where openness exists, trade is usually a more efficient way to acquire stocks than war. Goods transferred without war have fewer social costs. Flows of production (under conditions of openness) are better than flows of armies. This is particularly true in modern times.

All nations produce goods and therefore have access to stocks. The countries that excel are those that know how to influence or control the flows of goods and factors of production from one economy to another. In this sense mastery of flows assures an access to stocks that local production alone cannot possibly convey. One of the great advantages of the contemporary American economy has been its ability to attract flows of resources from elsewhere in the globe.

Robert Mundell, the noted economist, shows that movements of goods and movements of factors of production can substitute for one another.[16] Since this is true, the failure of trade is not always critical to economic welfare. If one's exports are not admitted to a foreign economy, a nation can produce the good abroad within the tariff zone of the target economy. In the absence of capital flows, a restriction on trade would be very important. The mobility of capital, however, can substitute for a failure in the mobility of goods. Thus President Clinton's initial inability to pass "fast track" legislation did not mean that U.S. goods could not be sold in Latin America, but merely that these goods had to be produced abroad. The opponents of "fast track" perhaps did not realize that the movement of jobs overseas would be greater without trade agreements than with them. They wanted goods to be produced at home and to reduce imports, but that was not the operative choice. Given their role in market decisions, major entrepreneurs would in fact choose between exports and foreign direct investment.

Economics and Nationalism

When Arnold J. Toynbee wrote *A Study of History* in the 1930s he observed that the nineteenth-century international economy was increasingly trapped within the nationalist confines of parochial states.[17] Rising nationalism, despite the progress of liberalism, democracy, and open trade, diverted commerce in a warlike direction. In late nineteenth-century Berlin, German trade was preferred to British trade; in London, the other way around. Imperial and colonial expansion distorted the prevailing openness into political closure.[18] The fin de siècle state still possessed the power to disrupt commerce and the flow of capital. This nationalistic tendency was carried further in World War I, in which previously liberal economies were captured by the state and mobilized for purposes of war. The state's role in economics continued after 1918 and during the Great Depression (1929–39). In World War II it reached its apotheosis. The Allied victory in 1945 was made possible by state economic planning as well as popular sacrifice.

States continue to possess the technical power to cut themselves off from worldwide flows—of production, capital, labor, and information. They can let economic nationalism determine affairs at home, but only at a considerable sacrifice in wealth and well-being. The incentives have been reversed since 1914. At that time a sacrifice in flows was necessary to augment stocks, and governments and peoples willingly made that exchange. Today, countries normally prefer flows to reliance on locally produced stocks. The stocks they accumulate as a result of international flows are far larger than they could produce at home. An incipient economic internationalism has dwarfed nationalism, except in areas based on the factor of land.

The reliance on international flows, however, has cost governments the ability to guarantee specific economic outcomes for their populations. Faced with globalization, governments negotiate with foreign factors of production but cannot dictate the result. There has been a sea change in economic and political practice since 1914. In a reversal of Toynbee, worldwide economics is no longer captured by the parochial organization of nationalist states. Rather, states are trapped in the international coils of economics.

Machine Production and the Worker

Historians of the Industrial Revolution have rightly observed that machine production and the factory system devalued the worker's individual initiative and creativity.[19] In the period of cottage industry and the "putting out system" households were organized as creative producing units. Household labor solidarity was high. Even though poverty was rampant, the worker did not have to leave home or gear his production to the revolutions of a steam-driven machine. Had the Industrial Revolution taken a different path, machines might have been decentralized to a greater number of small establishments so that aspects of cottage industry might have been retained within the industrial transformation.[20] The supervision of labor performance would have been weakened, so many claim. Since sources of machine power tended to be centralized, however, especially in the days before electricity, economies of scale demanded large, centrally located factories. In the factory system the human operations of the worker were entirely dictated by the repetitive motions of the machine. The worker for the most part became an ancillary adjunct to the machine, even though wealth in society and real wages increased.

The system of machine production on the factory floor has hardly disappeared; but things are beginning to change. Uneducated labor no longer puts screw number 75 on a repetitive series of washing machine assemblies. Machines, including robots, are increasingly doing the work that labor and machines used to do together. The worker in the future will have a more elevated role.[21] In time, labor will begin to perform functions previously undertaken only by management. The information the worker possesses will come to rival that of supervisors. The task of the worker-manager will be to regear machines to produce new products on a single assembly line or quality circle. Under these circumstances economies of scope will rise to compete with or even exceed economies of scale.

In Silicon Valley the distinction between workers and management has eroded. As computer programmers, workers are involved in the design as well as the production of new products. The dress code is not blue collar versus white collar; informality rules in both sectors. Routine production is likely to take place in another country, leaving U.S. "workers" to participate in higher-level functions.

This does not mean that the shift to services and production with high information content has entirely revolutionized the workplace. McDonald's and Burger King's food service jobs are almost as regimented as machine production and are not well paid. For most of the previously unemployed, new jobs are less well compensated than older, routine work; but change is in the air. For the first time since the early 1970s real wages are beginning to rise,[22] and the proportion of high-level services has grown. Better education will make possible an even more rapid increase.[23]

The Pivotal Role of Education

Education is an asset in two ways. First, a well-educated society is more effective as a competitor in the world economic marketplace. Second, education is the most appropriate way of remedying domestic inequality. This inequality has recently grown in North America. Economists agree that technological change and globalization are the two basic factors in loss of jobs internationally.[24] Technological change in this context refers primarily to the displacement of labor by more efficient means of production. Globalization explains why jobs are moved to low-wage contexts overseas or in Latin America. The remedy for domestic labor is to improve skills through education. The whole of international society is moving up the occupational ladder. South Korea used to be a country of farmers. Then it became a country of relatively skilled industrial workers. Soon it will have to recruit more highly trained technicians capable of designing products and regearing the assembly line to produce new goods. The answer to unemployment and inequality is to move up the education chain to a higher occupation in the technical scheme of things.

This will call for innovation in education in many countries and more spending to create distinctive human capital. While military expenditure is still necessary, national capacity in the future will reside increasingly in a well-educated citizenry. Economic competition will come to be more important than military competition because national outcomes will be decided on an economic rather than military battlefield.

Workers and Immigration

Most advanced industrial countries will recruit foreign labor to complement local production. Immigration will further be geared to fill gaps in the labor force.[25] Migrants will staff "niche" occupations in health care, day care, and routine service work. Filipinos perform such functions in many Southeast Asian countries. They also contribute language skills, teaching English to Asian children. Jamaicans have taken many home health care jobs in Florida. Mexican and Central American gardeners have replaced Japanese in southern California. Chinese restaurants are staffed by people from Hong Kong, Taiwan, or Canton. The children of these immigrants rise rapidly in the social scale. In fact the same transition within the workforce occurs internationally among countries. Immigrants recruited to perform manual functions quickly move (with education) to head functions, contributing new and intelligent cadres to universities, businesses, creative design establishments, and law firms.

In addition, immigrants, like the Jews who came to New York before the First World War, are likely to find their initial occupational choices limited. Confronting de facto restrictions on entering status occupations such as law, government, or the professions, migrants will innovate new economic functions, as the immigrants to England did in the early stages of the Industrial Revolution. The first English industrialists were largely non-Conformists, not members of the established Church of England. They capitalized on French and Dutch immigration of artisans and workingpeople to the British Isles.[26]

There is also a special rationale for migrants entering capital-rich countries. Since World War II, capital has not moved to labor-abundant societies in the Third World in sufficient amounts. Just before the Asian and Latin American financial crisis, it was beginning to do so. Less-developed countries can argue, however, that if capital does not move to areas of labor abundance, labor should have the right to move to regions of capital abundance. Such flows are needed to correct imbalances in the world economy. If existing workers suffer some dislocations due to immigration, a still greater social and international purpose is served. This dislocation should be temporary, because new migrants traditionally occupy "niche" job categories that do not compete with native workers.[27]

Japan as an International Stabilizer

The international crisis in Asia has placed a special responsibility on Japan. Since World War II, Japan has been content to play the role of number two to the United States both economically and politically. Yet Japanese capital has been critical to American economic growth and productivity. Japan has largely reinvested its balance of trade surplus back in the areas from which it was earned. In the future Japan will also need capital, and the flow should begin to reverse. This means that Japan will need to open up further to accommodate foreign investment in banking, services, pension funds, advertising, and the industrial sector. Japanese business will benefit from further industrial alliances with Western firms in technology and production.

Although Japan will need new capital at home, it will also assume greater responsibilities for the financial stability of the international economic system. In Asia, where Japanese industrial investment has been critical to local development, Japanese loans will help keep Thailand, Malaysia, Indonesia, Singapore, and Korea afloat. Not to invest in East Asia would be to sacrifice the whole notion of Japanese-led "flying geese."

Japanese trade surpluses will increasingly be reinvested in the countries that have deficits with Japan, initiating a new virtuous cycle. This cycle will be completed when Japan buys the products of these countries, allowing them to repay the loans and to finance Japanese investments.

In the past Japan has stood for "one-way" flows: goods from Japan and indebtedness from its export markets. Japan ploughed investment back into these markets, but did not allow other countries to earn returns by investing directly in Japan. In contrast, the United States and Europe have benefited greatly from inflows of capital, technology, and brainpower from other countries. In the future, Japan will no longer reject these incoming flows. The Japanese need for capital and technology in services as well as industrial innovation will permit foreigners to contribute to Japanese economic growth and to benefit accordingly.

If Japan moves to become a stabilizer, history will have a new pattern. The number-two nation has traditionally sought to defeat number one. In the seventeenth century, Britain went to war to challenge Holland. In the eighteenth and early nineteenth centuries, France challenged England. In the twentieth century, Germany warred twice with Britain. After 1945 the new number two, the Soviet Union, challenged the United States. According to this pattern, Japan might be expected to confront America in the early twenty-first century, yet it seems unlikely.

A Japanese–American conflict is unlikely not only because Japan and the United States increasingly share the tasks of international stabilization but also because China constitutes a looming uncertainty for both states. The United States and Japan see bringing China into an encompassing coalition of major nations as a better outcome than a direct test of economic or military strength between them. They both depend on an open international economy that would only be destroyed by a major war. Japan and the United States are fated to cooperate to prevent that outcome.

China's role, however, does not determine either Japan's or America's foreign policy. The common economic interests that unite Japan and the United States are stronger than any security uncertainties. Japan and the United States both have greatly benefited from an open international economy in the past fifty years. Each will cooperate with the other to maintain and strengthen that openness.

Services, Energy, and the Environment

The trend of the future shows country after country moving up the scale of high-level services. Even visible goods production has an increasing service (that is, information) component. Valued goods now weigh less than they used to. Hundreds of millions of dollars of American exports (semiconductors and microprocessors) can now travel on a single Boeing 747. The output of an information society based on high-level services will use less energy for the value it produces. In other words, the energy content of increases in GDP can be reduced. In the 1970s countries such as the United States found that each extra 1 percent of growth consumed an additional 1 percent of energy. Now in Europe and elsewhere each additional percent of growth requires only 0.3 percent of additional energy. If fewer individuals have to travel to work each day—communicating with their office by telephone, e-mail, fax, and the Internet—that number can be reduced further. Information services are environmentally friendly. World development can proceed at a decreasing rate of energy use.[28]

The Age of the Virtual State

This book began with an inquiry into the rise of the virtual state—a state increasingly based on intangibles and brainpower. Virtual states succeed if they can establish reliable ties with a production base located somewhere else. This institutes an interdependence of production that is far stronger than an interdependence of trade. It follows that intangible services are growing more important relative to visible trade, both nationally and internationally. Thus, states moving toward virtualization must greatly increase such services and continue to do so. Intangible services succeed as a national vocation only if the society creates new human capital to sustain them. Ultimately the strength of the national society is dependent on its education system and the ability of its economy to employ educated and trained workers. Education and its concrete applications are not the same thing. India has for years had a large population of educated individuals whom it could not employ in the civil service, academia, or industry. It is not surprising that many Indians have left for jobs in other countries. For years the same was true in China. Countries must organize themselves to make use of their educated citizens. Human capital thus is recruited through national education as well as migration. Both sources are necessary.

The education and technical revolution also affects the military. War can now be conducted electronically at a distance without great loss of life to the perpetrators. While countries can be disarmed or punished in this way, however, they cannot be occupied or administered electronically. Military punishment is relatively easy, but holding and controlling territory is not. A successful offensive war does not mean that one country can run another. Thus the technical revolution in military affairs does not obviate economics.[29] It makes economic activity ultimately more important, for economics—unlike military occupation—is a disinterested form of administration of social life. Foreign investors may be chastised for entering or leaving a market, as Mahathir Mohammed did in the wake of the Thai and Malaysian financial crisis. Yet no one believes that markets determine politics; they merely set standards of probity that countries can decide to meet or not meet. Within the context of national values, individuals can debate rights and wrongs, justice and injustice, but a government cannot obligate free markets to serve parochial national purposes. Traders and investors seek profits and do not care where they may be found. If, on the other hand, countries wish to attract foreign capital, they may have to run their economies more efficiently.

———————————

We are in the middle of a global economic revolution. The world economy has progressed from an emphasis on land to an emphasis on capital, labor, and information. Human capital today is more important than raw materials, agriculture, or oil: it makes possible the design and production of manufactured goods, but its work is not confined to this process. Machines used to gear labor to their operations. Now humans and their purposes have been put at the center—not the periphery—of the production process. People shape, redesign, or ignore machines. In the most advanced locations, such as Silicon Valley, Seattle, Bangalore, and Kaohsiung, creativity in the workplace is now rewarded instead of being punished as a deviation from established procedures. The human being has begun to emerge from the straitjacket of the industrial system.[30]

What does this foretell about the ultimate role of the national state? Despite economic globalization, religious fervor, and ethnic claims, the state has not succumbed to transnational or localist influences. It provides an arena in which individuals can decide or at least influence their collective fates. No other institution performs this paramount function. Despite Japanese employees' solidarity behind the banner of their corporations, companies are not run by their workers—or even their shareholders. Nation-states are at least broadly directed by the will of their citizens. Democracy does not exist in any other place—religious, corporate, or cultural. In the new virtualizing world, however, individual states are weaker than before. They cannot guarantee favorable economic outcomes for their peoples. They must cooperate with foreign factors of production economically and with other states politically. Politics must provide an umbrella under which economies can function—both nationally and internationally. Cooperation among states is essential to the functioning of the market.

In the twenty-first century, nation-states will remain the major organizing factor in international politics. Nations will continue to compete. As intangibles move to the fore, however, competition will not mean conflict over territory. Economic competition will reflect itself in flows of goods and key factors of production—flows that cannot take place unless societies and economies are open. These economies cannot perform unless there is some form of political coherence among great states, supervising and protecting the market. If such protection succeeds, the twenty-first century will be the first epoch in history to offer the prospect of peaceful transformation and enduring global stability.

International Theory:
A New Paradigm?

The study of international relations has been preoccupied with the attempt to find one single explanation of national behavior. Most theorists of international relations have supposed that states have only a single objective (to achieve national welfare or power) and that they pursue it relentlessly with a single strategy, economic or military. If nations seek these goals and apply these means, they improve their position. If they do not, they lose power and economic position.

At present there are two basic theoretical approaches that attempt to explain national goals and strategies: so-called realist and liberal theories.[1] Each approach seeks to discover uniform patterns of national action that would explain most of Western and international history. As we shall see, however, neither of these approaches is adequate.

The Realist Canon

According to the realists, nations are concerned to advance their position in international politics, absolutely and sometimes relative to others. In absolute terms, nations want to increase their power base through industrial growth or military expansion. Of course if one state goes up the scale, at least one other will go down in relative position.[2] Since all cannot advance simultaneously, realists see tension as a continual feature of international politics. The most powerful states rival for influence and perhaps dominance. This is why, some believe, the two leading states in the system must always be rivals.

Realists do not necessarily conclude, however, that these two states must fight.[3] War occurs when the balance between them becomes uncertain. As long as both know the likely outcome of a clash, war need not take place.[4] If one state seeks to expand the territory it controls, a balance of power may start to form against it. Other nations are then drawn into the power equation to restore equilibrium; yet tension remains. War can occur as a result of economic processes,[5] colonial acquisition, or territorial aggrandizement. The period in which one nation is poised to pass another in relative power is especially dangerous.[6] Then a beleaguered leader may lash out against a challenger. Or the challenger may directly seek to upset the previous hegemonic leader.[7] Ultimately, however, war cannot be avoided in a realist system of international relations, and balancing operations frequently take the form of military combat between states.

Realist approaches, it is said, explain the origins of World Wars I and II. In 1914 Germany was supposedly seeking greater power within Europe and greater territory outside. France, Russia, and then England formed a balance of power to prevent German expansion. The balance of Triple Entente (France, Russia, and Britain) against Triple Alliance (Germany, Austria, and Italy), however, was not strong enough to prevent war; the balance of power was only asserted through the waging of war.

In 1939 Nazi Germany was bent on expansion in Eastern Europe. Britain and France initially appeased Germany, returning previous German lands in Austria and Czechoslovakia to Hitler. After Germany had seized the rest of Czechoslovakia in March 1939, however, France and Britain came together to guarantee the territorial integrity of Poland, another country menaced by Germany. When Hitler attacked Poland on September 1, 1939, Britain and France declared war, unwilling to consent to a further increase in German power.

According to realists, states are bound to conflict with one another, and the two world wars were only manifestations of the underlying antagonism of conflicting interests that periodically bubble to the surface.

The Neo-Liberal Rejoinder

In contrast to realism, the liberal position asserts that conflict is not in-grained in the international system. Countries can go up and down the international scale without having to fight one another. Economic change, particularly, does not necessarily cause military attempts to re-store the status quo. This is because, in the liberal analysis, nations aim at two objectives. One is to distribute economic benefits to their own population;[8] the second is to maintain international stability. In most international circumstances the rise or fall of particular nations does not concern other countries or require a remedy. In this way the United States acknowledged the great relative gains made by Japan and Ger-many since World War II without seeking to redress them militarily. This was, so it is argued, because American liberal governments were content to achieve absolute, not relative, gains. They aimed at domestic social objectives and welfare for their population. If they were regularly or always to tailor their international policies to achieve relative gains against a rival, they would diminish economic welfare at home.

The cold war, however, did involve a relative competition against the Soviet Union, for even liberals believed that if the Soviet Union had suc-ceeded in conquering and assimilating Western Europe, the United States would not be left free to pursue unhampered economic growth at home. American markets, exports, and economic growth would suffer. Thus in certain circumstances liberals believe that victory for a key op-ponent could limit a country's future economic strength and vitality. Under these circumstances a vital competition takes place, and war re-mains a possibility.

Liberals also emphasize the role of institutions in safeguarding and extending liberal gains internationally.[9] An institutionalized interna-tional order will behave more predictably than undisciplined anarchy. Members of organizations will tend to favor "voice" within the institu-tion rather than "gains" outside it. They will frequently alter national policies to procure support within important international organiza-tions. In this way institutions not only affect the form in which national policy is expressed but also influence its content. The huge development of new institutions since World War II—the International Monetary Fund, the World Bank, the European Union, the new World Trade Organization—has assisted cooperation in world politics. Institutions reduce transaction costs, inculcate norms of behavior, and facilitate agreement. Adherents of liberalism believe that the development of institutions internationally can increase the amount of cooperation among states. Realists do not believe this.[10]

Liberals also explain national responses in terms of ruling economic factors and forces. When land was the major factor of production and power, war was endemic in the international system.[11] As more mobile factors (labor, capital, and information) have come to the fore, wars have declined in number, though not in destructiveness. Where land remains the major factor of production (in Eastern Europe, Central Asia, the Middle East, South Asia, and Africa), wars and civil conflicts have entailed enormous loss of life. In the future, however, liberal theorists contend, highly developed states may express conflicting national attitudes through economic rather than military competition.

Liberal-Realist Interaction in Historical Terms

The problem with both liberal and neorealist theories and approaches is that each assumes national behavior can be summed up in terms of uniform strategies or modes of action in international relations.

DYNAMICS

Most of world history does not support the notion of homogeneous national behavior. Sometimes states aim to improve their relative position. In other circumstances, however, states are content to earn absolute gains. Arthur Stein, an international theorist, observes that the choice between such strategies presents a dilemma.[12] Nineteenth-century Great Britain levied Corn Laws and Navigation Acts to protect its agricultural suppliers and shippers from foreign competition. In doing so it aimed to improve its relative position in the system as a whole. In economic terms Britain put on an "optimum tariff."[13] Later in the century, however, London repealed both acts and opened itself to foreign trade. It extended lower tariffs to states that did not necessarily reciprocate. It did not change its customs duties, even when foreigners raised theirs in the fourth quarter of the nineteenth century. Absolute gains had by then become the British objective. London was more concerned with bene-fits for its consumers (from low-priced agricultural and industrial im-ports) than with international advantage.

The United States underwent a similar evolution before and after World War II. America levied the highest tariff in U.S. history in the Smoot-Hawley Act of 1930, at a time when America's industries could easily have withstood foreign competition. After the Second World War the United States progressively reduced tariffs and even opened itself to tariff and currency discrimination enacted by other countries. Its initial preference to win relative gains changed to absolute gains, including concern for the economic development and rehabilitation of other countries.[14] In a host of negotiations with allies, the United States did not reply to the relative gains objectives of Europe and Japan with a stringent relative gains policy of its own.[15] More recently, however, while opening its market to North American Free Trade Area (NAFTA) and Asia-Pacific Economic Cooperation (APEC) partners, the United States has sought to even up the benefits gained. Relative gains issues have become more salient.

These episodes have led to theoretical disagreements about the im-pact of economic and political decline of a leading country on its cal-culations of gain. Do countries change to relative gains objectives when they see their position deteriorating? Didn't Britain finally take a stand against Hitler in 1939 when London witnessed its own power and in-fluence waning? If countries are about to be passed (economically, po-litically, and militarily) by another state, do they not then switch from absolute to relative objectives? The answer is far from clear. The United States passed Britain and Germany without either country changing its policy in the 1890s. The Soviet Union's rapid industrialization in the Five Year Plans allowed it to exceed Germany's GDP prior to World War

II. It seems unlikely, however, that Adolf Hitler's objectives were in any way affected by the change. Hitler already aimed at major gains relative to other powers. Japan's GDP surpassed the Soviet Union's in the early 1980s. Russia moved to reform its economy in response; but since 1917 the Soviet Union had always sought to achieve relative gains in respect to capitalist powers.

No single theory of relative versus absolute gains emerges from these examples. Sometimes countries pursue absolute gains (the preponderant liberal contention); other times they adopt relative criteria (a typical realist claim). No single pattern, however, tells us when they do.

STATICS

Dynamics are not the only issue. It does not follow that one country always proceeds through a particular evolution of relative and absolute gains concerns. Some countries pursue very different strategies from others. Certain nations are more cooperatively inclined in general terms. Some nations are more prone to conflict. Nor is it true that the weak are cooperative and the strong conflict-oriented. Strong states are frequently cooperative, and weak states combative. Eighteenth-century Prussia and late twentieth-century Iraq are both examples of weaker states that aspired to make great military gains. One succeeded, the other did not.

Powerful states also follow a mixed pattern of action. Napoleonic France was the leading power in the early nineteenth-century European system, and yet Napoleon sought an even greater dominance of the continent. Great Britain was the leading power in the period from 1840 to 1860, but made no great efforts to increase its primacy. The United States was the strongest state in the 1930s; America, however, did not seek to exercise (or even initially to defend) its position against others, but remained isolated.

Second-place powers also show no pattern of policy. Some number twos became challengers and sought to depose a hegemon, as Germany did after 1890. Yet others were not restive in their position. Japan has been second to the United States since the mid 1980s and demonstrates no will to take over international leadership from America. It is not clear what China, another second-ranked power, will do in the future. There is no pattern that irrevocably predicts hegemonic war to depose a declining leader.[16] Much depends on the benefits others gain under that leadership.

Liberal-Realist Interaction in Analytic Terms

What is true historically is also true in terms of game theory. Game theory enables us to depict national incentives in a simple and direct manner. A typical international game is one in which two countries can do well by cooperating, but each can do better if the other cooperates and they defect. This set of incentives is represented by the well-known Prisoner's Dilemma.[17] Since there is no way to bind the parties to live up to their agreements in international relations, nations (which are the players in international relations) are tempted to take advantage of the cooperation of the other player.[18] If both defect, of course, they are worse off than if they had cooperated. These incentives can be seen in trade or arms control negotiations. Both countries can do better through free trade (a reduction of tariffs on both sides—the cooperative outcome), but one country can improve its terms of trade by maintaining tariffs while the other dismantles them. Equally, nations can both benefit from arms reductions and controls. Yet if one disarms and the other maintains its military forces, the latter will do better still.

Much of the literature shows that continued cooperation is possible only if future gains are not discounted heavily and if the game is of indefinite duration.[19] This conclusion, however, is subject to the well-known Folk Theorem, which states that many different strategies can emerge from iterated playing of the Prisoner's Dilemma.[20] There is no single evolutionarily stable strategy that works for all players under all conditions (noise, the "trembling hand," incomplete information, etc.) at all times and places. The same is likely true for nations.

One salient strategy that has relevance for interactions in the real world is Nice Tit for Tat. Pioneered by Anatol Rapoport and analyzed by

Robert Axelrod, the Nice Tit-for-Tat strategy involves cooperating on the first move and deciding one's subsequent play on the basis of the response of the opponent. If he also cooperates, then a sequence of cooperative moves can emerge, leading to relatively high payoffs as an outcome for both parties. If he doesn't cooperate, then the TFT player will defect on the second play and continue defecting until the second player returns to cooperation. Nice Tit for Tat works when there are other players playing Tit for Tat. A nucleus of cooperators can then emerge that not only gains absolutely but also relatively to players that select "All D" as their strategy.[21] The All D players continually defect, sanctioning each other. They earn lower payoffs than the cooperative players. This last conclusion has particular implications for international politics,[22] because realist theorists have believed that conflict in fact was profitable for the national players.

Dualism and International Politics

Theoretical monism—the attempt to explain all of international behavior or game theoretic interaction in terms of a single pure theory of action or strategy (under all conditions)—has not been successful, except where terms are defined so broadly that they lose analytical and empirical significance.[23] Liberal theories encounter cases where (according to their lights) states should have behaved more cooperatively than they actually did. Realists confront anomalies when states do not aim at relative gains or when they are willing to concede important national assets in order to keep cooperation alive with another country.[24] As examples: The United States gave important nuclear missile technology to Great Britain at the Nassau Conference in December 1962, when it was otherwise trying to stop the spread of nuclear weapons. The Soviet Union withdrew its occupation forces from Austria in 1955 to elicit cooperation from the United States when it did not need to do so.

In addition, neither liberal nor realist approaches have been able to claim that states following their prescribed policies have always achieved a high degree of evolutionary advantage. Realist states—by sanctioning other countries—frequently undermine their own position. They are so cautious and unbending that other more cooperative states do much better. In contrast, liberal states—by extending cooperation—frequently become vulnerable to predators. They may succeed with other cooperators, but they can fail if they cooperate too much with relative gains players.

It is therefore plausible to suggest[25] that no single (monistic) strategy or systemic orientation can hold without modification in international relations. It is equally important to observe that relentless pursuit of a single strategy is likely to be self-defeating. Predators may make signal gains by exploiting a cooperative system of liberal states. Cooperators may accumulate benefits playing each other on the fringes of a system in which two (mutually defecting) powers are locked in bipolar struggle. In such circumstances, without actually aiming at them, cooperators may achieve gains relative to the conflictual players.

A number of game theoretical studies attest to the plausibility of these outcomes. Jack Hirshleifer offers a series of models in which players of one stripe are vulnerable to invasion by players of another stripe. In one example, ranchers are countered by rustlers, who in turn are preyed on by bounty hunters. In a paper with Juan Carlos Martinez Coll, Hirshleifer observes that cooperation among TFT players is unlikely to be sustained in real-world conditions, where there is uncertainty as to precisely what the opposite player is doing. Even where no uncertainties exist, All D defeats Nice TFT in an elimination contest.[26] For cooperative stability to continue, there must be a way of disciplining potential defectors. Hirshleifer suggests the addition of "punisher" players, who make their most significant gains against defectors. These players also win benefits (of a somewhat lesser degree) in games against cooperators or TFT players. The addition of punisher strategies makes cooperation in a PD game more stable, because punishers sanction those who are tempted to revert to defection at high levels of systemic cooperation.[27]

In a complex game theoretic simulation, Bjorn Lomborg[28] offered a game in which players might modify their strategy in response to success and failure over a very long period of iterations. The system started with players using the All D (all defect) strategy. Progressively the players modified their strategies in a more cooperative direction to make greater gains. Tit for Tat then successfully invaded All D. In turn, Tit for Tat was eventually invaded by an even more cooperative strategy: Tit for Three Tats (this strategy specifies that cooperation be given three times in a row in response to defection by the other player. Only after that does the TF3T player choose "defect" in retaliation). In Lomborg's simulations, the amount of cooperation rose systemically (over 450,000 iterations). Eventually, however, when almost everyone was using a very cooperative strategy, new predatory strategies seeking to capitalize on the cooperation of others emerged. Then wholesale reversion to All D brought the downfall of cooperation in the system. No punishers were available in Lomborg's game to discipline the defect players. Gains plummeted, and systemic cooperation vanished.

Lomborg's simulation illustrates again the truth that no single strategy is adequate in the Prisoner's Dilemma game (or in international relations more generally). The initial cooperation of liberal-type states is ultimately shattered by the invasion of realist predators. Thus stability requires a means of preventing breakdown when cooperation reaches high systemic levels. Neither Tit for Tat, TF3T, nor any other strategy performs this function.

Dualism in International Politics

Dual strategies may succeed, however, where univocal strategies fail. Historically there are justifications for a dualistic approach. As we have already seen, very cooperative strategies are subject to invasion by predatory players. On the other hand, very tough or conflictual (relative gains) strategies earn little playing each other. In Western international history, preparations for war initially helped states to organize themselves administratively.[29] The continuance of war and conflict in Western history, however, has retarded economic progress.[30] Neither monistic strategy—liberalism or realism—has been successful historically.[31]

Equally important, monistic approaches do not describe the actual variety of state policies. Few states are rigid liberal cooperators or—alternatively—relative gains players. In practice, countries follow dualistic strategies, frequently altering their behavior. Systemic stability also depends on a mixture of strategies: monism does not suffice. Neither the liberal theory nor realism offers an evolutionarily stable strategy. Dualism is required for stability.

This proposition cannot be investigated exhaustively here, but signal examples of its operation can be mentioned. In the 1930s, France and England, two liberal states, were unprepared to meet the relative gains strategies of Adolf Hitler's Germany. For a long period they believed that Hitler would not go to war—that Germany's losses would be as great or greater than theirs. They were therefore unprepared for war and spent an inordinate amount of time and energy seeking to appease Hitler—trying to get him to become an "absolute gains" player. This strategy failed. The reasons for failure can be understood in terms of game theoretic simulations. Once the international system reached high levels of cooperation (or at least low levels of conflict) in Europe, a resolute relative gains player (Nazi Germany) could reenter the system and make signal advances. In the 1930s there were no punishers (or shields) available to take away the gains of Hitler's All D strategies. The system became very unstable as a result, and World War II occurred. Had punishers or guardians been available to police the system, the German chancellor's early gains would not have occurred, and the cooperation of the liberal nucleus—France and Britain—might have been prolonged.

In contrast, the international system after 1945 contained a punisher equivalent in the international strategy of the United States. The United States played relative gains against the Soviet Union, but absolute gains vis à vis its European partners and Japan. The European and Far Eastern nucleus was protected, and the Soviet Union deterred. It was America's dualistic strategy that made the difference.[32] On the Soviet side, the Russians not only played relative gains vis à vis the West, they also sought to advantage themselves relatively against their own allies in

Eastern Europe. As a result, Eastern Europe remained very weak—both economically and politically—and could not help the Soviet Union sustain its position against the West. With U.S. encouragement Western states and Japan played relative gains against the United States, further improving their position and gaining rapid economic growth.

The end of the cold war is inexplicable in monistic terms: (1) relative gains did not decide the contest, and (2) absolute gains were not universally applied. It was the mixture of the two strategies that made the difference. By cooperating with its allies, the United States rehabilitated Europe and Japan and brought them into the balance against the Soviet Union. By failing to cooperate with its allies, the Soviet Union weakened them and, ultimately, itself. These changes did not lead to overall cooperation. Cooperation did not emerge until the end of the cold war. Such dualistic strategies, however, did produce a stable and cooperative system on the Western side of the cold war ledger.

Dualism in the Post–Cold War System

The basic difference between the cold war and post–cold war systems is that the Western and democratic system of international relations has been extended in principle to the rest of the world. There is no single guarantor or guardian of the system, such as, for example, the quasi-hegemonic United States acting within the Western group of nations after 1945. Instead there are a group of potential guardians.[33] These great powers, consisting of key European nations, the United States, Japan, and possibly China and Russia have protected the system as a whole. In ways first adumbrated by Duncan Snidal in 1985, a group of great power cooperators has supplanted a single hegemonic provider of the "K-group"—that is, the minimum number of cooperators that can gain a positive return.[34] The political and military protections of this encompassing coalition liberate the economic opportunities of other states in pursuing investment, trade, and development. The encompassing coalition's relative gains strategy against possible disruptors facilitates the pursuit of absolute gains elsewhere in the system. At the core level, the emerging rapprochement that has been achieved among great powers permits them to seek absolute gains among themselves and to aim at economic improvement and development, even under conditions of financial uncertainty.

If the theory and its applications are valid, it would appear that the search for a single strategy or pattern of behavior in international politics is vain. Nations use at least two different strategies historically, and stability in the system is a function of their continued presence. Both cooperators and protectors are necessary for stability in international relations.

The virtual state lodging production abroad is protected by an encompassing coalition of great powers that maintains general peace and safeguards trade routes. International trade and production require an agreement among major powers. If this agreement holds, predators will not scuttle the stability of the cooperative international system.

Notes

Chapter 1

1 This is a novel development. When negotiating peace treaties, diplomats traditionally have been hesitant to create new states unless they are economically "viable." The newly constructed states thus had to possess well-defined products they could export to others and a distinct comparative advantage; but this requirement defines *viability* too narrowly.

2 Technically, a virtual state is a country in which services total as much as 80 percent of GDP and manufacturing less than 20 percent (with the remainder in primary products).

3 *The Economist* wrote recently: "So should the rich world worry that its manufacturing sector now seems to be migrating to low-wage competitors? Without big factories that ship steel, cars, machine tools and television sets to foreign customers, how can rich countries earn their keep in the world . . . ?" The answer given was: "A household can use only so many cars and refrigerators and dishwashers in its members' lifetimes. As countries get richer, a rising share of income goes on holidays, health, and education. Busy people want to hire other people to clean their homes, launder their clothes, and so on. Anyway, many jobs traditionally thought of as part of 'manufacturing' such as the design and marketing of products, are really service jobs. As the demand for them increases, these service jobs become better paid and more interesting compared with the drudgery of factory work . . ." ("Meet the Global Factory," *The Economist*, 20 June 1998, 4).

4 Richard Brown and DeAnne Julius question whether manufacturing matters as much as it once did. They point out:

> Many of today's high-technology activities are in the service sector, and they are driving research in new products. The communications industry creates the market for the fax machine and the cellular phone. The health industry shapes the

227

research of pharmaceutical companies. The transport industry drives aerospace development. These examples further illustrate the growing interdependence between manufacturing and services—large corporations are contracting out important activities such as marketing and computing to the service sector, and are buying high-technology intermediate inputs such as just-in-time distribution systems and computer-aided design (hence the rapid growth of business services). The growth of services is a natural and necessary concomitant to increased economic specialisation and sophistication.

Richard Brown and DeAnne Julius, "Is Manufacturing Still Special in the New World Order?" in Richard O'Brien, ed., *Finance and International Economy.* Vol. 7 (Oxford: Oxford University Press, 1993), 14.

5 See Richard Rosecrance, *The Rise of the Trading State: Commerce and Conquest in the Modern World* (New York: Basic Books, 1986); P. Katzenstein, *Small States in World Markets: Industrial Policy in Europe* (Ithaca, NY: Cornell University Press, 1985); and R. Rogowski, "Structure, Growth, and Power: Three Rationalist Accounts," *International Organization* (Autumn 1983): 713–38.

6 This transformation was foreshadowed in the 1970s in Raymond Vernon's "product life cycle" argument. Vernon foresaw the process by which export trade in a new product would turn into import of the same product. American pioneers of a new product such as television sets first would manufacture them at home, then sell abroad. After a time they would face competition for overseas markets. At the next stage, late-coming competitors from other countries would begin to produce at home and then export their product to America. In a final stage of the process U.S. and foreign producers would make their television sets in Asia or Mexico and ship them to the United States and other countries. As flows of goods gradually changed into flows of production, the role of the state would shift from promoter of exports to facilitator of capital movements. See Raymond Vernon, *Sovereignty at Bay* (New York: Basic Books, 1971). *The Economist* observed recently: "over the past decade, trade has been growing twice as fast as output and foreign direct investment three times as fast" (28 September 1996), 2.

7 For American practice see particularly *The Big Emerging Markets: 1996 Outlook and Source Book* (U.S. Department of Commerce, International

Trade Administration, Lanham, MD). French activities are briefly treated in "Closing the Deal," *Newsweek*, 6 March 1995.

8 In the nineteenth century the terms of trade for agricultural commodities held up well vis à vis manufactures (i.e., agricultural prices maintained their position as compared to the increasing prices of manufactured goods). In the twentieth century, however, an opposite situation obtained. Taking 1975 as 100, the terms of trade for developing countries fell from 121 in 1955 to 90 in 1981. (International Monetary Fund, International Financial Statistics, various years.)

9 See J. D. Gould, *Economic Growth in History: Survey and Analysis* (London: Methuen, 1972).

10 This outcome was understood relatively early; see particularly G. N. Clark, *The Balance Sheets of Imperialism* (New York: Russell and Russell, 1937), but see also Peter Liberman, *Does Conquest Pay?* (Princeton, NJ: Princeton University Press, 1996).

11 The argument is analogous to one of the essential theses of Immanuel Wallerstein, who sees as early as the "long seventeenth century" an imperial inability to engross the commerce of key commercial cities such as Venice, Genoa, Antwerp, and Amsterdam. When the territorial empire captured a trading city, the commerce migrated away. See Immanuel Wallerstein, *The Modern World System*, vols. 1 and 2 (New York: Academic Press, 1974).

12 The relative decline in the value of the products of land is confirmed in a whole series of IMF and World Bank studies, including E. Grilli and M. C. Yang, "Primary Commodity Prices, Manufacturing Goods Prices, and the Terms of Trade of Developing Countries: What the Long Run Shows," *World Bank Economic Review 2*, 1 (1988): 1–47. They write: "Our data indicate from the beginning of the present century to date, a cumulative trend fall of about 40 percent in the market prices of nonfuel primary commodities relative to those of manufactured products and a cumulative trend decline of about 36 percent in the market prices of all primary commodities" (p. 9). Similar conclusions are reached in E. Borensztein, M. S. Khan, C. Reinhart, and P. Wickham, *The Behavior of Non-Oil Commodity Prices* (Washington, DC: International Monetary Fund, 1994), and C. Reinhart and P. Wickham, "Commodity Prices: Cyclical Weakness or Secular Decline?" *IMF Staff Papers 41*, 2 (June 1994). In addition, since 1994, oil and commodity prices have further declined relative to manufactured goods.

13 Oil prices have greatly declined as well.

14 See Rosecrance, *Rise of the Trading State*.

15 Even the U.S. Bureau of Labor Statistics now admits that its measure of "productivity" has understated results since 1973 (*New York Times*, 31 March 1999).

16 This does not mean that unemployment rises. Laid-off production workers become effective service workers.

17 Many firms accordingly have set up virtual operations. SCI Systems, Solectron, Merix, Flextronics, Smartflex, and Sanmina turn out products for Digital Equipment, Hewlett-Packard, and IBM. AT&T, Motorola, MCI, and Dow-Corning meet part of their production needs through other suppliers. TelePad, a company which makes pen-based computers, was launched with no manufacturing capability at all. Compaq's latest mid-range computer is to be produced on another company's production line. Cadence software creates its latest designs on the producing units of its customers. As Cadence helps Motorola design the latter's newest chip, Cadence's customers become the producing unit.

18 A study by Braxton Associates and Booz, Allen, and Hamilton indicates that the companies most active in forging strategic alliances (to have their goods produced by another company) receive returns 50 percent higher than those of traditional companies. See *Financial Times*, 2 October 1995.

19 For an alternative view see Stephen Cohen and John Zysman, *Manufacturing Matters* (New York: Basic Books, 1987).

20 As a proportion of foreign direct investment, service exports have grown strikingly in most highly industrialized societies. According to a 1994 World Bank report, "The reorientation of [foreign direct investment] toward the services sector has occurred in almost all developed market economies, the principal exporters of services capital; in the most important among them, the share of the services sector is around 40 percent of the stock of outward FDI and that share is rising."The World Bank, *Liberalizing International Transactions in Services: A Handbook* (New York: The World Bank, 1994), 10–11.

21 See José Ripoll, *The Future of Trade in International Services*, Center for International Relations Working Paper, UCLA, January 1996.

22 Service prices have increased by more than 9 percent a year, industrial prices by 7 percent.

23 Pam Woodall contends:

Perhaps the most important characteristic of information technology (IT) is that it deals with knowledge. More and more
knowledge can now be codified: information whether in the
form of numbers, letters, pictures, or voice can be reduced to
digital form and stored in computers as a series of zeros and
ones. This allows knowledge to be diffused more rapidly and
so makes it easier for developing countries to catch up.

The Economist, 28 September, 1996, 4.

24 This does not mean that emerging nations should cease exploiting their
advantages in land. Their errors in the past largely stemmed from import-
substituting industrialization—that is, trying to build up an inefficient
and protected manufacturing sector at home in preference to relatively
efficient agriculture. Rather, like Australia and Canada, they should move
toward a combination of raw materials production and higher-valued services. As their population becomes better trained, they also could move
toward manufacturing.

25 Deepak Lal, *Unintended Consequences: The Impact of Factor Endowments,
Culture, and Politics on Long Run Economic Performance* (Cambridge, MA:
MIT Press, 1998).

26 This may be because such countries must export to live; they cannot afford inefficient import-substituting industrialization. Lal and Myint
argue: ". . . if the country is small, the limited size of the domestic market makes reliance upon foreign trade inevitable. This makes it less likely
that any grave departures from the free-trade resource allocation will
emerge . . ." (398). Deepak Lal and H. Myint, *The Political Economy of
Poverty, Equity, and Growth* (Oxford: Clarendon Press, 1996).

27 See Jeffrey Sachs and Andrew Warner, "Natural Resource Abundance and
Economic Growth," mimeo, Harvard University, September 1995. They
write: "It is possible then that the full effect of the one-shot resource boom
is to raise the level of GDP initially, but reduce the growth rate by enough
that the level of GDP eventually falls below that of a non-booming economy" (Appendix B, 7). They also point out: "economies with a high ratio
of natural resource exports to GDP in 1971 (the base year) tended to have
low growth rates during the subsequent period 1971–89" (Abstract).

28 See particularly Paul Krugman and Elhanan Helpman, *Trade Policy and
Market Structure* (Boston: MIT Press, 1989).

29 World Bank study cited in the *New York Times*, 19 September 1995, B12.
The study estimates world wealth at $86 trillion, of which $55 trillion resides in human capital.

30 One paradox is that past discrimination against women in the workforce
probably improved U.S. schools. As intelligent women have been freed to
pursue careers in medicine, law, and business, U.S. children have been
taught by less intelligent men!

31 This was shown to be true for many Far Eastern nations during the recent financial crisis.

32 This is the essential argument of Anthony Lake in "Future Political-
Military Challenges to the World and the United States." (Bernard Brodie
Lecture, UCLA, Berkeley, April 1998.)

33 This is the essential thesis of Susan Strange's pathbreaking work *The Retreat of the State: The Diffusion of Power in the World Economy* (Cambridge: Cambridge University Press, 1996).

34 *The Economist* (28 September 1996) writes:

> Production is increasingly in the form of intangibles based on
> the exploitation of ideas rather than material things. The
> fashionable talk is about the "weightless" or "dematerialised"
> economy. As production has shifted from steel, heavy copper
> wire, and vacuum tubes to microprocessors, fine fibre-optic
> cables, and transistors, and as services have increased their
> share of the total, output has become lighter and less visible.
> In a speech earlier this year the Fed's Alan Greenspan pointed
> out that America's output measured in tons is barely any
> heavier now that it was 100 years ago even though real GDP
> has increased twentyfold.

35 The issue of proper state and market roles is a long and controverted one.
See inter alia, Edward Lindblom, *Politics and Markets: The World's Politi-
cal Economic System* (New York: Basic Books, 1977), Susan Strange,
States and Markets (London: Pinter, 1988), and especially Jane Jacobs,
*Systems of Survival: A Dialogue on the Moral Foundations of Commerce and
Politics* (New York: Vintage Books, 1994).

36 Despite protagonists of the "unipolar moment," the United States cannot
do this alone.

Chapter 2

1 See Edward Fox, *History in Geographic Perspective: The Other France* (New York: Norton, 1971), 24.

2 David Landes explains why geologic and geographic influences made Europe an ideal spot for cultivation. "This geologic good fortune gives western Europe warm winds and gentle rain, water in all seasons, and low rates of evaporation—the makings of good crops, big livestock, and dense hardwood forests." *The Wealth and Poverty of Nations: Why Some Are so Rich and Some so Poor* (New York: W. W. Norton: 1998). See also p. 37.

3 See Fox, *History in Geographic Perspective*, 35.

4 See John R. Hicks, *A Theory of Economic History* (Oxford: Oxford University Press, 1969), chap. 4.

5 John Hicks emphasized the issue of trust in terms of the enforcement of contracts (ibid., 46–47), but see also Francis Fukuyama, *Trust: The Social Virtues and the Creation of Prosperity* (New York: The Free Press, 1995), part 1.

6 Their reaction against foreign rule did not occur generally, however, until the eighteenth century and after.

7 See Hicks, *Theory of Economic History*, 37.

8 See J. H. Parry, *The Age of Reconnaissance* (London: Weidenfeld and Nicolson, 1963), 97–99, and Dava Sobel, *Longitude: The True Story of a Lone Genius Who Solved the Greatest Scientific Problem of His Time* (New York: Walker, 1995).

9 See the brilliant account in Landes, *Wealth and Poverty of Nations*, chaps. 8 and 9.

10 This does not mean that they do not use strongly competitive techniques in dealing with each other.

11 As one example, in the case of the United States, services now total 70 percent of U.S. GDP.

12 Because of Japan's invasion of China, the United States, Holland, and Britain had barred the sale of critical raw materials to Japan.

13 See Richard Rosecrance, *The Rise of the Trading State: Commerce and Conquest in the Modern World* (New York: Basic Books, 1986).

14 See Arthur I. Bloomfield, *Patterns of Fluctuation in International Investment Before 1914* (Princeton, NJ: Princeton University Press, 1968); and Peter Svedberg, "The Portfolio-Direct Composition of Foreign Investment in 1914 Revisited," *Economic Journal 88*, 352 (December 1978).

15 See Shoshona Zuboff, *In the Age of the Smart Machine: The Future of Work and Power* (New York: Basic Books, 1988).

16 Charles Tilly, ed., *The Formation of National States in Western Europe* (Princeton, NJ: Princeton University Press, 1975).

17 World War II was not started for this purpose, but after it ended, Stalin seized the opportunity to cart factories and industrial capital away from defeated Germany. The United States took the even more radical step of bringing German scientists and rocket engineers to America—one of the few instances of capturing creative expertise by military means.

Chapter 3

1 See Robert Rowthorn and Ramana Ramaswamy, *Deindustrialization: Causes and Implications* (Washington, DC: Research Department, International Monetary Fund Working Paper, April 1997), who conclude:

> Employment in manufacturing now constitutes only a small fraction of civilian employment in most of the "old" industrial economies. The dynamic economies of East Asia also appear to have embarked on the process of deindustrialization in recent years. An important conclusion of this paper is that deindustrialization, unlike the problems of rising income inequalities and unemployment, is not a negative phenomenon, but a natural consequence of the process of economic development in an already highly developed economy. (p. 22)

2 See particularly Michael Piore and Charles Sabel, *The Second Industrial Divide: Possibilities for Prosperity* (New York: Basic Books, 1984).

3 The *Financial Times* (4 September 1998) writes:

> FDI doubled in the five years to 1997, after doubling in the previous five-year period, a rate of growth far surpassing the increase in world output or trade. While the share of trade in GDP has remained broadly constant since 1980, that of FDI flows has risen from 1 percent in 1980 to 2.3 percent in 1996 and that of FDI stock from 10 percent to 21 percent. "This demonstrates that [global economic] integration is being accelerated more through investment than trade," UNCTAD says. (p. 4)

4 For divergent perspectives on the Third World's prospects see "Economic Growth: The Poor and the Rich," *The Economist*, 25 May 1996, 23–25, and *World Development Report, 1995*, chap. 7.

5 Chapter 7 deals specifically with virtual states.

6 See Robert Reich, *The Work of Nations: Preparing Ourselves for 21st Century Capitalism* (New York: A. A. Knopf, 1991).

7 See Brian Healy, "Economic Power Transition in the International System: The Translation of Economic Power into Political Leverage in the International Monetary System" (Ph.D. diss., Cornell University, 1973), and William Gutowitz, "The Interrelationship of Economic Factors and Political Relations among Nations—A Quantitative Analysis" (Honors essay, Ithaca, Cornell University, 1978).

8 See Susan Strange and Roger Tooze, eds., *The International Politics of Surplus Capacity: Competition for Market Shares in the World Recession* (Boston: Allen & Unwin, 1984).

9 Peter Cowhey and Jonathon Aronson write: "[The Daimler-Chrysler] decision to merge shows that management has learned that international strategic alliances allowing firms to pool resources to tackle global markets and technologies, while maintaining corporate independence, are fragile." ("Do Mergers Threaten Nations?" *Los Angeles Times*, 28 June 1998, M6.)

10 Technically the German firm was called Daimler-Benz, and the new firm will be designated Daimler-Chrysler.

11 Equally important, the merger positioned the two companies to be ready to build a dramatically redesigned car, necessary to meet new fuel and environmental standards. See Cowhey and Aronson, "Do Mergers Threaten Nations?" M6.

12 See Francis Fukuyama, *Trust: Social Virtues and the Creation of Prosperity* (New York: The Free Press, 1995).

13 "India has endured a 20 percent drop in share prices since the nuclear tests, a 7 percent fall in the value of the rupee against the dollar and a flight of foreign investments." (*New York Times*, 7 July 1998, A7.)

14 See José Ripoll, "The Future of International Services," UCLA Center for International Relations Working Paper No. 10, 1996.

15 See Christopher Patten, *East and West: China, Power, and the Future of Asia* (New York: Random House, 1998).

16 Jeffrey Sachs and Steven Radelet have been critical of IMF "conditionality" programs, arguing that IMF strictures sometimes force recession on im-

poverished debtor nations. Instead, they argue, the IMF should allow some depreciation of the local currency so the debtor can reestablish its balance of payments and attract investors. High interest rates alone will not do this. See "Next Stop Brazil," *New York Times*, 14 October 1998, A25.

Chapter 4

1 See Stephen Rock, *Why Peace Breaks Out: Great Power Rapprochement in Historical Perspective* (Chapel Hill: University of North Carolina Press, 1989).

2 See Robert Gilpin, *The Political Economy of International Relations* (Princeton, NJ: Princeton University Press, 1987), and Comment on "Economics and Security," in Richard Schultz, Jr., Roy Godson, and George Quester, eds., *Security Studies for the 21st Century* (Washington, DC: Brassey's, 1997), 238.

3 See Ludwig Dehio, *The Precarious Balance: Four Centuries of the European Power Struggle,* trans. Charles Fullman (New York: A. A. Knopf, 1962).

4 Personal communication from N. J. Richardson, April 1998.

5 Tensions along these lines are forecast in Matt Connelly and Paul Kennedy, "Revisiting the Camp of the Saints or, Further Thoughts on 'The West Against the Rest'," mimeo, New Haven, Yale University, 1994.

6 In other words, they claim that governments and factors of production will not work together to attain "virtual" ends.

7 See Fred L. Block, *The Origins of International Economic Disorder: A Study of United States International Monetary Policy from World War II to the Present* (Berkeley: University of California Press, 1977).

8 Evidence of this alliance and its refractory aspects is provided in Peter F. Cowhey and Jonathon D. Aronson, "Do Mergers Threaten Nations?" *Los Angeles Times*, 28 June 1998, M6.

9 See also Jeffrey E. Garten, *The Big Ten: The Big Emerging Markets and How They Will Change Our Lives* (New York: Basic Books, 1997).

10 See Wayne Cornelius, "The Role of Immigrant Labor in the United States and Japanese Economies: A Comparative Study of San Diego & Hamamatsu Japan," Center for U.S.-Mexican Studies, University of California, San Diego, 1 April 1998.

11 This is particularly true where, as in the United States, the growth of new jobs exceeds those entering the labor market by nearly two to one.

12 For an overview of the problem of ethnic conflict see Donald Horowitz, *Ethnic Groups in Conflict* (Berkeley: University of California Press, 1985),

and Michael Brown, *The International Dimensions of Internal Conflict* (Cambridge, MA: MIT Press, 1996). More recently, see the passionate essay by Michael Ignatieff, *The Warrior's Honor: Ethnic War and the Modern Conscience* (New York: Metropolitan Books, 1998). See also John Lewis Gaddis, "Living in Candlestick Park," *Atlantic Monthly*, April 1999.

13 See William Greider, *One World, Ready or Not: The Manic Logic of Global Capitalism* (New York: Simon & Schuster, 1997). See also "Stop the World, I Want to Get Off," *The Economist*, 28 September 1996, 45–46.

14 See particularly Susan Woodward, *Balkan Tragedy: Chaos and Dissolution after the Cold War* (Washington, DC: Brookings Institution, 1995).

15 Michael Ignatieff discusses how and when to reconstitute federal states whose destruction has brought ethnic conflict:

> Making the right choice depends on understanding the history of the region in question. If minority or majority have slaughtered each other in the recent past, it is unrealistic to expect them to live together in the future. A history of bad blood—of real and recurrent killing—does justify a claim to secession and self-determination if—and it is a critical rider—the territory claimed is defensible and economically viable and if the seceding party is prepared to guarantee the minority rights of those who remain within their state.

Michael Ignatieff, *The Warrior's Honor: Ethnic War and the Modern Conscience* (New York: Metropolitan Books, 1998), 101–2.

16 See particularly Samuel P. Huntington, "The Clash of Civilizations," *Foreign Affairs* 72, 3 (April 1993).

17 John Lewis Gaddis, "Living in Candlestick Park," *Atlantic Monthly* (April 1999).

18 A balanced view of the ethnicity problem and its effect on conflict is presented by Susanne Hoeber Rudolph in "Religion, the State, and Transnational Civil Society," in S. Rudolph and J. Piscatori, eds., *Transnational Religion, the State, and Global Civil Society* (forthcoming). She writes: "Religion is no master-variable that will determine the political cleavages that lead to war or the solidarities that promote peace. Religions are themselves internal contests" (p. 50).

19 Though how far this will proceed in the Indian case, given the restrictionist impulses of the BJP government, is not yet clear.

20 Despite the presence of KFDR. See Michael Brown and Richard Rose-crance, eds., *The Costs of Conflict: Prevention and Cure in the International System* (New York: Rowman and Littlefield, 1999).

21 See particularly the new book by Richard Holbrooke, *To End a War* (New York: Random House, 1998). Holbrooke warns: "There will be other Bosnias in our lives, different in every detail but similar in one overriding manner; they will originate in distant and ill-understood places, explode with little warning, and present the rest of the world with difficult choices—choices between risky involvement and potentially costly neglect," pp. 368–369.

22 Inequality does not necessarily mean gross inequity. Higher-income groups have done better but the poor have not suffered. Michael Cox and Richard Alm observe in the United States that "poor households of the 1990s in many cases compared favorably with an average family in the early 1970s in owning the trappings of middle class life. For example, almost half of the poor households had air conditioners in 1994, compared to less than a third of the country as a whole in 1971. The pattern holds true for dryers, refrigerators, stoves, microwaves, and color televisions." W. Michael Cox and Richard Alm, *Myths of Rich and Poor* (New York: Basic Books, 1999), 14–15.

23 See Robert H. Frank and Phillip J. Cook, *Winner-Take-All Markets* (New York: The Free Press, 1995).

24 Historically of course many societies were stable in the absence of social mobility.

25 See University of Michigan Index of Consumer Sentiment.

26 In fact, since 1992, real wages in the United States have substantially increased.

27 None of these conditions hold according to Cox and Alm; see *Myths of Rich and Poor*, particularly chaps. 6 and 8.

28 See the work of Susan Strange here.

29 But see Steve Weber in "The End of the Business Cycle?" *Foreign Affairs* 76, 4 (July-August 1997).

30 See Lester Thurow, *The Future of Capitalism: How Today's Economic Forces Will Shape Tomorrow's World* (New York: William Morrow, 1996).

31 See John M. Keynes, *The General Theory of Employment, Interest, and Money* (New York: Harcourt Brace, 1935).

32 In September 1998 a 20 percent fall in the New York stock market apparently did not greatly worry investors. While the consumer sentiment index

of the University of Michigan slipped from 104.1 in August to 100.1 in September, the overall index was upbeat; the average consumer sentiment since 1947 was only 85. (*New York Times*, 19 September 1998, A1.)

33 See R. Taggart Murphy, "Power Without Purpose: The Crisis of Japan's Global Financial Dominance," *Harvard Business Review* 67, 2 (March–April 1989): 71–83.

34 See Brad De Long, "The Role of International Economic Institutions," paper presented at UCLA Colloquium on War and Peace, Berkeley, November 7–8, 1997.

35 See J. B. Say, in Robert L. Heilbroner, *The Great Economists: Their Lives and Their Conceptions of the World* (London: Eyre & Spottiswoode, 1955).

36 See the work of Ravi Batra, *The Great Depresion of 1990* (New York: Simon & Schuster, 1987).

37 This is an argument against using income disparities as the single measure of economic stability.

38 Recessions typically see 10 percent unemployment. The Great Depression of 1929–39 witnessed 20 percent unemployment.

39 This argument is based on comments by N. J. Richardson.

40 Stimulating the flow of repatriated profits, for example.

41 The killings of President Anwar Sadat (Egypt) and Prime Minister Itzhak Rabin (Israel) are examples.

42 The World Health Organization estimates that 50 kilograms of anthrax, if properly dispersed on a city of one million, could kill 36,000 and incapacitate another 54,000. Cited in Seth Carus, "The Threat of Bioterrorism," *Strategic Forum*, 127 (September 1997): 2.

43 See Roy Godson, "Transstate Security," in R. Schultz, R. Godson, and G. Quester, eds., *Security Studies for the 21st Century* (Washington, DC: Brassey's, 1997).

44 Cited in Ehud Sprinzak, "The Great Superterrorism Scare," *Foreign Policy* (Fall 1998).

45 See *The Economist's* special survey, "Manufacturing," 20 June 1998, 5, which shows (since 1970) the volume of foreign direct investment (measured by jobs) on a worldwide basis to be rising much more rapidly than either exports or GDP.

46 Ehud Sprinzak suggests that bloated counterterrorism budgets could distort national priorities. He writes: "There is neither empirical evidence nor logical support for the growing belief that a new 'postmodern' age of terrorism is about to dawn, an era afflicted by a large number of anonymous

mass murderers toting chemical and biological weapons" (p. 127). He deplores "irresistible demands to fortify the entire United States against future chemical and biological attacks, however absurd the cost" (p. 127).

47 "Remarks by Dr. John Hamre, Deputy Secretary of Defense at the Council on Foreign Relations," New York, 5 June 1998, 9.

48 See Kenneth Waltz, *Man, the State, and War: A Theoretical Analysis* (New York: Columbia University Press, 1959).

49 See Richard Rosecrance and Arthur Stein, "Beyond Realism: The Study of Grand Strategy," in R. Rosecrance and A. Stein, eds., *The Domestic Bases of Grand Strategy* (Cornell University Press, 1993).

50 See particularly Richard Rosecrance and Chi-cheng Lo, "The Mysterious Case of the Napoleonic International System," *International Studies Quarterly 40*, 4 (December 1996): 479–500.

51 See Stephen D. Krasner, "State Power and the Structure of International Trade," *World Politics 28*, 3 (April 1976): 317–47; and Duncan Snidal, "The Limits of the Hegemonic Stability Theory," *International Organization 39*, 4 (Autumn 1985): 579. See also Edward Ingram, "Hegemony, Global Power, and World Power: Britain Two as World Leader," paper presented at the Conference on History and International Relations Theory, Arizona State University, Tempe, AZ, January 15–17, 1998.

52 Some think that it can. Thomas Friedman writes: "The hidden hand of the market will never work without a hidden fist—McDonald's cannot flourish without McDonnell Douglas, the designer of the F–15. And the hidden fist that keeps the world safe for Silicon Valley's technologies is called the United States Army, Air Force, Navy and Marine Corps." *New York Times Magazine*, 28 March 1999, 61.

53 See Rosecrance and Stein, "Beyond Realism."

54 See Hans J. Morgenthau on "nationalistic universalism" in *Politics Among Nations: The Struggle for Power & Peace*, 2d ed. (New York: A. A. Knopf, 1954).

55 See Farheed Zakaria, "The Rise of Illiberal Democracy," *Foreign Affairs 73*, 2 (March-April 1994).

56 See Nazli Choucri and Robert C. North, *Nations in Conflict: National Growth and International Violence* (San Francisco: W. H. Freeman, 1975).

57 Under these circumstances, international influences would be exerted within the foreign society, not external to it.

58 This is not the same thing, however, as the new empire recommended by John Lewis Gaddis.

59 See Michael Doyle, "Kant and Liberal Legacies in Foreign Affairs," *Philosophy and Public Affairs* (Summer and Fall, 1983): parts 1 and 2; and Zeev Maoz and Bruce Russett, "Alliance, Contiguity, Wealth and Political Stability: Is the Lack of Conflict Among Democracies a Statistical Artifact?" *International Interactions* 17 (1992).

60 Michael Doyle, *Ways of War and Peace: Realism, Liberalism, and Socialism* (New York: Norton, 1997), chap. 8.

61 Edward Mansfield and Jack Snyder, "Democratization and the Danger of War," *International Security* 20, 1 (Summer 1995).

62 See Zakaria, "Rise of Illiberal Democracy."

63 See the work of Etel Solingen, particularly "The Political Economy of Nuclear Restraint," *International Security* 19, 2 (1994).

64 See Peter Beinart, "An Illusion for Our Time," *New Republic*, 20 October 1997.

65 Ibid.

66 See Samuel P. Huntington, "Transnational Organizations in World Politics," *World Politics* 25, 3 (April 1973): 333–68.

67 See Paul M. Kennedy, *The Rise of the Great Powers: Economic Change and Military Conflict from 1500 to 2000* (New York: Random House, 1987); E. J. Hobsbawn, *Industry and Empire* (Harmondsworth, UK: Penguin Books, 1969).

68 See Kenneth Waltz, *Theory of International Politics* (Reading, MA: Addison-Wesley, 1979), p. 118.

69 See particularly Kenneth Waltz, "The Myth of Interdependence," in Charles Kindleberger, ed., *The International Corporation: A Symposium* (Cambridge, MA: MIT Press, 1970).

Chapter 5

1 It should be noted that this dependence is a surprising result in international relations. Enduring economic relationships require trust on both sides. See Francis Fukuyama, *Trust: The Social Virtues and the Creation of Prosperity* (New York: The Free Press, 1995). Yet nations have traditionally violated trust, forming alliances only to break them. Historically, the callings of "national interest" have overriden cooperative alignments. Moving one's production abroad then is a major step. It requires dependable cross-boundary relations between states as well as their corpo-

rations, and therefore posits a new international atmosphere. Chapter 5 continues this discussion.

2 See Laura D'Andrea Tyson's address at the University of Vienna, "Globalization and Unemployment: American and European Trends," Bruno Kreisky Forum for International Dialogue, 26 June 1997, 8.

3 See Bob Herbert's column in the *New York Times*, 4 June 1998. Pam Woodall contends in *The Economist*:

> There is no justification for the apocalyptic predictions of mounting joblessness and shrinking wages as workers in rich economies are replaced by computers or foreign labor. Some workers and firms will indeed be squeezed out but in aggregate the information age like every technological revolution before it will generate at least as many jobs as it destroys and on the whole the new jobs will be better paid than the old ones.

"A Survey of the World Economy: The Hitchhiker's Guide to Cybernomics," *The Economist*, 28 September 1996, page 7 of special report.

4 James Flanigan contends: "The leading U.S. industries today are the related fields of computer electronics, telecommunications and software, now employing 4.5 million. It is in those industries that new service jobs have grown up, such as computer programmer, network manager, and so forth. Often derided as low-wage, such service jobs in fact pay more than $50,000 a year on average" (*Los Angeles Times*, 7 July 1998, D6).

5 See Robert Brenner, "The Economics of Global Turbulence," A Special Report on the World Economy, 1950–98, *New Left Review*, 229 (May-June 1998).

6 Anthony P. Carnevale and Stephen J. Rose, *Education for What?—The New Office Economy* (Princeton, NJ: Educational Testing Service, 1998).

7 See ibid., 22, fig. 9.

8 The aforementioned ETS study observes:

> In the past, most of the effort was concentrated on production—getting the product out the door. Productivity advances, especially in transportation and communication, led to economies of scale, larger organizations, and mass markets. Today, further technological gains have made production much easier and more dispersed. Actual factory work, especially low skilled, has tended to flow toward countries with cheap labor. . . . At the same time, consumption is mov-

ing away from cheap, standardized goods to more customized products and services (p. 32).

9 Two measures of the movement away from economies of scale is plant size and the decentralization of production. Sukkoo Kim points out that average plant size in the U.S. economy has declined since the 1940s. He also observes that particular industrial activities have become less regionally localized since then. See Sukkoo Kim, "Expansion of Markets and the Geographic Distribution of Economic Activities: The Trends in U.S. Regional Manufacturing Structure, 1860–1987," *Quarterly Journal of Economics* (November 1995): 903–4.

10 See particularly Charles F. Sabel, *Work and Politics: The Division of Labor in Industry* (Cambridge, MA: MIT Press), and Charles Sabel and Michael Piore, *The Second Industrial Divide: Possibilities for Prosperity* (New York: Basic Books, 1984). Economies of scope occur when the cost of producing units separately is greater than the cost of producing them in one assembly process or line. Both Sabel and Piore believe that "flexible specialization" favors economies of scope, as compared with the mass production function involved in economies of scale. See *Second Industrial Divide*, 258–63.

11 One outstanding bakery in Los Angeles produces thirty-two different breads ranging from 3 ounces to 3 pounds every day. There is no apparent loss due to product differentiation.

12 *The Economist*, 28 September 1996. The same customers' daughters can go online to order their own custom-designed Barbie dolls, p. 44.

13 "A Survey of the World Economy." Page 15 of special report, *The Economist* (28 September 1996) points out:

> In many services it is hard even to define the unit of output partly because higher output often comes in the form of quality improvements. In such areas as finance, health care, and education, government statisticians typically assume that output rises with the number of hours worked. The bizarre effect is that measured productivity growth is zero by definition.

14 Silicon Valley executive Gordon Moore suggests that computer power quadruples every thirty months. *The Economist* observes: "If cars had developed at the same pace as microprocessors over the past two decades a typical car would now cost less than $5.00 and do 250,000 miles to the gallon" (28 September 1996).

15 Alan Blinder contends:

> It is well known that the Consumer Price Index, or any price
> index, is biased upward, i.e., it exaggerates the rate of infla-
> tion. That means that the real growth rate is being under-
> stated. Because labor input (the other factor in the growth
> rate) is measured fairly accurately, . . . that implies an error in
> productivity measurement. The more accurate productivity
> growth rate is probably 0.5 to 1.0 percent higher than the of-
> ficial numbers—although this is a matter of great dispute.

The Aspen Institute, *Work & Future Society: Where Are the Economy and
Technology Taking Us?* (Washington, DC: The Aspen Institute, 1998), 13.

16 See Michael Boskin Report by the Congressional Advisory Commission
on the Consumer Price Index, to the Senate Finance Committee, December 1996.

17 See speeches by Alan Greenspan, 1997–98.

18 See particularly Greenspan here.

19 Remarks by Chairman Alan Greenspan at the 15th Anniversary Conference of the Center for Economic Policy Research at Stanford University
(5 September 1997), 5. More recently, he contended: "Signs of a major
technical transformation of the economy are all around us, and the benefits are evident not only in high-tech industries but also in production
processes that have long been part of our industrial economy." Testimony
by Chairman Alan Greenspan before the Joint Economic Committee,
U.S. Congress, 10 June 1998, 4. Richard K. Lester observed that where
quality of the product is improving, government statisticians have had
great difficulty in correcting productivity estimates. See Lester, *The Productive Edge* (New York: Norton, 1998), 330.

20 Stephen Roach of Morgan Stanley, for example, has argued on both sides
of the issue. When the computer was initially incorporated into the
workplace, it did not lead immediately to a decline in the number of
clerks or secretaries. Inputs were high, but they did not produce a commensurately higher output. In time, however, mechanical word processing has freed erstwhile secretaries to become personal assistants and
office managers, adding value to output.

21 *The Economist* (28 September 1996), writes that Leonard Nakamura,

> an economist at the Federal Reserve Bank of Philadelphia, es-
> timates that America's inflation rate has been overstated by an

average of two or three percentage points a year since 1974 mainly because new products or product improvements have been neglected. If this is correct, then productivity growth in the rich industrial economies has been much higher than the official figures suggest. This would matter less if new products and quality changes were introduced at a constant pace. The overstatement of inflation (and hence the understatement of growth) would be constant over time, so it would not distort relative productivity growth between two periods and hence could not explain the productivity paradox. However, there is good reason to believe that the degree of mismeasurement has worsened as product cycles have shortened. Mr. Nakamura estimates that the mismeasurement of inflation has been 1.7 percentage points a year higher since 1974 than in the previous 15 years. The greater understatement of growth that this implies would be almost enough to explain all of the apparent slowdown in America's productivity growth in the past two decades. "Survey of the World Economy." *Paradox Lost*, p. 16.

22 By mid 1998 Bureau of Labor Statistics productivity increases were reaching nearly 2 percent per year. *New York Times*, 15 August 1998, B2.

23 Jane Jacobs, *Systems of Survival* (New York: Random House, 1992).

24 Martin Wolf, *Financial Times*, 26 August 1997.

25 Ibid.

26 Yet we know that social orders cannot be purely economic in character. The social obligations linking parents and children cannot be reduced to the cash nexus. One family does not invite another over for dinner, expecting to be paid for the service, although there is some assumption of reciprocity. See Michael Anderson, *Family Structure in 19th Century Lancashire* (Cambridge: Cambridge University Press, 1971), who describes families in the late 1830s depression actually bartering (or even selling) dinners with one another.

27 For the importance of property rights see the work of Douglass North, *Structure and Change in Economic History* (New York: Norton, 1981), chap. 5.

28 This is the thesis of Christopher Patten in *East and West: China, Power, and the Future of Asia* (New York: New York Times Books/Random House, 1998).

29 Unemployment may derive from corporate downsizing and investment abroad. It may stem from international competition in the particular product line.

30 See Robert Reich, *The Work of Nations: Preparing Ourselves for 21st Century Capitalism* (New York: A. A. Knopf, 1991), chap. 25.

31 For an account of their domestic economic effects see Norman J. Glickman and Douglas P. Woodward, *The New Competitors: How Foreign Investors Are Changing the U.S. Economy* (New York, Basic Books, 1989).

32 Yet one of the surprising results has been the rise in status of the least well-off workers. "Jared Bernstein, an economist with the Economic Policy Institute in Washington, DC, noted that from 1996–1997 the hourly wages of the bottom 20 percent of workers increased by 3.2 percent in real terms. That compared with a 1.5 percent increase in the top 20 percent of wage and salary workers" (*New York Times*, 4 June 1998, A27).

33 It also is important to recall that "in the developed world, thanks to that all-too-rapid change, today's average citizen enjoys a higher standard of living than a king did 200 years ago. Only more often than not, he is not enjoying it as much as he might: he is too worried that it might all disappear at the click of a mouse" (*The Economist*, 28 September 1996, p. 45).

34 For those in trouble there are a number of obvious governmental remedies. Peter Passell (*New York Times*, 13 August 1998) writes:

> The earned-income tax credit could be expanded. State and Federal tax systems could be tilted, effectively eliminating taxes on the bottom third of the income distribution and making up the lost revenue with modest increases on the top third. Government could take some of the sting out of private income inequality by increasing outlays for communal services—day care, early childhood education, mass transit, recreation. (p. C2)

35 See Economic Expectations poll data in Gallup Opinion Index for the 1960s.

36 See Shoshona Zuboff, *In the Age of the Smart Machine: The Future of Work and Power* (New York: Basic Books, 1988). She writes: "The rigid separation of mental and material work characteristic of the industrial division of labor and vital to the preservation of a distinct managerial group (in the office as well as in the factory) becomes not merely outmoded, but perilously dysfunctional" (p. 393).

37 *The Economist* (28 September 1996) writes that

> A study by MIT economists Erik Brynjolfsson and Thomas
> Malone found that the size of the average American firm
> whether measured by number of employees, sales, or value
> added has shrunk since the 1970s and that firms that in-
> vested most in Information Technology tended to be smaller
> than others. Over the past two decades the average number
> of employees per firm in America has fallen by a fifth. An
> analysis by the OECD shows that in most rich industrial
> countries the average firm size has declined in most sectors
> except for computer services, drugs, and supermarkets.
> (p. 36)

See also E. Brynjolfsson, T. Malone, V. Gurbaxani, and A. Kambil, "Does
Information Technology Lead to Smaller Firms?" *Management Science 40*,
12 (December 1994).

38 Cited in the *Financial Times*, 11 August 1998, 3.

39 The defeat of one Russian prime minister does not solve Russia's economic problems with the world. Chernomyrdin, Kiriyenko, or Primakov
each faced an essentially intractable world economic environment.

40 See Louis Pauly, *Who Elected the Bankers?* (Ithaca, NY: Cornell University
Press, 1997), esp. chap. 1. Pauly puts the dilemma nicely:

> citizens in democratic societies continue to hold the govern-
> ment of their own state—alone—responsible for widening
> economic prosperity. If that government cannot deliver pros-
> perity, it may be replaced. If, however, those same citizens
> ever perceive effective governing authority to have somehow
> dissipated into a supranational ether, they would find them-
> selves up against the legitimacy crisis that theorists have been
> speculating about for years. Attempting to respond to the ris-
> ing anxieties of its citizens, a government might make des-
> perate moves to wrest control back, only to find that
> economic catastrophe has umasked the true nature of the cri-
> sis. The state itself has become obsolete. (p. 16)

See also Susan Strange, *The Retreat of the State: The Diffusion of Power in
the World Economy* (Cambridge: Cambridge University Press, 1996).

41 See Joel D. Aberbach, *Keeping a Watchful Eye: The Politics of Congressional Oversight* (Washington, DC: Brookings Institution, 1990).

42 Richard Lester, in *The Productive Edge*, writes:

> Take the new information technologies, for example. Job-destroying, occupation-reshaping, wage polarizing "agents of change"? Perhaps. But that is only one side of the story. The other emphasizes the unprecedented opportunity afforded by these technologies to move beyond the production systems of the past, systems that offered intrinsic satisfactions only to people at the top of the pyramid. This aspect of the story highlights the potential of these technologies to eliminate much of the rigid, narrow, repetitive work of today, and more broadly to provide personal and professional satisfaction for a far greater number of workers than ever before. (p. 326)

Chapter 6

1 Virginia Haufler, *Dangerous Commerce: Insurance and the Management of International Risk* (Ithaca, NY: Cornell University Press, 1997). See also Kenneth Arrow, *Optimal Insurance and Generalized Deductibles: A Report Prepared for the Office of Economic Opportunity* (Santa Monica, CA: RAND 1973).

2 Economic deterrence is discussed in Richard Rosecrance, "International Interdependence," in Geoffrey L. Goodwin and Andrew Linklater, eds., *New Dimensions in World Politics* (New York: Wiley, 1975).

3 See James Cable, *Gunboat Diplomacy, 1919–1991: Political Applications of Limited Naval Force*, 3d ed. (New York: St. Martin's Press, 1994).

4 Gary Clyde Hufbauer, Jeffrey J. Schott, and Kimberly Ann Elliott, *Economic Sanctions Reconsidered* (Washington, DC: Institute for International Economics, 1990). See also Zachary Alan Selden, "Economic Coercion in Theory & Practice: The Utility of Economic Sanctions in American Foreign Policy" (Ph.D. diss., Berkeley, UCLA, 1995). For a contrary view see David A. Baldwin, *Economic Statecraft* (Princeton, NJ: Princeton University Press, 1985). Lisa Martin points out that cold war factors strongly influenced the success of sanctions. She writes: "U.S. sanctions against Cuba in the 1960s, for example, should have had a

good chance of working because of Cuba's dependence on the United States. Once the Soviet Union came to Cuba's aid, however, such sanctions were much less likely to be effective" (p. 35). See Martin, *Coercive Cooperation: Explaining Multilateral Economic Sanctions* (Princeton, NJ: Princeton University Press, 1992).

5 For a general inquiry into the problem of building cooperation among states in the absence of hegemony see Robert Keohane, *After Hegemony: Cooperation and Discord in the World Political Economy* (Princeton, NJ: Princeton University Press, 1984).

6 See UCLA 1992 Conference paper, "Cooperation in a World Without Enemies: Solving the Public Goods Problem in International Relations," UCLA, Center for International Relations.

7 On the other hand, if powers are ideologically at odds, one group may not act to counterbalance a state holding a similar ideological view.

8 See Richard Rosecrance and Chih-cheng Lo, "Balancing, Stability, and War: The Mysterious Case of the Napoleonic International System," *International Studies Quarterly 40*, 4 (December 1996): 479–500.

9 Richard Rosecrance and Arthur Stein, "Beyond Realism: The Study of Grand Strategy," in R. Rosecrance and A. Stein, eds., *The Domestic Bases of Grand Strategy* (Ithaca, NY: Cornell University Press, 1993).

10 See Hedley Bull, *The Anarchical Society: A Study of Order in World Politics* (New York: Columbia University Press, 1977).

11 See also Richard Rosecrance and Peter Schott, "Concerts," in D. Lake and P. Morgan, eds., *Building Security in a New World* (University Park: Pennsylvania State University Press, 1997).

12 North writes: "Ideology is an economizing device by which individuals come to terms with their environment and are provided with a 'world view' so that the decision-making process is simplified. Ideology is inextricably interwoven with moral and ethical judgments about the fairness of the world the individual perceives." Douglass North, *Structure and Change in Economic History* (New York: Norton, 1981), 49.

13 In 1998 shares of world GDP were:

USA 25.2%   Europe 29.3%   Japan 17.4% = 71.9%
Source: *The Financial Times*, 15 September 1998, 12.

14 Carl Kaysen, "War, Peace and Politics: The U.S. and New World Order," UCLA, Center for International Relations Working Paper no. 2, February 1994.

15 This insight differs with "minimum winning coalition" arguments, in which small but winning coalitions strive to hold down membership in order to increase total gains and gains per player. The assumption of these studies is, of course, that the winners win only what the losers lose. See William Riker, *The Theory of Political Coalitions* (New Haven: Yale University Press, 1962).

16 For an overview of the impact of the world economy on domestic politics and economics see Jeffry Frieden and Ronald Rogowski, "The Impact of the International Economy on National Policies: An Analytical Overview," in Robert Keohane and Helen Milner, eds., *Internationalization and Domestic Politics* (Cambridge, UK: Cambridge University Press, 1996).

Chapter 7

1 In January 1998 labor costs in all three countries exceeded U.S.$1,000 on average per month as compared to a Chinese labor cost of about $100. (*The Economist*, 7 March 1998, 7.)

2 Taiwan's chip makers are quickly moving to new 0.18 micron line width technology. The previous standard (in Japan and Korea) was 0.25. So while Korean and Japanese production will stall (owing to the financial crisis), Taiwan will continue to expand production of the latest designs. (*Financial Times*, 12 October 1998, iii.)

3 See Robert Rowthorn and Ramana Ramaswamy, *Deindustrialization: Causes and Implications* (Washington, DC: Research Department, International Monetary Fund Working Paper, April 1997).

4 See Alwyn Young, "Lessons from the East Asian NICs: A Contrarian View," *European Economic Review* 38 (1994), and "The Tyranny of Numbers: Confronting the Statistical Realities of the East Asian Growth Experience," *Quarterly Journal of Economics* (August 1995). See also Paul Krugman, "The Myth of Asia's Miracle," *Foreign Affairs* 73, 6 (1994).

5 Paul Krugman, "First: What Ever Happened to the Asian Miracle?" *Fortune*, 18 August 1997. Krugman writes:

> By last year it became clear that South Korea's and Thailand's torrid growth rates of the first half of the 1990s had to end— wages were rising faster than productivity; overheated domestic markets were spilling over into imports, creating massive trade deficits. To perspiration theorists, these troubles were an early sign of the diminishing returns that will force a gradual slowdown in growth. The biggest lesson from

Asia's troubles isn't about economics; it's about governments. When Asian economies delivered nothing but good news, it was possible to convince yourself that the alleged planners of those economies knew what they were doing. Now the truth is revealed: they don't have a clue.

6 See Pam Woodall, "Frozen Miracle," *The Economist*, 7 March 1998. She writes: "Some myths about the tiger economies' success needed to be debunked, but the notion that the source of their rapid growth has permanently dried up is simply wrong. If governments grasp the opportunity to make long-needed economic reforms, the tiger economies could even end up stronger than before" (p. 17).

7 Susan Collins and Barry Bosworth, "Economic Growth in East Asia: Accumulation versus Assimilation," Brookings Papers on Economic Activity no. 2, 1996.

8 It is perhaps worth remembering that after the devaluation of 1994, Mexican exports in 1995 jumped by more than 40 percent in dollar terms. (*The Economist*, 7 March 1998, 8.)

9 *Wall Street Journal*, 15 May 1997, A18.

10 Greg Sheridan writes: "After the victory of the communists in mainland China in 1949, Hong Kong became a magnet for a million or more brilliant Chinese refugees, who brought to the small Crown colony their passionate commitment to work and family." Sheridan, *Leaders of the New Asia-Pacific Tigers* (London: Allen & Unwin, 1997), 234.

11 See Michael B. Yahuda, *Hong Kong: China's Challenge* (London: Routledge, 1996).

12 Rochelle L. Stanfield, "Excellence Goes Abroad: American Children Lag Behind in Science and Math," *National Journal* 28, 48 (30 November 1996): 2601.

13 Christopher Anderson, "Taiwan," *The Economist*, 7 November 1998, 16.

14 See particularly Stephan Gotz-Richter, "General Electric's Victory in Europe," *New York Times*, 30 November 1997, and Richard Waters, "Own Words: Jack Welch, General Electric," *Financial Times*, 1 October 1997.

15 See Rowthorn and Ramaswamy, *Deindustrialization*, 1.

Chapter 8

1 Chie Nakane, *Japanese Society* (Berkeley: University of California Press, 1970). She writes:

Competing clusters, in view of the difficulty of reaching agreement or consensus between clusters, have a diminished authority in dealing with the state administration. Competition and hostile relations between the civil powers facilitate the acceptance of state power, and, if that group is organized vertically, once the state's administrative authority is accepted, it can be transmitted without obstruction down the vertical line of a group's organization. In this way the administrative web is woven more thoroughly into Japanese society than perhaps any other in the world. (p. 102)

2 Shumpei Kumon, "Japan as a Network Society," in Shumpei Kumon and Henry Rosovsky, eds., *The Political Economy of Japan*. Vol. 3. *Cultural and Social Dynamics* (Stanford,CA: Stanford University Press, 1992), 130.

3 The *New York Times*'s Nicholas Kristof observed recently: "The emphasis on *wa* often impresses visitors, but it also results in paralysis. Japan has difficulty carrying out changes that benefit the majority but that are vigorously opposed by a small group of prospective losers." (*New York Times*, 26 October 1998, A10.)

4 Daniel Okimoto, "Political Inclusivity: The Domestic Structure of Trade," in Takashi Inoguchi and Daniel Okimoto, eds., *The Political Economy of Japan*. Vol. 2. *The Changing International Context* (Stanford, CA: Stanford University Press, 1988), 312.

5 See George Friedman and Meredith Lebard, *The Coming War with Japan* (New York: St Martin's Press, 1991).

6 Kenichi Ohmae argues, however, that Japanese superiority always rested on a few key manufacturing industries. See Ohmae, *The End of the Nation State: The Rise of Regional Economies* (New York: Free Press, 1996).

7 See Stephen Cohen and John Zysman, *Manufacturing Matters: The Myth of Post-Industrial Economy.* (New York: Basic Books, 1987). Also refer to Richard Baum and DeAnne Julius, "Is Manufacturing Still Special in the New World Order?" in Richard O'Brien, ed., *Finance and International Economy*, vol. 7 (Oxford, UK: Oxford University Press, 1993).

8 Robert Skidelsky writes: "Too much saving when consumer confidence is low could . . . lead to depression and unemployment. Japan is in this situation today. Its economy has been becalmed since 1991, and is still contracting, even though real interest rates are almost zero. This suggests that the Government should either cut taxes or spend more itself. It has promised to do both." (*New York Times*, 14 August1998, A23.)

9 Yen values may increase in the future. See Ronald I. McKinnon and Kenichi Ohno, *Dollar and Yen: Resolving Economic Conflict Between the United States and Japan* (Cambridge, MA: MIT Press, 1997).

10 See Table 8.1 in text. The Japanese surplus with Asian countries is largely based on *keiretsu* arrangements in Japan, which militate against the importation (into Japan) of Japanese products produced in East Asia. See the research by Dr. Kerry Chase, "Sectors, Firms, and Regional Trade Blocs: Building Blocks or Stumbling Blocks for the Liberalization of World Trade" (Ph.D. diss., Berkeley, UCLA, 1998); and Kozo Yamamura and Walter Hatch, "A Looming Entry Barrier: Japan's Production Networks in Asia," *Analysis: The National Bureau of Asian Research* 8, 1 (February 1997): 12.

11 See Mitchell Bernard and John Ravenhill, "Beyond Product Cycles & Flying Geese: Regionalization, Hierarchy and the Industrialization of East Asia," *World Politics* 47, 2 (January 1995): 171–209.

12 Yamamura and Hatch, "A Looming Entry Barrier," 24.

13 Lester Thurow, *The Future of Capitalism* (New York: William Morrow, 1996), 230–31. Robert Skidelsky, the biographer of John Maynard Keynes, recently observed:

> If people want a larger dinner today than they can afford, they saddle future generations with large debts. And if a country owes a lot to foreigners, they may flee in panic from a particular currency, as happened in Mexico in the early 1990s or to some East Asian countries more recently. This can start a chain reaction, like the one that brought down the world economy in the early 1930's. (*New York Times*, 14 August 1998, A23)

14 For further analysis see Steven Clemons, "A Constructive Agenda for Obuchi," *Yomiuri Shimbun*, 6 August 1998.

15 See Edward Lincoln, *Japan's Unequal Trade* (Washington, DC: The Brookings Institution, 1990).

16 See Yasusake Murakami, *An Anti-Classical Political-Economic Analysis: A Vision for the Next Century* (Stanford, CA: Stanford University Press, 1996), 315–20.

17 Such a strategy has been called for by many Japanese experts, including Takashi Inoguchi. See his "Japan's Foreign Policy in a Time of Global Uncertainty," *International Journal* (Autumn 1991): 581.

18 Ronald McKinnon and Kenichi Ohno, *Dollar and Yen: Resolving Economic Conflict Between the United States and Japan* (Cambridge, MA: MIT Press, 1997), 228–33.

19 Richard Cooper has investigated this possibility. He writes:

> Economists often argue that persistent yield differences on low-risk assets of comparable maturity must reflect expected movements in exchange rates, prospectively compensating for the differences in yield. That may be so, but forward exchange rates, which typically reflect yield differentials accurately, are notoriously poor (and biased) forecasters of future spot rates. (p. 16)

Cooper, "Key Currencies After the Euro," Working Paper no. 98–3, Weatherhead Center for International Affairs, Harvard University, February 1998.

20 Masatake Matsuda, president of the East Japan Railway Company, who is resisting a government proposal to levy more debt on his recently privatized company contends: "If we allow shareholders to be deprived of profits without rational reasons, it means the collapse of the modern state and the free economy set up with corporations at the core." (Quoted in the *New York Times*, 7 October 1998, C2.)

21 Peter Drucker points out that Japan and some European countries have relied entirely too much on government pension payments to finance retirement for the elderly. In the Japanese case, not only are the elderly becoming a larger fraction of the population, the birth rate has declined, forcing a smaller number of younger workers to finance the retirements of a large group of elderly. "Japan is badly hit because its pension system is entirely pay-as-you-go, and it has the largest budget deficit. Most of these state-run pension systems are heading for bankruptcy. With today's demographic situation these state systems cannot be saved. They can only be replaced." (*Forbes*, 7 September 1998, 116.) Younger people, however, are rebelling against paying for their retired elders, "and this has to lead to the emergence of managed plans so that individuals can make provision for a future that can no longer be guaranteed by governmental plans. So you have the emergence of funds managed increasingly by professionals, and those funds will put pressure for higher returns for the shareholder" (p. 116). Drucker also notes: "One of the biggest managers of money for well-to-do Japanese sits in London. Its typical customer is a successful Japanese sur-

geon with a net worth of $1 million or $2 million. This firm manages $20 billion of Japanese assets. Not one penny is invested in Japan. Not because it is bearish on Japanese stocks, but because the market in Japan isn't liquid, and also because many of its customers want income and Japanese companies don't pay dividends" (p. 118).

22 Eiji Hotopp Furukawa, "Down Market Helps Investors Speak Up: Japan's Major Shareholders Breaking Tradition of Silence as Corporate Wars Trim Their Portfolios," *Nikkei Weekly*, 22 June 1998, 7.

23 This conclusion is buttressed by data offered by Dr. Kerry Chase, "Sectors, Firms, and Regional Trade Blocs: Building Blocs or Stumbling Blocks for the Liberalization of World Trade" (Ph.D. diss., UCLA, 1998).

24 It is not clear, however, that any of the top twenty Japanese banks actually will be closed down.

25 Some disagree about the possible success of the "Big Bang." See inter alia, Takenak Heizo, "Prospects for the Japanese 'Big Bang'," *Japan Echo* (June 1997), and Saito Seiichiro, "Dont Expect a Big Bank from MOF," *Japan Echo* (August 1997).

26 At this point the de facto closure of the Japanese market for foreign merchandise trade becomes important. Raymond Vernon hypothesized that pioneer manufacturers eventually would face competition for their home markets. They would counter this by manufacturing abroad and reimporting the lower-cost television set or electronic appliance back into their own market. As Bernard Mitchell and John Ravenhill show, however, Japan never faced this problem because it did not allow foreign electrical equipment manufacturers to sell in Japan in the first place. Therefore it did not have to produce abroad for the Japanese public, and the result was that the "product life cycle" argument of Raymond Vernon did not apply to Japan. (Bernard Mitchell and John Ravenhill, "Beyond Product Cycles and Flying Geese: Regionalization, Hierarchy, and the Industrialization of East Asia," *World Politics* 47 (January 1995).

27 *International Financial Statistics*, June 1998, 742.

28 Recent statistics indicate that the aging of the Japanese workforce after 2000 will leave only two workers to pay for the retirement benefits of a single Japanese pensioner as compared with the five workers who used to do so.

29 *A New Japan? Change in Asia's Megamarket* (Canberra, Australia: East Asian Analytical Unit, Department of Foreign Affairs and Trade, 1997), 89.

30 *The Economist* has emphasized this long-term danger over the past several years.

31 See Friedman and LeBard, *The Coming War with Japan.* Walter Lafeber believes "that the causes of the U.S.-Japan clash have deep historical roots. The roots might be controlled. They will not be eradicated." Walter Lafeber, *The Clash: U.S.–Japanese Relations Throughout History* (New York: W. W. Norton, 1998), 398–99.

32 Some caution, however, that Japanese rates of growth may decline radically in the future. *A New Japan?* writes: "The International Monetary Fund estimates Japan's potential growth will be around 2.5 percent per year in CY–1995–2000, dropping gradually to around 1 percent per year by 2015 as growth in the working-age population slows" (p. 84).

33 He observes "the unparalleled competitive strength of many U.S. service-based industries. For Europe, Japan, and even the Asian tigers, however, the situation is altogether different. Unless their governments move rapidly to deregulate key service sectors so that sheltered domestic players can grow strong from more intense competition, these activities—by far the largest segment of their economies—will migrate cross-border in a very short period of time." Kenichi Ohmae, *The End of the Nation State: The Rise of Regional Economies* (New York: Free Press, 1995), 135.

34 Chalmers Johnson, "The Problem of Japan in an Era of Structural Change" (UC San Diego Research Report, 1989).

35 Japan also does not communicate as readily among its own citizens and with other nations via the Internet. One reason for this is too-high Japanese telephone charges. See particularly "Japan and International Society in the Age of Information Revolution," policy recommendations drafted by Shumpei Kumon, Tadao Saito, Tsuruhiko Nambu, Norimasa Shimada, Jiro Kikuryo, and Yasuhide Yamanouchi, *Japan Forum on International Relations*, Tokyo, August 1998, 54.

Chapter 9

1 See Stephen S. Cohen and John Zysman, *Manufacturing Matters: The Myth of the Post-Industrial Society* (New York: Basic Books, 1987). Also refer to Richard Brown and Deanne Julius, "Is Manufacturing Still Special in the New World Order?" in Richard O'Brien, ed., *Finance and International Economy*, vol. 7 (Oxford, UK: Oxford University Press, 1993).

2 As Paul Krugman points out, if productivity is undermeasured in the American economy, then growth is undermeasured. So defenders of ex-

isting statistics either have to revise productivity numbers upward or revise growth numbers upward. "If productivity growth had actually been
2.5 percent since 1990—or 1.5 percentage points higher than the official
statistics—then actual GDP growth would be understated by exactly the
same amount." Krugman, quoted in The Aspen Institute, *Work & Future
Society: Where Are the Economy and Technology Taking Us?* (Washington,
DC: The Aspen Institute, 1998), 13.

3 Former Under Secretary of Commerce for International Trade Jeffrey
Garten points out

> By the turn of the century, more than 16 million jobs will be
> supported by overseas sales. From Coca-Cola to Caterpillar,
> many U.S. companies are taking in more than 50 percent of
> their revenues abroad. From a foreign policy standpoint,
> moreover, America's links to most countries, and its potential
> influence on them, depend increasingly on commercial rela-
> tionships. Trade, finance, and business investment have be-
> come the *sine qua non* of links with Russia, China, Japan,
> Southeast Asia, the European Union, and the nations of the
> Western Hemisphere.

"Business and Foreign Policy," *Foreign Affairs* (May-June 1997): 69–70.

4 See W. J. Baumol, S. A. Batey Blackman, and Edward Wolff, *Productivity
and American Leadership: The Long View* (Cambridge, MA: MIT Press,
1989). Angus Maddison estimates productivity growth for major countries from 1973–1984 as follows:

France	Germany	Japan	Holland	U.K.	U.S.A.
3.4	3.0	3.2	1.9	2.4	1.0

Source: Baumol, Batey Blackman, and Wolff, *Productivity and American
Leadership*, 283.

5 The forecast deficit in the U.S. Balance of Payments for 1998–99 is
$224.8 billion (*New York Times*, 21 July, 1991, C1).

6 In the first half of 1998 U.S. investment surged to 26 percent of U.S. GDP,
a recent record. (*New York Times*, 15 August 1998, B2.)

7 Three individuals who did predict a U.S. renaissance include Joseph Nye,
Bound to Lead (New York: Basic Books, 1990), Henry Nau, *The Myth of
America's Decline: Leading the World Economy into the 1990s* (Oxford, UK:
Oxford University Press, 1990), and Richard Rosecrance, *America's Eco-
nomic Resurgence: A Bold New Strategy* (New York: HarperCollins, 1990).

8 In fact Japanese GDP has increased at 1.1 percent per year on average since 1990.

9 One exception of course, was Francis Fukuyama, *The End of History and the Last Man* (New York: Free Press, 1992).

10 *Federal Government Finances and Employment* No. 515—Federal Budget—Summary: 1945–1997, and *Federal Borrowing and Debt*—Foreign Holdings of Federal Debt. The difference between the value of foreign investment in the United States and U.S. investment abroad, however, was somewhat less at about $900 billion. In 1996 the market value of U.S. assets abroad was $4.2 trillion; the value of foreign assets in the United States was $5.1 trillion. (See Table B–107—International Investment Position of the United States at year-end, *Statistical Abstract of the United States* 1997, 403.)

11 Sukkoo Kim, "Expansion of Markets and the Geographic Distribution of Economic Activities: The Trends in the U.S. Regional Manufacturing Structure, 1860–1987," *Quarterly Journal of Economics* (November 1995).

12 See *New York Times*, 8 September 1997.

13 Testimony of Alan Greenspan before the U.S. Congress, Joint Economic Committee, 10 June 1998, 4.

14 In 1997 the deficit in (visible) goods trade was $197 billion. At the same time, however, there was a surplus in (invisible) services trade of $84 billion, leaving a net (deficit) balance on goods and services of just over $110 billion. (*International Financial Statistics*, June 1998, 742.)

15 This did not happen right away. The Johnson administration was still experimenting with an "interest equalization tax" as late as 1968. This tax made it difficult for foreigners to raise capital in the U.S. market and was shortly abolished. This openness occasionally has been criticized by economists (see, e.g., Jagdish Bagwati). Despite such views, former Secretary of the Treasury Robert Rubin, however, thinks open capital markets are a good idea. He told the *Financial Times*, "My views have not changed. I think opening capital markets is good" (*Financial Times*, 13 July 1998, 15).

16 For immigration benefits see two views: Julian Simon, *The Economic Consequences of Immigration* (Oxford, UK: Basil Blackwell, 1989 and 1991), and George Borjas, *Friends or Strangers: The Impact of Immigrants on the U.S. Economy* (New York: Basic Books, 1990).

17 See inter alia Norman Glickman and Douglas Woodward, *The New Competitors* (New York: Basic Books, 1989).

18 Jacob Weisberg, "Keeping the Boom from Busting," *New York Times Magazine*, 19 July 1998, 38.

19 Peter Ackerman, "The Revolution in Business Affairs: Bringing 21st Century Business Practices to Defense," Discussion paper, October 1997.

20 As Edmunds points out: "A small difference in the rate of return makes a big difference, because of compounding. In order to accumulate $750,000 by age 65 a person needs to save $500 a month if the rate of return is 10.7% per year, or $1,000 a month if the rate of return is 6.5% per year." (Personal communication to the author, 8 August 1997.)

21 Edmunds, personal communication to the author, 8 August 1997.

22 *New York Times*, 26 July 1998, 12.

23 See Saul Hansell, "Is This the Factory of the Future?" *New York Times*, 26 July 1998, sec. 3, 1. "Ingram's 40% annual growth rate far outpaces most of the rest of the technology industry, including networking (25%), software (20%) and hardware (15%). The company's work force has more than doubled in two years to 14,000, thanks to its aggressive hiring spree and the acquisition of nine distributor companies."

24 Ibid., 12.

25 See *Capitalism, Socialism, and Dictatorship*, the forthcoming book by Mancur Olson on this topic.

26 See Steven Solomon, *The Confidence Game* (New York: Simon and Schuster, 1995).

27 See particularly Richard Cooper, "Key Currencies After the Euro," Working Paper no. 98–3, Weatherhead Center for International Affairs, Harvard University, February 1998.

28 The measurement of savings of course does not include stock holdings. About 24 percent of U.S. household wealth was in the stock market in early 1999, but this was not counted as savings. There is a wealth effect that frequently leads to a decline in formally measured savings rates. This does not mean, however, that Americans are not saving for their retirement.

29 See *Financial Times*, 12 October 1998, 3.

Chapter 10

1 See Hajo Holborn, *The Political Collapse of Europe* (New York: A. A. Knopf, 1951).

2 See Richard Rosecrance, "The European Union: A New Type of International Actor," in Jan Zielonka, ed., *Paradoxes of European Foreign Policy* (The Hague: Kluwer, 1998).

3 Members of the EMU must limit government debt to no more than 60 percent of GDP, maintain current government deficits at no more than 3 percent of GDP, limit inflation, and achieve stable currencies.

4 The lack of ministerial responsibility to the European Parliament typically has been referred to as the "democratic deficit."

5 Even outsiders moved to put plants in Eastern Europe. General Motors built four identical plants abroad, in Argentina, Poland, Thailand, and China. Daewoo moved auto production to the Ukraine. Intel focused new production capability in Ireland.

6 See John Newhouse, *Europe Adrift* (New York: Pantheon Books, 1997).

7 This is the reflection of the operation of "the gravity model" observed in the work of Edward Leamer. See among others Edward Leamer, "U.S. Manufacturing and an Emerging Mexico," *North American Journal of Economics and Finance 4*, 1 (1993): 54–62.

8 See Ludwig Dehio, *The Precarious Balance: Four Centuries of the European Power Struggle*, trans. Charles Fullman (New York: A. A. Knopf, 1962), and Edward Vose Gulick, *Europe's Classical Balance of Power: A Case History of the Theory and Practice of One of the Great Concepts of European Statecraft* (Ithaca, NY: Cornell University Press, 1955).

9 This is not to say that they necessarily fail. After the Concert of Europe declined in the late nineteenth century, economic connections among nations continued and even increased, but they faced constant uncertainty. Most countries knew that another major European war had not been ruled out.

10 There has been much erroneous information on this topic. There was considerable portfolio investment in the late nineteenth century, but it is not clear how much direct investment there was (that is, productive investment in physical facilities and assets, constituting 15 percent or more of the value of a company). Arthur Bloomfield observes: "Before 1914, it might be noted, the concept of direct investment (in its present-day sense) was not clearly distinguished in the statistics from other (noncontrolling) equity investments in private foreign enterprises." See Arthur Bloomfield, *Patterns of Fluctuation in International Investment Before 1914*, Princeton Studies in International Finance no. 21 (Princeton, NJ: Princeton University Press, 1968), 3–4. Under these circumstances recent claims that foreign direct investment represented 11 percent or more of GDP seem questionable. Angus Maddison estimates that foreign investment constituted 16.6 percent of GDP. Two-thirds of this could not have been direct investment (see Bloomfield, *Patterns of Fluctuation*).

Even if this claim could be sustained, however, about one-half of all British foreign investments were in the empire. Thus the political conclusion reached by some (e.g., Peter Beinhart, "An Illusion for Our Time: The False Promise of Globalization," *The New Republic*, 20 October 1997) that globalization was greater in 1913 than it is today is almost certainly invalid. Investment in the colonies of one's own empire does not have the same globalizing effect as investing in other countries. Foreign direct investment in one's colonies is in effect domestic investment. There was no similar foreign direct investment in other potential great power rivals.

11 See Etel Solingen, "Democracy, Economic Reform, and Regional Cooperation," *Journal of Theoretical Politics* (January 1996).

Chapter 11

1 Hannibal, however, did sack Rome, and the Mongols carved out a large empire for a period of time.

2 This is one central thesis in Immanuel Wallerstein, *The Modern World System II: Mercantilism and the Consolidation of the European World Economy, 1600–1750* (New York: Academic Press, 1980).

3 See Arno J. Mayer, *The Persistence of the Old Regime: Europe to the Great War* (New York: Pantheon Books, 1981).

4 See James Harding, *Financial Times*, 4 September 1998, 4.

5 Technically, a country cannot be abundant in both land and labor.

6 See Chalmers Johnson, *MITI and the Japanese Miracle: The Growth of Industrial Policy, 1925–1975* (Stanford, CA: Stanford University Press, 1982).

7 I am indebted to Professor Richard Baum for this suggestion.

8 See Nicholas Lardy study published by Brookings, *China's Unfinished Economic Revolution* (Washington, DC: Brookings Institution, 1998).

9 See David Lake, "Anarchy, Hierarchy and the Variety of International Relations," *International Organization 50*, 1 (Winter 1996).

10 The growing Chinese trade surplus with the United States now exceeds that of Japan.

11 See James Harding, "China's Financial Sector Counts on a Slow Start from Abroad," *Financial Times*, 4 September 1998, 4.

12 One economist put the LDC plight in the following terms: "High interest rates have already hurt the [developing] economy. The key export sector has been hit particularly hard, making a difficult situation even worse. As

a result, most independent analysts have lowered their forecasts for [the developing economy's] economic growth in 1999 to the 2 per cent range, substantially below the 7.5 per cent average of the last decade" (Sebastian Edwards, "Barking Up the Wrong Tree," *Financial Times*, 7 October 1998, 10).

13 See Burton Malkiel and J. P. Mei, "Containing Chernobyl," *Financial Times*, 7 October 1998, 10.

Chapter 12

1 See Remarks by Alan Greenspan at Syracuse University, 3 December 1997.
2 Greenspan, op. cit., 2.
3 Bernard Hoeckman and Pierre Sauvé, "Liberalizing Trade in Services," World Bank Discussion Paper no. 243, Washington, DC, 1994.
4 Ibid., 5.
5 See Robert Strausz-Hupé and Stefan Possony, *International Relations in the Age of the Conflict Between Democracy and Dictatorship* (New York: McGraw-Hill, 1950); Brooks Emeny, *Mainsprings of World Politics* (New York: Foreign Policy Association, 1943); Frank Russell, *Theories of International Relations* (New York: Appleton-Century, 1936).
6 See also J. M. Clark, W. H. Hamilton, and Harold G. Moulton, *Readings in the Economics of War* (Chicago: University of Chicago Press, 1918), Part 2, "War as a Business Venture."
7 See Deepak Lal, "The World Economy at the End of the Millennium," in John Mueller, ed., *Peace, Prosperity, and Politics* (Boulder, CO: Westview Press, forthcoming).
8 Hoeckman and Sauvé, "Liberalizing Trade in Services," 5.

Chapter 13

1 See Steven Solomon, *The Confidence Game: How Unelected Central Bankers Are Governing the Changed Global Economy* (New York: Simon and Schuster, 1995).
2 Richard N. Cooper stresses that key currencies must provide liquidity to users. See his "Key Currencies After the Euro," Working Paper no. 98–3, Weatherhead Center for International Affairs, Harvard University, February 1998.

3 Alan Greenspan Speech before the Economic Club of New York, 2 December 1997, 7.

4 *New York Times*, 18 October 1998, sec. 3, 11.

5 Ibid.

6 See chap. 4.

7 This process influenced Malaysia's response to the 1997–98 financial crisis.

8 See Brad De Long, "The Role of International Economic Institutions," paper presented at the UCLA Colloquium on War and Peace, Berkeley, 7–8 November 1997.

9 See Barry Eichengreen, *Elusive Stability* (Cambridge: Cambridge University Press, 1990), chap. 11.

10 See Richard Rosecrance and Peter Schott, "Concerts and Regional Intervention," in David Lake and Patrick Morgan, eds., *Regional Orders* (University Park, PA: Pennsylvania State University Press, 1997).

11 The air war in Kosovo ultimately ended Serbia's control.

12 Syria, however, has been remarkably successful in its long-term intervention in Lebanon.

13 This belief lay behind the successful international attempt to overturn Iraq's invasion of Kuwait.

14 See Jack Hirshleifer, "The Dark Side of the Force," 1993 Presidential Address to the Western Economic Association, *Economic Enquiry 32*, 1 (January 1994): 1–10.

15 Adam Smith wrote in *The Wealth of Nations* (New York: Random House, 1937): "In the restraints upon the importation of all foreign commodities which can come into competition with those of our own growth, or manufacture, the interest of the home-consumer is evidently sacrificed to that of the producer. It is altogether for the benefit of the latter, that the former is obliged to pay that enhancement of price which this monopoly almost always occasions" (p. 625).

16 Robert A. Mundell, "International Trade and Factor Mobility," *American Economic Review 47*, 3 (June 1957): 321–35.

17 Arnold J. Toynbee wrote in volume 4 of his *A Study of History* (London: Oxford University Press, 1939): "Industrialism will not work freely or effectively or beneficently except in so far as the World is organized into one single field of economic activity—a single world-field in which everybody is at liberty to live and work and produce and consume and collect and distribute and sell and buy and travel and transact business without let or hindrance" (p. 169).

18 See John A. Kroll, *Closure in International Politics: The Impact of Strategy, Blocs, and Empire* (Boulder, CO: Westview Press, 1995).

19 See among others, Lewis Mumford, *Technics and Civilization* (New York: Harcourt, Brace, 1934).

20 See Michael J. Piore and Charles F. Sabel, *The Second Industrial Divide: Possibilities for Prosperity* (New York: Basic Books, 1984).

21 See Shoshona Zuboff, *In The Age of the Smart Machine: The Future of Work and Power* (New York: Basic Books, 1988).

22 In 1998 they rose by 2 percent.

23 The percentage of Americans with education beyond high school is now 50 percent as compared with 20 percent in 1970. *New York Times*, 18 October 1998, sec. 3, 11.

24 See Edward Leamer, "Wage Inequality from International Competition and Technological Change: Theory and Country Experience," *American Economic Review 86*, 2 (May 1996): 309–14.

25 The 1998 U.S. immigration bill pushes in this direction.

26 See Barbara Rosecrance and Richard Rosecrance, "British Vitality at Its Zenith: Explaining the Achievements of 1815–1851," in Armand Clesse and Richard Cooper, eds., *The Vitality of Britain* (Luxembourg: Institute for European and International Studies, 1997).

27 Wayne Cornelius writes: "The continuing need of even knowledge-intensive businesses for substantial numbers of relatively low-skilled production and maintenance workers helps to explain the pervasive demand for immigrant workers in large metropolitan areas like San Diego." See Wayne Cornelius, with the assistance of Yasuo Kuwahara, "The Role of Immigrant Labor in the U.S. and Japanese Economies: A Comparative Study of San Diego and Hamamatsu, Japan," Center for U.S.-Mexican Studies, University of California–San Diego, 1 April 1998, 29.

28 The rate of population growth will decline and world population may begin to stabilize in the mid twenty-first century, further reducing ecological and environmental problems. See Walt Rostow, *The Great Population Spike and After: Reflections on the 21st Century* (Oxford: Oxford University Press, 1998).

29 See Remarks by Secretary of Defense William S. Cohen, Center for International Relations, University of California, Los Angeles, 28 October 1998.

30 Piore and Sabel in *The Second Industrial Divide* write prophetically of a system of "flexible specialization" that allows workers to emancipate themselves from Fordist mass production:

Flexible specialization opens up long-term prospects for improvement in the condition of working life—regardless of this system's effect on the balance of power between currently existing organizations of capital and labor. Mass production is the least attractive on the shop floor. Even when shop-floor control is based on broad job classifications and substantive dispute resolution, mass production still invites as adversarial, hierarchical relation between workers and managers, and among the different units of an organization. Mass production's extreme division of labor routinizes and thereby trivializes work to a degree that often degrades the people who perform it. By contrast, flexible specialization is predicated on collaboration. And the frequent changes in the production process put a premium on craft skills. Thus the production worker's intellectual participation in the work process is enhanced—and his or her role revitalized. (p. 278)

Appendix

1 A third approach, called *constructivism*, will not be discussed here. According to this view, nations "construct" their own social-international order. They do not necessarily regard another state as a competitor or foe. The relations between countries may be of mutual assistance instead of strife. Constructivism, however, is consistent with a very wide range of de facto international behavior. It does not mandate particular national or systemic responses. See Alexander Wendt, "Anarchy Is What States Make of It: The Social Construction of Power Politics," *International Organization* 46, 2 (Spring 1992): 391–425.

2 Not all realists adopt this view, but see Grieco as one major example: Joseph M. Grieco, *Cooperation Among Nations: Europe, America, and Non-Tariff Barriers to Trade* (Ithaca, NY: Cornell University Press, 1990), and idem, "The Relative-Gains Problem for International Cooperation," *American Political Science Review* (September 1993).

3 Some realists conclude that hegemony by one power can only be terminated by "hegemonic war" launched by a challenger to end that rule. See George Modelski, *Long Cycles in World Politics* (Seattle: University of Washington Press, 1987), and Robert Gilpin, *War and Change in World Politics* (Cambridge, UK: Cambridge University Press, 1981).

4 See Geoffrey Blainey, *The Causes of War*, 3d ed. (New York: Free Press, 1988), who regards war as a dispute in the measurement of power.

5 See Nazli Choucri and Robert C. North, *Nations in Conflict: National Growth and International Violence* (San Francisco: W. H. Freeman, 1975).

6 See A.F.K. Organski, *World Politics* (New York: A. A. Knopf, 1958).

7 F. H. Hinsley, *Power and the Pursuit of Peace* (Cambridge, UK: Cambridge University Press, 1964).

8 See John Ruggie, "Continuity and Transformation in the World Polity: Toward a Neorealist Synthesis," *World Politics* (January 1983).

9 See Robert Keohane, *After Hegemony: Cooperation and Discord in the World Political Economy* (Princeton, NJ: Princeton University Press, 1984).

10 See John Mearsheimer, "The False Promise of International Institutions," *International Security* (Winter 1995): 5–49.

11 See Carl Kaysen, "Is War Obsolete?" (Review of John Mueller's *Retreat from Doomsday: The Obsolescence of Major War*, in *International Security* (Spring 1990), and Richard Rosecrance, "Economic Security," in R. Schultz, R. Godson, and G. Quester, eds., *Security Studies for the 21st Century* (London: Brassey's, 1998).

12 See Arthur Stein, "The Hegemon's Dilemma," *International Organization* (Spring 1984).

13 See also John Kroll, *Closure in International Politics: The Impact of Strategy, Blocs, and Empire* (Boulder, CO: Westview Press, 1995), and John Conybeare, *Trade Wars: The Theory and Practice of International Commercial Rivalry* (New York: Columbia University Press, 1987).

14 See Richard Rosecrance and Jennifer Taw, "Japan and the Theory of International Leadership," *World Politics* (January 1990).

15 Grieco, *Cooperation Among Nations*.

16 These contentions contrast with those expressed in Gilpin, *War and Change*.

17 A typical Prisoner's Dilemma game is as follows:

		Player B	
		Cooperate	Defect
Player A	Cooperate	3,3	1,4
	Defect	4,1	2,2**

**Solution outcome

"The prisoner's dilemma game has two characteristics. First, defection is the dominant strategy for each player. *Dominant* is the technical term used to indicate that following this strategy leaves each player better off *no matter what the opponent does.* Thus, defection is unconditionally the best strategy for each player. Second, by choosing the dominant strategy and defecting, both players find themselves in a suboptimal outcome, that is, they find themselves worse off than if they had chosen the cooperative strategy." G. Tsebelis, *Nested Games* (Berkeley: University of California Press, 1990), 62.

18 See John Harsanyi, "Game Theory and International Politics," in James Rosenau, ed., *International Politics and Foreign Policy: A Reader in Research and Theory* (New York: Free Press, 1969).

19 See Michael Taylor, *Anarchy and Cooperation* (New York: Wiley, 1976), and Robert Axelrod, *The Evolution of Cooperation* (New York: Basic Books, 1984).

20 See Rob Boyd and Jeff Lorberbaum, "No Pure Strategy Is Evolutionarily Stable in the Repeated Prisoner's Dilemma Game," *Nature*, 7 May 1987, and D. Fudenberg and E. Maskin, "The Folk Theorem in Repeated Games with Discounting or with Incomplete Information," *Econometrica* 54 (1986).

21 Jeff Lorberbaum shows that "Pavlov" can become a stable strategy under conditions of noise. See Lorberbaum (forthcoming).

22 Martin Nowak and Karl Sigmund have championed "Pavlov" (a strategy of win—stay, lose—shift) as a substitute for Nice Tit for Tat. In Pavlov a player takes into account his own and his opponent's last move. If Pavlov played D or C to the opponent's C on the last move, it will continue to make the same move (since it did not lose on these moves). If, on the other hand, Pavlov played C and received an opponent's D (thereby losing), it will shift to "Defect" on the next move. Unlike Nice Tit for Tat, Pavlov does not get stuck on a series of endless defections that might be the result of misunderstanding (or Selten's "trembling hand") among essentially cooperative players. It keeps trying to reinstate cooperation. Also Pavlov is not as easily invaded by highly cooperative strategies (such as TF3T or ALL C), since it readily takes advantage of an opponent's too generous cooperation. Since Pavlov is less likely to succumb to more cooperative strategies than Tit for Tat, systemic cooperation does not rise to a peak in which defection and All D strategies can temporarily take over. It is nonetheless true that Pavlov succumbs even more readily to All D than Tit for Tat (which loses only on the very first move). Nowak and Sigmund agree that Pavlov is better against cooperators while

TFT is better against defectors. See Martin Nowak and Karl Sigmund, "A Strategy of Win-Stay, Lose-Shift That Outperforms Tit-for-Tat in the Prisoner's Dilemma Game," *Nature 364*, 6432 (1 July 1993): 56–58.

23 See John Vasquez, "The Realist Paradigm and Degenerative versus Progressive Research Programs: An Appraisal of Neotraditional Research on Waltz's Balancing Proposition," *American Political Science Review* (December 1997) and the following debate. See also Vasquez, "The New Debate on Balancing Power: A Reply to My Critics," American Political Science Association paper, August 1998.

24 See Arthur Stein, *Why Nations Cooperate: Circumstance and Choice in International Relations* (Ithaca, NY: Cornell University Press, 1990), and Deborah W. Larson, "Trust and Missed Opportunities in International Relations," *Political Psychology 18*, 3 (September 1997).

25 See Richard Rosecrance, *The Rise of the Trading State: Commerce and Conquest in the Modern World* (New York: Basic Books, 1986).

26 Equally, "All C" also defeats TFT. See Jack Hirshleifer, "There Are Many Evolutionary Pathways to Cooperation," Working Paper no. 778A, Department of Economics, UCLA, May 1998, 16.

27 See Jack Hirshleifer and Juan Carlos Martinez Coll, "What Strategies Can Support the Evolutionary Emergence of Cooperation?" *Journal of Conflict Resolution 32* (1988): 367–98.

28 Bjorn Lomborg, "The Structure of Solutions in the Iterated Prisoner's Dilemma," UCLA Working Paper, Center for International Relations, 1993. See also idem, "Nucleus and Shield: The Evolution of Social Structure in the Iterated Prisoner's Dilemma," *American Sociological Review 61* (1996).

29 See Michael Mann, *The Sources of Social Power*, vol. 1 (Cambridge, UK: Cambridge University Press, 1986).

30 See the debate on the subject between Werner Sombart and John U. Nef. The relevant works are: Sombart, *Der Moderne Kapitalismus: Historische-Systematische Darstellung des Gesamteuropaischen Wirtschaftslebens von Seinem Anfrangen bis zur Gegenwart* (Munich & Leipzig: Duncker & Humblot, 1916), and J. Nef, *War and Human Progress: An Essay on the Rise of Industrial Civilization* (Cambridge, MA: Harvard University Press, 1950).

31 See Paul Kennedy on the longevity and success of Britain's appeasement policy in Kennedy, *Strategy and Diplomacy 1870–1945* (London: Allen & Unwin, 1983).

32 This argument accords well with Robert Gilpin's version of "hegemonic stability" as expressed in Robert Keohane and Joseph Nye, eds., *Transnationalism in World Politics* (Cambridge, MA: Harvard University Press, 1972).

33 See Richard Rosecrance, "A New Concert of Powers," *Foreign Affairs* (April 1992).

34 Duncan Snidal, "The Limits of Hegemonic Stability Theory," *International Organization* (Autumn 1985).

Index